Indexed in

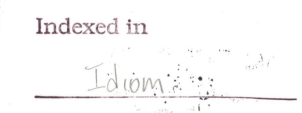

Idiom

INTIMATES IN CONFLICT:
A Communication Perspective

COMMUNICATION

A series of volumes edited by:
Dolf Zillmann and **Jennings Bryant**

INTIMATES IN CONFLICT:
A Communication Perspective

Edited by
Dudley D. Cahn
State University of New York
at New Paltz

 LAWRENCE ERLBAUM ASSOCIATES, PUBLISHERS
1990   Hillsdale, New Jersey   Hove and London

Lawrence Erlbaum Associates, Inc., Publishers
365 Broadway
Hillsdale, New Jersey 07642

Library of Congress Cataloging-in-Publication Data

Intimates in conflict : a communication perspective / edited by Dudley
   D. Cahn.
        p.   cm.—(Communication)
     ISBN 0-8058-0735-7
     1. Interpersonal conflict.   2. Interpersonal communication.
   I. Cahn, Dudley D.   II. Series: Communication (Hillsdale, N.J.)
     [DNLM: 1. Communication.   2. Conflict (Psychology).
   3. Interpersonal Relations.   BF 683 I61]
   BF637.I48I57   1990
   302.3′4—dc20
   DNLM/DLC
     for Library of Congress   89-71494
Printed in the United States of America   CIP
   10 9 8 7 6 5 4 3 2 1

Contents

Contributors

Janet K. Alberts is assistant professor in the Department of Communication, Arizona State University at Tempe.

Robert A. Bell is assistant professor in the Department of Rhetoric and Communication, University of California at Davis.

Judee K. Burgoon is professor in the Department of Communication, University of Arizona at Tucson.

Nancy A. Burrell is visiting lecturer in the Department of Communication at the University of Wisconsin, Milwaukee.

Dudley D. Cahn is professor in the Department of Communication, State University of New York at New Paltz.

Denise H. Cloven is a graduate student in the Department of Communication Studies, Northwestern University at Evanston, IL.

Paul de Mesquita is assistant professor in the Department of Educational and Counseling Psychology, College of Education, University of Kentucky at Lexington.

Mary Anne Fitzpatrick is professor and director of the Center for Communication Research in the Department of Communication Arts, the University of Wisconsin at Madison.

Gary Fontaine is associate professor in the Department of Communication, the University of Hawaii at Honolulu.

Jonathan G. Healey is a graduate student in the Department of Rhetoric and Communication, University of California at Davis.

Deborah A. Newton is assistant professor, Department of Communication, University of Arizona.

Rory Remer is associate professor in the Department of Educational and Counseling Psychology, College of Education, University of Kentucky at Lexington.

Michael E. Roloff is professor in the Department of Communication Studies, Northwestern University at Evanston, IL.

Dolf Zillmann is professor of communication and psychology and the associate dean for Graduate Studies and Research at the University of Alabama in Tuscaloosa.

Preface

After going through a period where it lacked differentiation, the field of interpersonal communication found a home in the study of relationship of growth and dissolution in books like Mark Knapp's (1984) *Interpersonal Communication and Human Relationships* and Don Cushman and Dudley Cahn's (1984) *Communication in Interpersonal Relationships*. Although a case has been made for the connection between interpersonal communication and human relationships, where does the field go from here? Although there are useful books of readings on interpersonal communication in general, there is a need for academic works that deal with specific problems such as conflict in interpersonal relationships.

Of the many books on the subject of conflict that take a communication perspective several works come to mind. In 1973, Fred E. Jandt wrote *Conflict Resolution Through Communication*, and, in 1974, Gerald R. Miller and Herbert W. Simons edited *Perspectives on Communication in Social Conflict*, which contains chapters written by communication scholars. More recently, Joseph Foger and Marshall S. Poole's (1984) *Working Through Conflict: A Communication Perspective*, Joyce L. Hocker and William W. Wilmot's (1985) *Interpersonal Conflict*, and Jandt's (1985) *Win—Win Negotiating: Turning Conflict into Agreement* identify general principles that may apply to a variety of different interpersonal relationships. However, due to the unique features of close, personal relationships, there is a need for a book that focuses specifically on interpersonal conflict in intimate relationships.

There is also a need to take an interdisciplinary approach and to add to the increasing dialogue between communication scientists and researchers in related fields who share an interest in this important subject. A vast number of empirical studies have been conducted in this decade alone and are reported in dozens of speech, communication, psychology, sociology, family studies, and other behavioral science journals. There is a need to synthesize these studies, identify key issues, and offer well-conceived empirical studies that clarify or advance understanding of these issues. Moreover, there are research camps that adhere to particular theories that need to be compared and contrasted. Finally, the subject needs re-examination by experts in the area to gain new insights.

Defining conflict as interaction between intimate partners expressing opposing interests, views, or opinions, *Intimates in Conflict* focuses on a form of communication that has an important role in the development and dissolution of intimate relationships. This edited book is intended to move forward the field of interpersonal communication theory and research in an important area of academic specialization. The work should appeal to current and new programs of research on interpersonal conflict in intimate relationships.

Primarily, the intended audience for this book consists of upper classmen, graduate students, teachers, social scientists, and clinical practitioners who are interested in interpersonal relationship growth and deterioration, intimacy, male–female communication, interpersonal communication, and conflict. The book is written from the viewpoint of the scholar–researcher and is designed to cross disciplines within the social sciences. Intended as required for courses on conflict in intimate relationships, the book should also work well as outside reading for advanced courses in interpersonal communication, male–female communication, marital communication, and conflict resolution. For example, newly developing courses in "advanced interpersonal communication" are finding few options available for higher level textbooks. The book is organized in such a way so that some chapters are more useful in some courses than others, but taken together the book should provide a useful collection for a variety of courses where intimacy or conflict is of interest.

Second, the book should also interest adult lay readers who were social science college graduates and are interested in improving their relationships or helping others. Third, because the area has experienced a great deal of activity especially during the past 10 years, the book's examination may also be of use to scholars who are interested in interpersonal conflict in other types of relationships.

Each chapter includes at least one author who has distinguished him or herself in a particular line of research that is now applied to conflict in close interpersonal relationships. By combining these contributions into a single volume, I hope to appeal to the scholar's practical and applied interests as well as theoretical and empirical.

In chapter 1, Dudley Cahn reviews a number of social science studies on conflict and methods for dealing with it. Given his definition of intimate relationships, intimates may be same- or opposite-sex close friends as well as lovers and mates. His review shows, however, that most of the research has been on married couples. In addition, his review shows that there is a great deal of interest in conflict management as well as conflict resolution.

Following the introductory chapter that reviews the literature, this book attempts to advance contemporary thinking on conflict management in Part I and conflict resolution in Part II. *Conflict management* refers to alternative ways of dealing with conflict, including sometimes avoiding it altogether. Believing that confrontation is not always necessary, useful, or beneficial, theorists suggest that conflict may be handled through a variety of coping mechanisms which in turn may be functional or dysfunctional. In chapter 2, to improve on present-day measures of responses to dissatisfying relationships, Jonathan Healey and Robert Bell examine the usefulness of Rusbult's four alternatives to conflict: exit, voice, loyalty, and partner neglect. Their work is particularly useful in the study of close friends in conflict. Roloff and Cloven, in chapter 3, report a study of dating couples in which they show how available alternatives and lack of commitment encourage intimates to avoid dealing with conflicts.

The alternatives that exist for managing conflict may be extended to the interaction itself. Deborah Newton and Judee Burgoon report a study in chapter 4 in which nonverbal behaviors were used to soften the impact of verbal conflicts among couples married or living together. In chapter 5, Janet Alberts describes how couples married or living together use humor to manage their interpersonal conflicts. Although it is generally believed that social networks influence the choice among alternatives to conflict, Jonathan Healey and Robert Bell question the role of social networks when conflicts occur among close friends in chapter 6.

Part II focuses on the idea that sometimes confrontation is desireable. The term *conflict resolution* is oriented toward the value of confrontation and bringing it successfully to an end. Because the relationship is a primary concern in intimate conflict, chapter 7 is devoted to a method for identifying verbal and nonverbal interpersonal communication behavior that produces perceived understanding and promotes relationship growth between intimates. Examining the psychological reality of spouses and how marital schema influence marital conflict, Nancy Burrell and Mary Anne Fitzpatrick describe interventionist strategies for helping couples adjust to their marriages in chapter 8. Dolf Zillmann, in chapter 9, presents a model of the interdependence of cognitive and excitatory processes in acute emotional conflict to shed insight into the escalation of conflict from rather trivial disagreements to destructive and sometimes violent behaviors and suggests ways to resolve conflicts that potentially involve serious emotional outbursts.

How do different cultural backgrounds complicate a couple's resolution of interpersonal conflict? Gary Fontaine, in chapter 10, describes methods for creating mutual or shared perspectives in intercultural couples. Finally, in chapter 11, Rory Remer and Paul de Mesquita describe a confrontation process complete with techniques for teaching and learning confrontation skills.

By examining the process of conflict itself, common alternatives to it, and its resolution through theory, supporting research, and applications, the editor and contributing authors intend this treatment to be comprehensive, suggestive, and useful. *Intimates in Conflict* promises a better understanding of an important event in everyday communication.

ACKNOWLEDGMENTS

I express my thanks to colleagues, especially Drs. Donald Cushman, Steve Duck, and Mark Knapp, for taking the time to discuss with me the initial ideas on which this book is based. I acknowledge the contributing authors' unwavering faith, cooperation at meeting deadlines, and endeavor to apply their knowledge and expertise to the study of conflict in intimate relationships. To the Communication Series editors, Drs. Dolf Zillmann and Jennings Bryant, and the editors at Lawrence Erlbaum Associates, particularly Jack Burton, I express appreciation for their support, encouragement, helpful suggestions, and efficient handling of reviews, editing of the manuscript, and publishing of the book. To David Bradler, I acknowledge his assistance in preparation of the author index. To the loved ones of the contributing authors and myself, I extend my thanks for their understanding, patience, help, and emotional support as we toiled to make this book a reality.

REFERENCES

Cushman, D. P., & Cahn, D. D. (1984). *Communication in interpersonal relationships.* Albany, NY: State University of New York Press.
Foger, J., & Poole, M. S. (1984). *Working through conflict: A communication perspective.* Glenview, IL: Scott, Foresman.
Hocker, J. L., & Wilmot, W. W. (1985). *Interpersonal conflict.* Dubuque, IA: Wm. C. Brown.
Jandt, F. E. (Ed.). (1973). *Conflict resolution through communication.* New York: Harper & Row.

Jandt, F. E. (1985). *Win–win negotiating: Turning conflict into agreement.* New York: Wiley.

Knapp, M. L. (1984). *Interpersonal communication and human relationships.* Boston, MA: Allyn & Bacon.

Miller, G. R., & Simons, H. W. (Eds.). (1974). *Perspectives on communication in social conflict.* Englewood Cliffs, NJ: Prentice-Hall.

Intimates in Conflict: A Research Review

Dudley D. Cahn
State University of New York at New Paltz

Although a great deal of research has been conducted in each of the subjects of interpersonal communication, intimate relationships, and interpersonal conflict, some researchers have chosen to concentrate on the intersection of these subjects because of its practical importance and common occurrence in everyday life. As much as intimates might like to avoid it, they often experience interpersonal conflict. *Intimacy* is by definition a close personal relationship in which two persons are mutually dependent and engaged in joint actions (Braiker & Kelley, 1979). Research reveals that intimate couples are more likely than acquaintances to experience frequent and intense disagreements.

According to Bell and Blakeney (1977), *interpersonal conflict* may be defined as interaction between persons expressing opposing interests, views, or opinions. This definition identifies interpersonal conflict as a form of human communication.

Interpersonal conflict between intimate partners goes beyond differences regarding a specific problem, issue, or argument because of the emotional nature of their relationship. Couples who experience more frequent and severe interpersonal conflicts tend to be more unhappy and dissatisfied than couples who engage in fewer and less severe conflicts.

Alternatives to constructive conflict management are detrimental for several reasons (Barry, 1970). First, they create stress. Unresolved conflicts leave couples unhappy, doubting, and irritated (Duck, 1988; Lloyd & Cate, 1985). Moreover, according to Rusbult, Johnson, and Morrow (1986), exiting from the relationship and partner neglect are destructive problem-solving responses and were more powerfully predictive of couple distress than are giving voice to problems and passive loyalty.

Second, alternatives to constructive conflict management make matters worse. For example, conflict is negatively related to feelings of love during relational dissolution (Braiker & Kelley, 1979; Canary & Spitzberg, 1989; Lloyd & Cate, 1985). Moreover, Schafer, Braito, and Bohlen (1976) found that marital conflicts and tensions contribute to a lack of self-concept support and accurate role-taking.

It is also common for negative acts from one partner to be reciprocated by negative acts from the other. In both distressed and nondistressed couples, negative communication behavior is more likely to be reciprocated than positive (Gottman, Markman, & Notarius, 1977; Margolin & Wampold, 1981; Wills, Weiss, & Patterson, 1974). Of course, there is greater negative reciprocity for dissatisfied couples than for happy ones (Gottman, 1982a, 1982b; Margolin & Wampold, 1981; Pike & Sillars, 1985).

Because destructive conflict behavior may harm intimate relationships, it is important to better understand interpersonal conflict. Numerous studies by empirical researchers and counselors appearing in several related disciplines, especially in psychology, communication, and family studies, have attempted to answer the question: What are the bases, processes, and outcomes of interpersonal conflict in intimate relationships? The problem is that these different lines of research lack coordination. Some studies merely duplicate those in other fields. Some are undertaken without awareness that the same questions are being asked in related disciplines and therefore do not benefit from insights and progress being made there. Even in cases where researchers in different disciplines attempt to answer some of the same questions using experimental methodology, each researcher deals with a discipline's unique issues and writes in its jargon.

There is a need for a review that pulls together loose ends as a step toward building a consensus among social scientists. Although reviews exist on each of the subjects of interpersonal communication, intimate relationships, and conflict, there is no comprehensive review of empirical studies on interpersonal conflict in intimate relationships. By examining research on intimates in conflicts, a review may provide an answer to the question, "Where do researchers go from here?"

In keeping with this book's purpose to cut across the social sciences in the study of intimates in conflict, this chapter interrelates the empirical findings of numerous studies in a way that charts progress toward answering the following basic questions: What is unique about conflict in intimate relationships? How might intimate conflicts be classified? What are the bases of destructive conflict between intimates? In the final section, answers to these questions lead to a discussion of the implications of past empirical findings for future research.

WHAT IS UNIQUE ABOUT CONFLICT
IN INTIMATE RELATIONSHIPS?

Conflict As a Process

Different theorists argue that interpersonal conflict is a process consisting of three stages. According to Gottman (1982a, 1982b), distressed couples appear to respond verbally with complaints and criticism in the first phase and nonverbally with hostile behaviors in the second phase. In the third phase, distressed couples find it difficult to agree on a solution.

Another three-stage process is proposed by Coombs (1987). First, *potential* interpersonal conflict is experienced within a person when faced with a choice between two or more incompatible options or goals (Type I). Second, the interpersonal conflict becomes an *actuality* when interaction reveals that the partners want different things, but they think that these differences can be resolved (Type II). Third, the conflict becomes *more serious* when the parties perceive that there is no mutually acceptable outcome and unwanted sacrifices must be made for resolving their differences (Type III). At the third level, self-interests usually replace mutual interests; there are winners and losers; and exercises of power likely dominate the process. For intimates, this stage of the conflict process may significantly alter or even destroy the nature of the relationship. Coombs observed that self-interest drives the individual from Type II to Type III levels, whereas common interest drives a couple from Type III level to Type II or I.

Multidimensionality

Research indicates that the conflict process is multidimensional. Argyle and Furnham (1983) reported that conflict between intimates and nonintimates consists of emotional conflict and criticism factors.

Emotional Conflict. This conflict, which is greater in more intimate relationships, consists of competing for attention/affection and control as well as conflict over money/possessions, beliefs/values, independence from each other, emotional help and support, normal daily activity, and being able to understand and empathize with each other.

Criticism. This factor, based primarily on problems with the partner's behaviors, includes a concern that the other is behaving unwisely, conflict over each other's habits and lifestyle, and not being able to discuss personal problems.

According to Argyle and Furnham, these factors are greater in intimate than in nonintimate relationships.

The emotional and critical dimensions of conflict pertain to three different lines of research on intimate partners. Lewis and Spanier (1979) showed that marital happiness and interaction form one dimension of marital quality, whereas a separate dimension included three intimate conflict subgroups—on-going marital problems, specific disagreements, and marital instability. When studying the dimensions of marital quality, Johnson, White, Edwards, and Booth (1986) discovered three intimate conflict factors: (a) the amount and severity of conflict between the spouses, (b) the extent to which personal traits and behaviors of either spouse has led to problems in the marriage, and (c) the views and behaviors directed toward termination of the marriage. Thus, it appears that interpersonal conflict between intimates is a multidimensional construct consisting of emotional and critical aspects of specific disagreements, on-going problems, and changing intimate relations.

Levels of Conflict

Interpersonal conflicts also occur at different levels depending on the topic (Braiker & Kelley, 1979).

Behavioral Conflicts (Level 1).   These conflicts include conflict over specific behaviors, such as different preferences for popular music, current arts entertainment and dance, discussion topics, recreational activities, and sexual behaviors.

Normative Conflicts (Level 2).   Involved here are conflicts over the unique norms and rules of the relationship such as different preferences for household duties, economic-support responsibilities, and authority relations between partners.

Personal Conflicts (Level 3).   Level 3 conflicts concern a partner's characteristics, dispositions, and attitudes including life values, selfishness, inconsiderateness, and affectional relations.

Of course not all conflicts are limited to only one level. For example, problems like excessive drinking and sexual promiscuity can relate to all three levels. In addition to these three levels of conflicts, couples describe a fourth (the *conflict process* itself), the necessity of resolving metaconflicts about how to deal with conflicts at lower levels. At this level, arguments are about the partner being argumentative, critical, nagging, complaining, quick-tempered, or oversensitive (Braiker & Kelley, 1979).

These categories of conflict actually represent levels because there is a tendency for individuals to raise conflict to higher levels than seemingly justified. For example, when specific behaviors are actually "the problem," partners tend to describe the problem at a higher level, namely at the normative or personal levels. This escalation to higher levels may have incentive value. Where criticism of specific behaviors may not achieve results, expressed disagreement on relationship rules and personality are more likely to get the partner's attention. Thus, conflict at higher levels may motivate constructive work on the problems that exist at a lower level.

In summary, intimate conflict is an emotional and critical process consisting of specific disagreements, on-going problems, and/or relationship instability involving different levels. The complex nature of intimate conflict has resulted in three different types of research studies discussed next.

HOW MIGHT INTIMATE CONFLICTS BE CLASSIFIED?

Across a wide diversity of studies, intimate interpersonal conflicts are of three different sorts that may be grouped according to the nature of the type of communication involved.

Specific Disagreements. Some researchers focus on a specific communication act or interaction, namely, an argument over a particular issue. Sometimes this disagreement is referred to as a difference of opinion or view, a complaint, criticism, hostile/coercive response, defensive behavior, or unpleasant action. In any case, a couple overtly disagrees on some issue.

Problem-Solving Discussion. Other researchers focus on a more encompassing communication situation known as a negotiation or bargaining session or problem solving discussion that may deal with an on-going problem—consisting of more than one conflicting issue.

Unhappy/Dissolving Relationships. Finally, still other researchers study the general pattern of communication characteristic of dysfunctioning couples, stormy marriages, and couples who report that they are unhappy, dissatisfied, maladjusted, or seeking counseling.

Although research on intimate interpersonal conflict frequently makes clear which of these types of conflicting couples are being studied making classification straightforward, many studies examine different ways these couples respond as alternatives for dealing with conflict. The problem is that, without comparisons across these studies, one is easily confused by the many options available to intimates presented in the literature. It is helpful to know that each type of conflict varies in degree and complexity (Weingarten & Leas, 1987) and that different alternatives exist for different degrees and complexities of conflict.

Specific Disagreements

Couples of the first type of conflict have a specific disagreement. According to Weingarten and Leas (1987), although real differences exist and relational tensions stem from the fact that people perceive their goals, needs, action plans, values, and so on to be conflicting, most conflict of this type does not threaten a relationship. Anger when it is expressed is short-lived. Frequently, these couples are able to work through their differences without the help of a third party.

What specific acts function as alternatives when partners disagree with each other about a particular issue? Obviously, they may ignore one another or resort to physical abuse, but if they choose to argue with one another what are their options? Utilizing Kipnis' (1976) Interpersonal Conflict Scale, Fitzpatrick and Winke (1979) surveyed single and married subjects' uses of communication tactics in their relationships. They found that the more favorable strategy of empathic understanding was not as popular as the alternative negative strategies. In opposite-sex relationships, respondents who showed the most commitment to the relationship (i.e., the married ones) indicated that they were more likely to use the strategies of emotional appeal or personal rejection to gain their own way. Those who indicated the least involvement in the relationship were more likely to use the strategies of manipulation and non-negotiation. In any case, when confronted with conflict, partners were most likely to resort to more negative strategies for dealing with interpersonal conflict. To avoid escalation to more serious conflict stages, couples need to rely more on empathic understanding.

Problem-Solving Discussion

Whereas a single issue is at stake with the first type of conflict, the next type involves several issues, although they may be reduced to a single complex problem. Weingarten and Leas (1987) pointed out that partners may be motivated more by a need for self-protection than they are by a need to solve particular problems. Or, more seriously, they may be motivated by a power motive where "winning" becomes the key dynamic of the conflict. The emotional climate is one of frustration and resentment, and anger erupts easily often over trivial matters and usually dissipates slowly. Although the partners feel ambivalent about the personal compromises they perceive are required, they would like to resolve their differences, but do not know how. For this type, although real differences often exist, an interpersonal communication problem usually exists as well. Improving communication can make it easier to solve the real problems and to negotiate differences. Presumably, for this type, education, training, or counseling are needed to help couples develop constructive communication attitudes and problem solving skills.

What specific acts function as alternatives when partners experience *problems* of the second type? For this type of conflict, partners may: (a) *compete–force* (argue the strongest), (b) *accommodate–smooth* over (give in), (c) *avoid–withdrawal* (not argue or deal with the issue), (d) *compromise* (wheel-and-deal; give and take), and (e) *collaborate–confront* to reach a mutually satisfying solution (Bell & Blakeney, 1977; Blake & Mouton, 1964; Thomas & Kilmann, 1974).

Fitzpatrick (1988) examined couples' interactions for examples of conflict avoidance, accommodating, collaborating, and competing strategies for managing conflict and found that "traditional couples" were more cooperative and conciliatory and engaged in avoidance more than they claimed, "independent couples" tended to be more confrontative, and "separate couples" were more likely to engage in hostile acts and avoidance. Ideally, these couples should work toward identifying mutually satisfying (i.e., "win–win") as opposed to more frequent individually satisfying (i.e., "win–lose") agreements.

Unhappy (Dissolving) Relationships

Couples experiencing the third type of conflict have had it with one another. Outsiders, friends, or lovers are enlisted, not in support of the relationship, but as an alternative to it. Weingarten and Leas (1987) claimed that these couples are known for their willingness to hurt one another and view defeat of the partner as more important than either winning issues or solving particular problems. They may become physically violent. The emotional climate ranges from one of alienation and antagonism to one charged with volatility, rage, and hopelessness. No reconciliation is possible until the intensity of the conflict is reduced through therapy, or steps toward disengagement are taken.

For the third type of conflict, what general categories of acts function as alternatives when a marriage or serious long-term relationship is in

serious trouble? Rusbult and Zembrodt (1983) discussed four characteristic reactions:

Exit, actively ending the relationship, destroying the relationship.

Voice, actively and constructively expressing dissatisfaction, with the
intent of improving conditions.

Loyalty, remaining passively loyal to the relationship.

Neglect, ignoring the partner, spending less time together, allowing
the relationship to atrophy.

These behaviors vary in destructiveness (Rusbult et al., 1986). Exit and
neglect are destructive, whereas voice and loyalty are constructive. In
comparison with men, women engage in somewhat higher levels of voice
and loyalty and may behave less neglectfully.

Other researchers have found four types of conflicts and outcomes.
As part of a study of fertility decision making, Rands, Levinger, and
Mellinger (1981) asked 244 California married couples to respond to
questions about the kinds of conflicts they encountered, their conflict
style, their expected outcome of the conflict, and their marital satisfaction. Four main ways of dealing with interpersonal conflict were found
that varied along dimensions of aggressiveness and intimacy. The four
patterns were:

1. a nonintimate-aggressive pattern, about 30% of the sample, least
   satisfying especially when the partner is seen as uncompromising,
2. a nonintimate-nonaggressive one, about 20% of the sample,
3. an intimate-aggressive pattern, about 20% of the total,
4. an intimate-nonaggressive one, about 30% of the sample, which
   couples found the most satisfying.

In the second subtype, some spouses appeared to tolerate their relationship rather well, even though it was unexciting. For some of the spouses
in the third subtype who achieved intimacy after a confrontation, spouses'
high intimacy seemed to counteract their attacking behavior. The researchers found that perceptions of conflict outcome varied from one
extreme in which there was less intimacy following the conflict and the
other in which the spouses felt closer, understood each other better, had
fun making up, and tended to compromise. It is useful to note that Rands
et al. (1981) observed that 30% of the couples in their study tended to
select less intimate and more aggressive ways of dealing with conflict
situations that resulted in less satisfaction.

Finally, Cahn (1987) has observed that couples may continue, repair, renegotiate, or disengage from an intimate relationship depending on four factors: relationship (dis)satisfaction, availability of more desirable alternatives, size of investments in the relationship, and social system constraints (family, friends, boss, etc.). Couples may ignore or tolerate problems in their relationship due to investments and social system constraints, engage in outside affairs rather than improve their primary relationships, or disengage without attempting to resolve the problems.

In many cases, partners experiencing the third type of conflict (unhappy relationship) are better off separated at least temporarily while individuals undergo therapy and job training. Helping individuals gain control over their own lives and enlarging their perceived arena of independent choice seems both to lessen the dependency that underlies their tolerance of abuse or dissatisfaction and to diminish their need to oppress others. If partners learn to exist on their own, they may then choose to work on their relationship or end it.

Thus, studies of intimate interpersonal conflict may be classified as dealing with different communication patterns, namely, specific verbal disagreements, problem-solving discussions, or unhappy (dissolving) relationships. Each line of research has its own alternatives, some more destructive than others. Interestingly, research shows that couples are more likely to resort to destructive alternatives than choose constructive ones. The reason for the popularity of more destructive approaches is the subject of the next section.

Interrelationship Among Types of Conflict

Often times, the three types of conflict studies (specific disagreements, problem-solving discussions, and unhappy relationships) are interrelated. Rausch, Barry, Hertel, and Swain (1974) observed husbands in unhappy marriages and determined that they used more coercive strategies and fewer reconciling acts in response to coercive strategies. Unhappy couples were found to be more coercive and less cognitive in their disagreements and conflict discussions (Billings, 1979). Meanwhile, Fitzpatrick (1988) and Pike and Sillars (1985) discovered that more satisfied couples used conflict avoidance to a greater extent than did the dissatisfied couples.

Moreover, dissatisfied couples appear to engage in particular destructive communication behaviors when engaging in specific disagreements. Studying satisfied and dissatisfied couples, Gottman (1979) found that unhappy couples were more likely to engage in cross-complaining sequences and less likely to engage in validation sequences. According to

Ting-Toomey (1983), partners may choose among the following alternatives that may be classified as disintegrative or integrative.
Disintegrative communication options are as follows:

Confronting directly attacks, criticizes, or negatively evaluates the other's feelings/ideas, and consists of negative evaluations, loaded questions, and direct rejection.

Complaining discloses discontent and resentment through indirect
strategies of blame aimed at the other, a third party, and/or the situation.

Defending persists in clarifying one's own position in spite of other's
feelings/ideas and involves justifying one's own actions, those of others,
and/or the situation.

Integrative communication options are as follows:

Confirming reveals one's understanding of the situation and openly
conveys acknowledgment, empathy and/or acceptance of partner's
feelings/ideas.

Socioemotional description refers to descriptive statements made in a
leveling manner.

Instrumental questioning consists of task-oriented questions for factual
information or further elaboration.

Ideally, intimate partners who value their relationship should argue
in a way that contributes to integration of the relationship and avoid
statements and nonverbal communications that lead to disintegration,
but unfortunately the latter course is the more common. According to
Ting-Toomey, marital partners typically begin a conflict in a manner
directly attacking one another with criticism and negatively loaded statements, followed by attempts to justify oneself and blame the other.
    Although the research just described on destructive communication
behavior during specific disagreements has not established a causal link
with relationship dissatisfaction, it is known that conflict escalates. Thus,
it might be argued that partners may start out with specific disagreements
that may lead to problem solving discussions and may terminate in unhappy relationships. Rands et al. (1981) described a nonintimate-aggressive pattern that escalates to include other issues. Once hostility is expressed by either partner, Gaelick, Bodenhausen, and Wyer (1985)
showed that it is likely to escalate in frequency over the course of the
interaction. Similarly, Menaghan (1982) linked the level of problems to
the choice of coping efforts suggesting a worsening spiral. She concluded

that as problems mount, typical coping choices may actually exacerbate distress and relationship problems.

WHAT ARE THE BASES OF DESTRUCTIVE
CONFLICT BETWEEN INTIMATES?

Although there may be many more bases for intimate conflict, recent empirical investigation has focused on two types, psychological variables that should be included in research on conflict and social contexts in which conflicts occur. The psychological variables include romantic involvement, relationship dissatisfaction, gender and sex type, and personality. These psychological variables are discussed here.

Psychological Factors

Romantic Involvement. Ironically, one of the bases for destructive conflict styles is the nature of the intimate relationship itself, namely, the romantic, passionate dimension. Fry, Firestone, and Williams (1983) assessed the influence of romantic involvement on the integrative bargaining of dating couples. The bargaining process and outcomes of 74 dating couples was compared with that of 32 mixed-sex stranger pairs. Although the stranger dyads indicated zero romantic involvement, dating couples were distributed over a broad range of degrees of romantic feelings for their partners. Romantic involvement was found to detract from the dyad's ability to discover mutually advantageous outcomes.

Relationship Dissatisfaction. Much of the research on destructive interpersonal conflict uses couples seeking counseling. Such couples are usually functioning at low levels; they are often unhappy, dissatisfied, maladjusted, distressed, or unstable.

Genshaft (1980) found that distressed couples are more defensive than nondistressed. Birchler, Weiss, and Vincent (1975) obtained data that showed that distressed couples engaged in fewer positive and more negatives during casual conversation and problem solving than did nondistressed couples. Gottman et al. (1977) observed that distressed couples were likely to begin a discussion by cross-complaining, followed by negative exchanges without ending with a contract sequence. Rands et al. (1981) discovered a nonintimate-aggressive pattern. Margolin and Wampold (1981) reported less problem solving, and more verbal and nonverbal negative behaviors in distressed couples than in nondistressed, although there were male–female differences in communication conflict patterns (Margolin & Wampold, 1981). According to Ting-Toomey (1983), low marital adjustment interaction was mainly characterized by unique reciprocal patterns of confront → confront, confront → defend, complain → defend, and defend → complain verbal interacts.

Gender and Sex Differences.   Barry (1970) investigated the health of spouses' personalities and found that the husband's personality was a greater factor in a happy marriage than the wife's. The "healthier" the husband's personality, the more capable he is of being emotionally supportive of his wife and thus less likely to engage in severe and destructive conflict. Belsky, Lang, and Rovine (1985) observed that the decline of marital quality during the first 6 months is worse for wives than for husbands. Women experience negative relationships between length of marriage, elation, and absence of anxiety (Mathes & Wise, 1983). Negative affect reciprocity upsets husbands more than wives who appear to want a response to the expressions of their negative feelings. As Levenson and Gottman (1985) reported, martial satisfaction declines most when husbands do *not* reciprocate their wives' negative affect, and when wives *do* reciprocate their husbands' negative affect.

Sex differences in perception and interpretation may function as another source of conflict in intimate relationships. Men (and not women) tend to interpret their female partners' lack of love expression as an indication of hostility, whereas women (not men) tend to interpret their male partner's lack of hostility as an indication of love (Gaelick et al., 1985). According to White (1985), wives tend to perceive much more agreement than husbands despite the actual state of affairs.

For males, the most salient aspect of conflict (in terms of relationship quality) is the stability of the conflict issue. Greater perceived stability of conflict issues is related to lower levels of love and commitment to the relationship. The more females bring up the same issue, the more the males want to disengage. For females the number of conflicts is most salient to the relationship quality (Lloyd, 1987).

Demands on women differ from those placed on men in intimate relationships. As a consequence of demands external to their marriage that are different for husbands and wives, men and women follow different paths of personal development that makes intimacy difficult later (Swensen, Eskew, & Kohlhepp, 1984). For example, according to Berryman-Fink and Brunner (1987), men are more likely than women to compete in conflicts, whereas women are more likely than men to use a compromising style. It should be noted that, conflict or not, sex-typed spouses (traditional man–woman roles) best understand each other, whereas undifferentiated mates least understand their spouses (Indvik & Fitzpatrick, 1982).

Women also differ from men in conflict communication behavior. Women disclose significantly more about their problems and tensions than do men (Burke, Weir, & Harrison, 1976). Gottman (1982a, 1982b) found that men are less responsive to negative affect from their spouses than women are. Levenson and Gottman (1985) found that men are more likely than women to withdraw and avoid conflicts. Moreover, women are more likely than men to offer accounts to their children for seeking divorce (Cushman & Cahn, 1986). Finally, women tend to reciprocate men's negative communication more than vice versa.

According to Hawkins, Weisberg, and Ray (1980), men and women differ in what they prefer from men in conflict communication. Women prefer less control, more openness, and more sharing of deep emotions than men do. Men prefer less conventional style expressions and more speculative and analytic behavior from women than women prefer to engage in. Also, men tend to value the instrumental dimension of a romantic relationship, while women value the affectional dimension (Rettig & Bubolz, 1983).

Personality. Personality variables are linked to the conflict management modes/styles of confronting, smoothing, and forcing.

Confronting: Exploring options, redefining problems, and finding productive solutions.

Smoothing: playing down the conflict or giving into the other to keep everyone happy.

Forcing: employing power; believing that victory goes to the strongest.

Achievement motivation was linked to confronting and aggression to forcing (Bell & Blakeney, 1977). Positive correlations were found between affiliation-smoothing, deference-forcing, succorance-smoothing, nurturing-smoothing, dogmatism-confronting, and Machiavellianism-confronting. Negative correlations were found for affiliation-forcing and Machiavellianism-smoothing (Jones & Melcher, 1982).

Individuals were found to be quite consistent in their conflict management styles or modes both within and across content domains, and the mode of conflict management could be predicted quite well from knowledge of certain intellectual and personality characteristics (Sternberg & Soriano, 1984). Moreover, strong consistencies in conflict management styles were observed by individuals across different situations, and at the same time, widespread differences were observed across individuals (Sternberg & Dobson, 1987). It should be noted, however, that although personality measures continued to correlate with the style/mode of conflict management, little association was found between preference for particular styles/modes and actual observed conflict behavior (Kabanoff, 1987).

If depression is viewed as a personality variable, Kahn, Coyne, and Margolin (1985) found that couples with depressed spouses engaged in more destructive problem-solving behavior than normal couples.

In addition to including psychological variables in studies of conflicts, researchers should also attend to the social contexts in which the conflicts occur. These social contexts are discussed next.

Social Contexts

Marital Stages. Some stages of a couple's marital career also act as an antecedent to conflict by making the relationship temporarily unhappy. Belsky et al. (1985) examined marital quality and found that it declines especially over the first 6 months after the wedding ceremony. Swensen et al. (1984) investigated changes in love and marital problems and found that younger married couples appeared to have more marriage problems than older couples. Also, in comparison to retired and middle-aged couples, younger couples had a comparatively intense engagement style of interaction, characterized by alternation between analytic confrontation and humorous remarks (Zietlow & Sillars, 1988).

Why should younger marriages have more problems than older marriages? In studies conducted by Burr (1972) and Miller (1976), children were shown to interfere with couples' companionship activities and reduce marital satisfaction. This was especially true for two working parents. Others have also reported that the more hours wives worked and the presence of school-age children in the family contributed significantly to marital instability, problems, and disagreements, (Johnson et al., 1986; Munro & Adams, 1978; Schumm & Bugaighis, 1985). Researchers reported, however, that the trend toward greater problems and decreasing marital satisfaction reverses itself in later years (Anderson, Russell, & Schumm, 1983).

Exceptions should not go unnoticed. In spite of a large literature that demonstrates correlations between the presence of children, marital problems, and relationship dissatisfaction, White and Booth (1985) found that the transition to parenthood did not seem to affect marital happiness, interaction, disagreements, or number of marital problems. The effects of children and working parents may depend more on the attitudes, needs, and goals of a couple. Some couples may find the presence of children or a working wife an added asset to the couple's relationship satisfaction, whereas others do not.

Low Family Strengths. Due to lack of family strengths, some couples are ill prepared to deal with conflicts (Birchler et al., 1975; MacKinnon, MacKinnon, & Franken, 1984). Compared to a high family strengths group identified by an empirical measure, the low family strengths group reported less satisfaction with the family and with the quality of life, health, home, time, financial well-being, and the overall quality of life. This group was more likely to acquire social support and resort to passive appraisal. It was also found to display lower scores on idealistic distortion, marital satisfaction, personality issues, *communication, conflict resolution,* financial management, leisure activities, sexual relations, children and marriage, family and friends, and religious orientation. Because past negotiations and outcomes provide the context for future renegotiations (Scanzoni & Polonko, 1980), couples may be ill equipped for constructively managing conflicts.

Power Differences. Power differences may precede conflicts and make them harder to resolve. The structure of decision-making power is significantly related to effective marital and family functioning. For example, wife-dominated partners are least satisfied; next is the husband-dominant group (Ting-Toomey, 1984). Men and women who are not equitably treated are less content in their marriages and perceive the marriage as more unstable than men and women in equitable marriages (Utne, Hatfield, Traupmann, & Greenberger, 1984). Relative to androgynous gender couples, couples with undifferentiated or dominant, aggressive partners reported the lowest relationship quality (Kurdek & Schmitt, 1986). However, in contrast to the commonly supported egalitarian finding, Kolb and Straus (1974) found that families above the median in husband-to-wife power tend to be high in marital happiness.

Unequal couples are more likely to want to dissolve than egalitarian partners. Hill, Rubin, and Peplau (1976) found that 54% of the unequal couples broke off their relationships within 2 years, where as only 23% of the equal couples were disengaged. In another study, 75% of those who under- or over-benefitted in their relationship disengaged from it, but only 25% of the equitable couples broke up (Cody, 1982). Again, not all studies support the egalitarian principle, however. According to Chafetz (1980), the more equal partners are to one another, the higher the rate of marital dissolution.

Cultural Difference and Social Changes. According to Cahn (1985), couples who have different cultural perspectives experience more frequent and intense interpersonal conflict than couples from the same culture. Moreover, Swensen and Trahaug (1985) reported that the move from "institutional" marriages (for convenience of society) to "intrinsic" marriages (based on love; for convenience of individuals) has increased marital satisfaction and decreased marital problems. However, Rausch et al. (1974) argued that this cultural swing has resulted in couples demanding more of their relationship than a comfortable stasis.

Consequently, among the factors researchers have identified as bases of interpersonal conflict are psychological variables of romantic involvement, unhappy or dissolving relationships, gender differences and sex type, personality variables, and social contexts such as some marital stages like younger marriages with children and working parents, lack of family strengths, power differences, cultural differences and social changes.

IMPLICATIONS FOR RESEARCH

According to the Braiker and Kelley's (1979) definition of intimate relationships, intimates may be same- or opposite-sex close friends as well as lovers and mates. A review shows, however, that most of the research has been on married couples. Thus, there is a need for more studies of close friends and lovers as well as mates. Moreover, following Bell and Blakeney (1977), this chapter identifies interpersonal conflict as a form of human communication—that is, interaction between persons expressing opposing interests, views, or opinions.

This chapter includes studies that extend research on conflict resolution and conflict management processes. The term *conflict resolution* is oriented toward the value of confrontation and bringing it successfully to an end. The term carries with it the idea that sometimes confrontation is desirable. This chapter suggests that conflict resolution is most useful in cases where relationships have broken down.

Conflict management, however, refers to alternative ways of dealing with conflict, including avoiding it altogether. This chapter suggests that, in newly formed or growing intimate relationships, the relationship itself may take precedence over resolving the conflict, so managing conflict is key rather than necessarily resolving it. Believing that confrontation is not always necessary, useful, or beneficial, theorists suggest that conflict may be handled through a variety of coping mechanisms that in turn may be further categorized as functional or dysfunctional.

Although the study of interpersonal conflict attempts to better understand an important element in the development of intimate relationships, the uncoordinated research efforts across disciplines has resulted in problems of generalizability and usefulness. One of the main sources of difficulty may be attributed to the different concepts of interpersonal conflict used by different researchers that lead to confusion over the nature of the communication processes involved.

Intimate interpersonal conflict may be fruitfully viewed as a communication process with multiple dimensions and levels. Typically, researchers categorize as conflict a wide range of phenomena that vary in seriousness, dimensionality, and levels. Researchers should determine more precisely the dimension and level in their study, limit their generalizations accordingly, and where possible compare and contrast their findings with other studies. Along these lines, some useful questions might be:

How does a couple keep a conflict from escalating to higher levels or stages?

How can the discovery of the dimensions of conflict (Argyle & Furnham, 1983) benefit research on interpersonal conflict?

How might couples be trained to avoid disintegrative communications and to use integrative communications (Ting-Toomey, 1983)?

How might couples be trained in constructive communication attitudes and skills that underlie successful problem-solving discussions (Weingarten & Leas, 1987)?

Conflicts may be usefully categorized according to one of three types of communication situations: (a) verbal disagreements, (b) problem-solving discussions, and (c) unhappy (dissolving) intimate relationships. Researchers need to clearly identify the type of conflict under examination, restrict their generalizations to that type, and compare/contrast their findings to those of the other types. For example, researchers have shown that unhappy relationships of the third type manifest particular patterns of negative communication and negotiation practices of the first and second types (Fitzpatrick, 1988; Gottman, 1979; Pike & Sillars, 1985; Rausch et al., 1974; Ting-Toomey, 1983). Other questions that might be asked are: (a) under what conditions do particular patterns of negative communication of the first type contribute to unhappy relationships of the third type? and (b) How do particular problem solving approaches of the second type result in unhappy relationships of the third type?

Future research should also give attention to conflict as a symptom of a problem and conflict as a cause of a problem. Interpersonal conflict may reflect factors that underlie dissatisfying relationships. In this case, both the relationship dissatisfaction and the interpersonal conflict are effects of deeper problems in an intimate relationship. For example, a couple may be both unhappy and argue frequently because a partner often wastes money on pornography. Meanwhile, interpersonal conflict may be the cause and differentiate happy from unhappy couples. For example, a couple may be dissatisfied because a partner is argumentative, quick-tempered, or oversensitive. Consequently, the following questions are in need of answers:

Are patterns of conflict as a cause and as an effect both equally destructive in intimate relationships?

Are negative patterns of conflict as a cause and as an effect similar?

There are many bases or antecedents to destructive conflict in intimate relationships, including romantic involvement, relationship (dis)satisfaction, gender differences and sex-type, and personality. Thus, researchers need to include these psychological variables in their experimental designs or restrict their generalizations accordingly. When collecting data from subjects, researchers should ask themselves:

How romantically (Fry et al., 1983) involved are the partners?

How satisfied (i.e., Ting-Toomey, 1983) with their intimate relationship are the partners?

Are the partners male or female? What psychological gender and sex type are they?

Are the partners' personality types identified as affiliation, succorance, and nurturing or are they identified more as deference, dogmatic, and machiavellian?

What are other personality variables that function as antecedents in intimate conflict?

Research shows that certain social contexts also function as antecedents and influence the nature of conflict, its bases, processes, and outcomes. Therefore, researchers need to compare/contrast subjects from different social contexts or restrict their generalizations accordingly. Some questions to keep in mind when collecting data from subjects include:

At what marital stage (i.e., Zietlow & Sillars, 1988) are the partners?

Are the partners as a unit high or low in family strengths (i.e., MacKinnon et al., 1984).

Are the intimate partners egalitarian in their relationship with each other, or are there significant power differences between them?

Are the partners from the same or different racial or ethnic groups in a country? Are they from the same cultural group as those in studies used for comparison?

Are the partners from the same time period or social era as those in studies used for comparison?

What are other social contexts that function as antecedents in intimate conflict?

REFERENCES

Anderson, S. A., Russell, C. S., & Schumm, W. R. (1983). Perceived marital quality and family life-cycle categories: A further analysis. *Journal of Marriage and the Family, 45,* 127–139.

Argyle, M., & Furnham, A. (1983). Sources of satisfaction and conflict in long term relationships. *Journal of Marriage and the Family, 45,* 481–93.

Barry, W. A. (1970). Marriage research and conflict: An integrative review. *Psychological Bulletin, 73,* 849–857.

Bell, E. C., & Blakeney, R. N. (1977). Personality correlates of conflict resolution modes. *Human Relations, 30,* 849–857.

Belsky, J., Lang, M. E., & Rovine, M. (1985). Stability and change in marriage across the transition to parenthood: A second study. *Journal of Marriage and the Family, 47,* 855–865.

Berryman-Fink, C., & Brunner, C. (1987), The effects of sex of source and target on interpersonal conflict management styles. *Southern Speech Communication Journal, 53,* 38–48.

Billings, A. (1979). Conflict resolution in distressed and nondistressed married couples. *Journal of Consulting and Clinical Psychology, 47,* 368–376.

Birchler, G. R., Weiss, R.L. & Vincent, J. P. (1975). Multimethod analysis of social reinforcement exchange between maritally distressed and nondistressed spouse and stranger dyads. *Journal of Personality and Social Psychology, 31,* 349–360.

Blake, R. R., & Mouton, J. S. (1964). *The managerial grid.* Houston, TX: Gulf.

Braiker, H. B., & Kelley, H. H. (1979). Conflict in the development of close relationships. In R. L. Burgess & T. L. Huston (Eds.) *Social exchange in developing relationships* (pp. 135–168). New York: Academic Press.

Burke, R. J., Weir, T., & Harrison, D. (1976). Disclosure of problems and tensions experienced by marital partners. *Psychological Reports, 38,* 531–542.

Burr, W. (1972). Satisfaction with various aspects of marriage over the life cycle: A random middle class sample. *Journal of Marriage and the Family, 32,* 29–37.

Cahn, D. (1985). Communication competence in the resolution of intercultural conflict. *World Communication, 14,* 85–94.

Cahn, D. (1987). *Letting go: A practical theory of relationship disengagement and reengagement.* Albany, NY: SUNY Press.

Canary, D. J., & Spitzberg, B. H. (1989). A model of the perceived competence of conflict strategies. *Human Communication Research, 15,* 630–649.

Chafetz, J. (1980). Conflict resolution in marriage: Toward a theory of spousal strategies and marital dissolution rates. *Journal of Family Issues, 1,* 397–421.

Cody, M. (1982). A typology of disengagement strategies and an examination of role intimacy, reactions to inequity, and relational problems play in strategy selection. *Communication Monographs, 49,* 148–170.

Coombs, C. H. (1987). The structure of conflict. *American Psychologist, 42,* 355–63.

Cushman, D. P., & Cahn, D. D. (1986). A study of communicative realignment between parents and children following the parents' decision to seek a divorce. *Communication Research Reports, 3,* 80–85.

Duck, S. (1988). *Relating to others.* Chicago: Dorsey.

Fitzpatrick, M. A. (1988). *Between husbands and wives: Communication in marriage.* Beverly Hills, CA: Sage.

Fitzpatrick, M. A., & Winke, J. (1979). You always hurt the one you love: Strategies and tactics in interpersonal conflict. *Communication Quarterly, 27,* 3–11.

Fry, W. R., Firestone, I. J., & Williams, D. L. (1983). Negotiation process and outcome of stranger dyads and dating couples: Do lovers lose? *Basic and Applied Social Psychology, 4,* 1–16.

Gaelick, L., Bodenhausen, G. V., & Wyer, R. S. (1985). Emotional communication in close relationships. *Journal of Personality and Social Psychology, 49,* 1246–1265.

Genshaft, J. L. (1980). Perceptual and defensive style variables in marital discord. *Social Behavior and Personality, 8,* 81–84.

Gottman, J. M. (1979). *Marital interaction: Experimental investigations.* New York: Academic Press.

Gottman, J. M. (1982a). Emotional responsiveness in marital conversations. *Journal of Communication, 16,* 108–119.

Gottman, J. M. (1982b). Temporal form: Toward a new language for describing relationships. *Journal of Marriage and the Family, 44,* 943–962.

Gottman, J. M., Markman, H., & Notarius, C. (1977). The topography of marital conflict: A sequential analysis of verbal and nonverbal behavior. *Journal of Marriage and the Family, 39,* 461–477.

Hawkins, J. L., Weisberg, C., & Ray, D. (1980). Spouse differences in communication style: Preference, perception, behavior. *Journal of Marriage and Family, 42,* 585–593.

Hill, C., Rubin, Z., & Peplau, L. (1976). Breakups before marriage: The end of 103 affairs. *Journal of Social Issues, 32,* 147–68.

Indvik, J., & Fitzpatrick, M. A. (1982). "If you could read my mind, love. . ." Understanding and misunderstanding in the marital dyad. *Family Relations, 31,* 43–51.

Johnson, D. R., White, L. K., Edwards, J. N., & Booth, A. (1986). Dimensions of marital quality. *Journal of Family Issues, 7,* 31–49.

Jones, R., & Melcher, B. (1982). Personality and the preference for modes of conflict resolution. *Human Relations, 35,* 649–658.

Kabanoff, B. (1987). Predictive validity of the MODE conflict instrument. *Journal of Applied Psychology, 72,* 160–163.

Kahn, J., Coyne, J. C., & Margolin, G. (1985). Depression and marital disagreement: The social construction of despair. *Journal of Social and Personal Relationships, 2,* 447–461.

Kipnis, D. (1976). *The power-holders.* New York: Academic Press.

Kolb, T., & Straus, M. (1974). Marital power and marital happiness in relation to problem-solving ability. *Journal of Marriage and the Family, 36*, 756–766.

Kurdek, L. A., & Schmitt, P. (1986). Interaction of sex role self-concept with relationship quality and relationship beliefs in married, heterosexual cohabiting, gay, and lesbian couples. *Journal of Personality and Social Psychology, 51*, 365–370.

Levenson, R. W., & Gottman, J. M. (1985). Physiological and affective predictors of change in relationship satisfaction. *Journal of Personality and Social Psychology, 49*, 85–94.

Lewis, R., & Spanier, g. (1979). Theorizing about the quality and stability of marriages. In W. Burr, R. Hill, F. Nye, & I. Reiss (Eds.), *Contemporary theories about the family* (pp. 268–94). New York: The Free Press.

Lloyd, S. A. (1987). Conflict in premarital relationships: Differential perceptions of males and females. *Family Relations, 36*, 290–294.

Lloyd, S. A., & Cate, R. M. (1985). The developmental course of conflict in dissolution of premarital relationships, *Journal of Social and Personal Relationships, 2*, 179–194.

MacKinnon, R., MacKinnon, C., & Franken, M. (1984). Family strengths in long-term marriages. *Lifestyles: A Journal of Changing Patterns, 7*, 115–126.

Margolin, G., & Wampold, B. (1981). Sequential analysis of conflict and accord in distressed and nondistressed marital patterns. *Journal of Consulting and Clinical Psychology, 49*, 554–567.

Mathes, E. W., & Wise, P. S. (1983). Romantic love and the ravages of time. *Psychological Reports, 52*, 839–846.

Menaghan, E. (1982). Measuring coping effectiveness: A panel analysis of marital problems and coping efforts. *Journal of Health and Social Behavior, 23*, 230–234.

Miller, B. C. (1976). A multivariate developmental model of marital satisfaction. *Journal of Marriage and the Family, 38*, 643–657.

Munro, B., & Adams, G. R. (1978). Love American style: A test of role structure theory on changes in attitudes toward love. *Human Relations, 3*, 215–228.

Pike, G., & Sillars, A. L. (1985). Reciprocity of marital communication. *Journal of Social and Personal Relationships, 2*, 303–324.

Rands, M., Levinger, G., & Mellinger, G. D. (1981). Patterns of conflict resolution and marital satisfaction. *Journal of Family Issues, 2*, 297–321.

Rausch, H., Barry, W. Hertel, R., & Swain, M. (1974). *Communication, conflict and marriage.* San Francisco, CA: Jossey-Bass.

Rettig, K. D., & Bubolz, M. M. (1983). Interpersonal resource exchanges as indicators of quality of marriage. *Journal of Marriage and the Family, 45*, 497–509.

Rusbult, C. E., Johnson, D. J., & Morrow, G. D. (1986). Impact of couple patterns of problem solving on distress and nondistress in dating relationships. *Journal of Personality and Social Psychology, 50*, 744–753.

Rusbult, C. E., & Zembrodt, I. M. (1983). Responses to dissatisfaction in romantic involvements: A multidimensional scaling analysis. *Journal of Experimental Social Psychology, 19*, 274–293.

Scanzoni, J., & Polonko, K. (1980). A conceptual approach to explicit marital negotiation. *Journal of Marriage and the Family, 42*, 31–43.

Schafer, R. Braito, R., & Bohlen, J. M. (1976). Self-concept and the reaction of a significant other: A comparison of husbands and wives. *Sociological Inquiry, 46*, 57–65.

Schumm, W. R., & Bugaighis, M. A. (1985). Marital quality over the marital career: Alternative Explanations. *Journal of Marriage and the Family, 48*, 165–168.

Sternberg, R. J., & Dobson, D. M. (1987). Resolving interpersonal conflicts: An analysis of stylistic consistency. *Journal of Personality and Social Psychology, 52*, 794–812.

Sternberg, R. J., & Soriano, L. J. (1984). Styles of conflict resolution. *Journal of Personal and Social Psychology, 47*, 115–126.

Swensen, C. H., Eskew, R. W., & Kohlhepp, K. A. (1984). Five factors in long-term marriages. *Lifestyles, 7*, 94–106.

Swensen, C. H., & Trahaug, G. (1985). Commitment and long-term marriage relationship. *Journal of Marriage and the Family, 47*, 939–945.

Thomas, K.W., & Kilmann, R. H. (1974). *Thomas-Kilmann conflict mode instrument.* Tuxedo, NY: Xicom.

Ting-Toomey, S. (1983). An analysis of verbal communication patterns in high and low marital adjustment groups. *Human Communication Research, 9*, 306–319.

Ting-Toomey, S. (1984). Perceived decision-making power and marital adjustment. *Communication Research Reports, 1*, 15–20.

Utne, M. K., Hatfield, E., Traupmann, J., & Greenberger, D. (1984). Equity, marital satisfaction, and stability. *Journal of Social and Personal Relationships, 1*, 323–332.

Weingarten, H., & Leas, S. (1987). Levels of marital conflict model: A guide to assessment and intervention in troubled marriages. *American Journal of Orthopsychiatry, 57*, 407–417.

White, J. M. (1985). Perceived similarity and understanding in married couples. *Journal of Social and Personal Relationships, 2*, 45–57.

White, L. K., & Booth, A. (1985). The transition to parenthood and marital quality. *Journal of Family Issues, 6*, 435–449.

Wills, T. A., Weiss, R. L., & Patterson, G. R. (1974). A behavioral analysis of the determinants of marital satisfaction. *Journal of Consulting and Clinical Psychology, 42*, 802–811.

Zietlow, P. H., & Sillars, A. L. (1988). Life-stage differences in communication during marital conflicts. *Journal of Social and Personal Relationships, 5*, 223–245.

I

CONFLICT MANAGEMENT: ALTERNATIVES TO CONFLICT

Assessing Alternative Responses to Conflicts in Friendship

Jonathan G. Healey
University of Southern California

Robert A. Bell
University of California, Davis

No matter how close we are to a friend, it is inevitable that he or she will occasionally say and do things that upset us. From forgotten birthdays to overt acts of hostility, distressing events occur in most, and probably all, close friendships. Given the countless ways in which friends can disappoint us, it is not surprising that we are frequently confronted with the task of dealing with conflicts in our friendships.

Although most disappointments and conflicts with friends are not serious enough to lead to a severing of ties, many friendships do end. The sad fact is that most of our intimates come into our lives, visit for a relatively small portion of our lifespan, and then move on (Johnson, 1982). Stueve and Gerson (1977), for example, found that very few of the friendships of male adolescents extend into adulthood and that young adults change their "best friends" very often. The high incidence of conflict among friends is illustrated by the investigation we report in this chapter. Over 300 persons were asked to describe a recent incident in which a friend disappointed them during the previous five-week period. Although the episodes described appear to have varied considerably in seriousness, *every* person was able to report such an event.

RESPONDING TO DISSATISFACTION WITH A CLOSE FRIEND

The great frequency with which problems arise between friends reflects, in part, the dialectical nature of human relationships (Stueve & Gerson, 1977). Baxter (1988) identified three contradictions in close relationships that virtually guarantee occasional disruptions in a friendship: autonomy–connection, novelty–predictability, and openness–closedness. The autonomy–connection dialectic is central to friendship because the development of a relationship requires the sacrifice of some independence. Although too much autonomy will dissolve the bond that connects friends, too little of it will disrupt the friendship by destroying individuals' identities. Rawlins (1983a) has vividly demonstrated how the task of balancing the vitally important but conflicting needs for autonomy and connection in friendship is extraordinarily difficult. The novelty–predictability dialectic also creates great potential for dissatisfaction in friendship. The establishment of predictability is a central goal in relationship development (Berger, 1987), but too much predictability can damage a relationship through repetitiveness, boredom, and tedium. Two individuals must negotiate those areas in which predictability is valued over spontaneity through an indirect process of trial and error that may be ridden with conflict. The openness–closedness dilemma highlights the opposing needs for open disclosures that cultivate intimacy and for privacy. Rawlins (1983b) has illustrated specific ways in which needs for openness and closedness may clash.

Of course, conflicts may emerge in friendships for reasons that have nothing to do with the paradoxical requirements of close relationships. For example, friends may do intolerable things, such as violate important friendship rules; the criteria used for selecting friends may change as one's interests and values evolve; a friend may be displaced by another who better meets one's needs or by a romantic relationship that interferes with the friendship; or a friend may be unable to provide support for one's self-concept (Argyle & Henderson, 1984; Bailey, Finney, & Helm, 1975; Cahn, 1987; Rose, 1984; Rose & Serafica, 1986). In short, dissatisfying events are an inherent feature on the typography of friendship.

The primary goal of our research, which is described in greater detail later, is to come to a better understanding of how friends respond to conflict in their relationships. Although much has been learned over the past few years about interpersonal conflict and relational maintenance, most studies have examined these topics within the context of premarital and marital heterosexual relationships. Surprisingly little is known about how friends deal with their differences. Just how do people deal with dissatisfaction with their friends? This question can be broken down into two more specific issues. First, from what kinds of responses does a person choose when he or she becomes dissatisfied with a friend? Second, what factors inspire his or her selection of a particular response over other courses of action?

We have looked for answers to the first question in the work of Rusbult and her colleagues (Rusbult, 1987). Rusbult's model of responses to conflicts in close relationships has received much empirical attention.

Unfortunately, her typology has been used only in studies of romantic relationships. Given the important differences between romantic and friendship bonds, such as the absence of an exclusivity expectation in friendship, we are hesitant to draw conclusions about conflict management in friendship on the basis of such research. Nevertheless, Rusbult's typology does offer a useful starting point for our investigation. We thus attempted to extend her typology beyond romantic relationships to friendships by developing measures of the responses to dissatisfaction she has identified that are relevant to friendships.

An answer to the second question requires a model for predicting how people will make strategic choices from among possible responses. Once again, we turned to Rusbult's work, more specifically to her Investment Theory, in our efforts to predict friends' responses (Rusbult, 1980a, 1980b, 1983). Although Rusbult's typology has not been examined within the context of friendship, Investment Theory has been so applied (Rusbult, 1980b). However, no investigation to date has attempted to *integrate* these two lines of work by accounting for the selection of responses to dissatisfaction via Investment Theory propositions within the context of friendship. The remainder of this section briefly reviews Rusbult's impressive program of research.

The Exit–Voice–Loyalty–Neglect Typology

When one encounters conflict with a friend, there are several responses upon which a course of action might be constructed. Rusbult and her colleagues classify these responses into the categories exit, voice, loyalty, and neglect (Rusbult, 1980a, 1987; Rusbult, Johnson, & Morrow, 1986; Rusbult, Zembrodt, & Gunn, 1982). *Exit* includes telling the partner that the relationship is over, threatening to end the relationship, thinking about terminating the bond, or drastically deescalating the relationship through minimization of communication. *Voice* refers to problem-solving responses in which one expresses concerns to the partner with the intent of improving the situation. *Loyalty* entails passively waiting for conditions to improve, with the hope that the relationship's quality can be restored. For instance, one might be silent about his or her dissatisfaction or avoid topics that are likely to lead to conflict. *Neglect* encompasses aversive actions that do not address the problem at hand, and thus allow the relationship to atrophy; examples include being uncooperative when the friend seeks to resolve problems, criticizing the other for things unrelated to the cause of the dissatisfaction, and spreading negative gossip about the friend.

As shown in Fig. 2.1, Rusbult and her colleagues believe that these responses can be differentiated along the dimensions constructive–destructive and active–passive. The first dimension discriminates voice and loyalty responses, which are intended to repair the relationship, from exit and neglect responses, which threaten the relationship. The active–passive dimension distinguishes exit and voice from loyalty and neglect. Exit and voice are active in that both involve taking actions that directly impact on the problem causing conflict. Loyalty and neglect are considered passive because each consists of responses that do not directly pertain to the problem. Rusbult and Zembrodt (1983) found that the constructive–destructive dimension may weigh more heavily on people's assessments of responses to dissatisfaction than the active–passive dimension.

In this chapter, Rusbult's classification system is used in lieu of other typologies that can be found in the communication literature for four reasons. First, the model is more parsimonious than many of the typologies advanced to date (e.g., Cody, 1982). Second, the model has a theoretical foundation in Investment Theory that has had considerable success in predicting people's behavior in close relationships. Third, the exit–voice–loyalty–neglect model assumes that individuals in such relationships can take both constructive and destructive courses of action, in sharp contrast to other typologies that have incorporated only termination responses to relational difficulties (e.g., Baxter, 1982; Cody, 1982; Miller & Parks, 1982). Fourth, each of the four responses is clearly communicative in nature.

Investment Theory

Given the many factors that can tear a relationship apart, just what is it that holds one together? The answer to this question is central to Rusbult's (1980a) Investment Theory. Although initially developed as a means

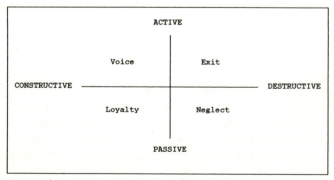

FIG. 2.1. Rusbult's typology of responses to dissatisfaction.

of describing satisfaction and commitment in romantic relationships, Investment Theory has demonstrated considerable heuristic value when applied to friendships (Rusbult, 1980b). The theory is based on several principles borrowed from Interdependence Theory (Thibaut & Kelley, 1959), which asserts that the essence of any relationship is resource exchange. When two friends interact they engage in behaviors that have consequences for each other. Positive consequences are *rewards,* whereas negative consequences can be considered *costs.* A person determines the value of the friendship by comparing it to two personal points of reference: *comparison level* and *alternative quality.* One's comparison level is the baseline of rewards, relative to costs, that he or she feels deserving of. A satisfying relationship is characterized by a reward–cost ratio that exceeds comparison-level expectations. Alternative quality defines the lowest level of outcomes a person will accept from the relationship in light of his or her beliefs about available alternative relationships.

Investment Theory builds on Interdependence Theory by distinguishing between *satisfaction* with a relationship and *commitment* to it. Satisfaction is based exclusively on the extent to which one's relationship has a reward–cost ratio that exceeds his or her comparison level. Although satisfaction is assumed to increase one's commitment to a relationship, satisfaction is only one of three determinants of commitment, according to the theory. In addition to satisfaction, commitment is assumed to result from low alternative quality and numerous investments in the relationship (Rusbult, 1980a). As an individual's investment size increases, commitment to the relationship also increases because severing the relationship results in a costly loss of many of these investments.

Integrating Investment Theory and the Exit–Voice–Loyalty–Neglect Model

Rusbult et al. (1982) have used Investment Theory to predict exit, voice, loyalty, and neglect responses with the variables satisfaction, alternative quality, and investment size in romantic attachments. They argued that satisfaction and investment size determine if a person will use a constructive response (i.e., voice and loyalty) or a destructive response (i.e., exit and neglect). Specifically, satisfaction should foster constructive responses to dissatisfaction and deter destructive actions because people will be motivated to preserve a relationship if it is rewarding. Likewise, the greater a person's investment size, the more likely he or she is to use constructive approaches in lieu of destructive ones in order to protect these investments. Thus, satisfaction and investment size should both be positively related to the use of voice and loyalty and inversely related to the use of exit and neglect. On the other hand, these scholars posited that alternative quality should determine if a person actively deals with the dissatisfaction or adopts a passive strategy. In essence, having alternatives to a relationship empowers a person ("I don't have to put up with you, so get your act together or we're through!"). Thus, having an attractive alternative should lead to an active response (i.e., voice or exit). When quality alternatives are not available, a passive tack of loyalty or neglect should be expected.

Application of Investment Theory to the exit–voice–loyalty–neglect model thus leads to the following predictions: (a) exit should be most likely when satisfaction and investment size are low and when alternative quality is high. (b) Voice should be expected when satisfaction, investment size, and alternative quality are all high. (c) Loyalty should be preferred when satisfaction and investment size are high and when alternative quality is low. (d) Neglect behaviors should be enacted when satisfaction, investment size, and alternative quality are all low. The findings of Rusbult et al. (1982) are consistent with these predictions for satisfaction and investment size. Furthermore, alternative quality does appear to encourage exiting, and deter loyalty responses. However, contrary to expectations, there was little relationship between alternative quality and the selection of voice or neglect reactions. It remains to be seen if these predictions hold for friendships.

Public Presentation of The Conflict

In addition to applying Rusbult's exit–voice–loyalty–neglect model and Investment Theory to conflicts between friends, we sought a better understanding of the extent to which friends in conflict collaborate to develop strategies for presenting their conflict and their relationship to other people. Many scholars have noted that intimates undergoing relationship troubles are often faced with the task of working out the social consequences of their problems (e.g., Duck, 1982; La Gaipa, 1982; McCall, 1982). Because it is often difficult to hide problems from mutual friends, two intimates in conflict may find it desirable to discuss the ways in which the situation will be presented to the network. They may hold discussions to construct accounts of the nature of the conflict that preserve both friends' integrity and promote the well-being of the network. If the conflict weakens or destroys the friendship, the two antagonists should be especially motivated to create a story that provides a background of understanding that allows network members to cope with the redefinition. Second, the individuals may collaborate to create rules of civility to guide the manner in which they will conduct their subsequent interactions when in the presence of mutual friends. To make possible the study of the presumed tendency of feuding friends to engage in such public relations activities, we attempted to develop measures of collaboration on accounts and collaboration on future interaction.

Beyond simply examining the degree to which friends in conflict collaborate in the construction of accounts and the negotiation of interaction rules, we also explored the relationships of these collaborative efforts to exit, voice, loyalty, and neglect. It was our expectation that collaboration on accounts and interaction rules, being essentially proactive, would accompany use of the active response of voice. After all, talking with one's friend about ways of resolving a conflict and talking with that person about ways to minimize the effects of the conflict on others reflects problem-solving orientations that should co-occur. We also expected positive relationships between the two collaboration variables and exit because a relationship on the verge of disengagement may have the most aversive impact on the larger social network—effects that must be managed. Negative correlations were expected between the two forms of collaboration and loyalty because it makes no sense for the person who does not wish to discuss a problem with his or her friend in hopes that it may go away by itself to be willing to talk with that individual about ways of presenting the conflict to third parties. Likewise, the person who opts for enacting destructive behaviors of neglect that are not relevant to the causes of the problem should be equally unwilling to talk with that friend about ways of managing the effects of the conflict on mutual friends and acquaintances.

A study was conducted to address five sets of concerns. First and most basic, we attempted to develop reliable measures of exit, voice, loyalty, and neglect responses to dissatisfying events so that Rusbult's typology could be examined in conjunction with Investment Theory to cast light on interpersonal conflict between friends. Second, we sought to develop measures of collaboration on accounts and collaboration on future interaction to make possible an examination of their associations with the four responses. Third, we attempted to replicate the structure of Rusbult's typology to determine if the active–passive and constructive–destructive dimensions assumed to underlie it held for friendly relations. Fourth, we tested the predictions derived from Investment Theory concerning the relationships of satisfaction, alternative quality, and investments to exit, voice, loyalty, and neglect responses. Fifth, we explored the effects of gender on responses to dissatisfaction and on Collaboration.

THE STUDY

Subjects

Participants in the study were 327 students enrolled in undergraduate courses at a large public West Coast university; 207 of these students were females, and the remaining 120 were males. These students were recruited from the university's Psychology Department subject pool.

Measures

Exit, Voice, Loyalty, and Neglect Scales. Twelve items were written to represent each of the four responses identified by Rusbult and her colleagues. When constructing these items, close attention was given to Rusbult's (1987) descriptions of each response. Exit was assessed with items such as "I told my friend that I no longer wanted to be friends with him/her" and "I threatened to end our relationship if my friend did not change his/her ways." The scale for measuring voice was comprised of statements such as "We solved our problems by talking things over in a calm and polite manner" and "We worked together to settle our differences." Loyalty tendencies were measured with items like "I said nothing and waited for things to get better" and "I tried to pretend that the incident never occurred out of concern for the friendship." The neglect scale was comprised of statements such as "I said nasty things about my friend to other people" and "While in the presence of my friend, I acted as though he/she did not even exist." Subjects' responses to these 48 items were made on 7-point disagree–agree Likert scales. The factor structure of these items was assessed in a series of confirmatory factor analyses that are reported in the next section, along with the final version of each instrument.

Collaboration on Accounts and Future Interaction. Five items were written to assess collaboration on accounts, an example of which is "I talked with my friend about how we would explain our conflict to other friends." Five items were also written to assess collaboration on future interaction (example: "We made an agreement to be polite to each other so that others would not feel uncomfortable around us"). Responses were made on 7-point disagree–agree Likert scales. These items were subjected to a confirmatory factor analysis to determine if they tapped unique dimensions of collaboration.

Investment Theory Variables. Satisfaction, alternative quality, and investment size were each measured by summing across three items adapted from Rusbult (1980b). Responses were made on 9-point bipolar scales tailored to the wording of each item. Satisfaction was assessed with the following items: (a) "All things considered, how much did you like your friend *prior* to the incident that upset you?"; (b) "How satisfying was your friendship *prior* to the incident that upset you?"; and (c) "Prior to the incident that upset you, how would you have compared this friendship to the ideal friendship?" Alternative quality was measured with the following three items: (a) "Whenever we become dissatisfied with a friend, we always have alternatives to the friendship. These alternatives range from replacing the friend with a new one to spending time alone. All things considered, how appealing is your best available alternative to this friend?"; (b) "How difficult would it be to replace this friend with another one?"; and (c) "How does this friendship compare to your available alternatives to it?" Investment size was assessed with these three items: (a) "To what extent are there important objects, events, persons, or activities that are in some sense 'lost' to you if this friendship ended?"; (b) "All things considered, what is the size of your investment in this friendship?"; and (c) "All things considered, how much time and energy have you put into this friendship?"

Procedure

After signing a consent form, each participant was given a questionnaire that asked him or her to think of a situation that took place sometime during the past 5 weeks in which a friend said or did something that was upsetting in some way. "Friend" was described as a person to whom the participant felt close who was not a relative or romantic partner. After describing the situation in as much detail as possible, the participant responded to the 9 items included in the questionnaire to assess satisfaction, alternative quality, and investment size; the 48 items written to represent the exit, voice, loyalty, and neglect constructs; and the 10 collaboration items.

Findings

Development of Instruments

Responses to Dissatisfaction Scales. The factor structure of the 48-item questionnaire designed to assess each of the four responses described by Rusbult was analyzed in four steps to develop the final measure. First, the 12 items written to represent each of the four responses to dissatisfaction were subjected to item analyses. Any item that lowered the overall *alpha* reliability of the scale was discarded. The effect was that two items were deleted from each of the four scales.

Second, the factor structure of the remaining 40 items was examined via confirmatory factor analysis. A four-factor model was tested using the LISREL VI program (Jöreskog & Sorbom, 1984), with one factor representing each of the four responses. The results of the statistical test of fit of the model to the data was $\chi^2(734) = 2,148.03$ ($p < .001$). The χ^2/df ratio was 2.93. Wheaton, Muthen, Alwin, and Summers (1977) suggested that a ratio smaller than 5.0 indicates a reasonably good fit of the model to the data. Although this ratio suggests an acceptable overall fit, the model was rejected after an examination of the factor loadings and modification index values of the items revealed that several parameters were misspecified in the model. The modification index is an estimate of the expected decrease in chi-square if a single constraint in the model is relaxed.

The third step of the analysis involved identifying the item with the largest modification index, deleting that item, and then repeating the confirmatory analysis. This iterative procedure led to the rejection of two additional items for each of the four scales. The final factor solution was thus based on a four-factor model, with eight items loading on each factor. The goodness of fit χ^2 value for this solution was 1,333.12, with 458 degrees of freedom ($p < .001$). With a χ^2/df ratio of 2.91, the model provides a good fit to the data.

Fourth, this model was tested against three alternative ones. The first competing model was one in which items written to assess the active strategies of voice and exit were allowed to load on just one factor, and the passive strategies of loyalty and neglect were assigned to a second factor. This active-versus-passive model had a poor fit to the data [$\chi^2(463) = 2,803.68$, $p < .001$; χ^2/df ratio = 6.06].

The second competing model was a two-factor model in which the 16 items written to represent the constructive responses of voice and loyalty were allowed to load on one factor, whereas the destructive strategies of exit and neglect were assigned to the second factor. Although the overall fit of the model was adequate [$\chi^2(462) = 1,859.00$, $p < .001$], with a χ^2/df ratio of 4.02, an examination of the modification index for each item revealed that many of the parameters were misspecified. Furthermore, when this two-factor model was compared to the four-factor model using the χ^2 difference test (Loehlin, 1987), a highly significant χ^2_{diff} value of 525.88 was obtained ($df = 4$, $p < .001$). This indicates that the four-factor model was superior to the constructive versus destructive two-factor model. This alternative model was thus rejected.

The third competing model, which was suggested by an examination of the correlations among the exit, voice, loyalty, and neglect scales, was one in which the exit and neglect items were assigned to one factor, voice items to a second factor, and loyalty items to a third factor. This voice-loyalty-disengagement model, with an overall fit of $\chi^2(461) = 1,419.25$ ($p < .001$), and a χ^2/df ratio of 3.08, provided a good fit to the data. It did not, however, fit the data as well as the four-factor solution ($\chi^2_{diff} = 86.13$, with 3 df: $p < .001$). Thus, the four-factor model based on Rusbult's typology proved to be superior to all other models examined. Table 2.1 reports the factor loadings, means, and standard deviations for each item, as well as the *alpha* reliabilities for each scale. These results suggest

TABLE 2.1
Confirmatory Factor Analysis of the Responses to Dissatisfaction
in Friendship Instrument

Factor/Item	Loading	Mean	SD
Exit (α = .85)			
1. I told my friend that I no longer wanted to be friends with him/her.	.63	1.46	.90
2. I told my friend that I was thinking seriously about ending the relationship.	.65	1.66	.99
3. I permanently cut off all contact with my friend.	.69	1.65	1.03
4. I told other people that my friend and I had gone our separate ways.	.63	2.03	1.19
5. I walked away from the friendship.	.69	2.02	1.20
6. I told my friend that we were not suited to each other and should give up trying to be friends.	.73	1.55	.87
7. I let my friend know that I did not want him/her to ever talk to me again.	.73	1.43	.87
8. I threatened to end our relationship if my friend did not change his/her ways.	.58	1.56	.92
Voice (α = .91)			
1. We solved our problems by talking things over in a calm and polite manner.	.74	3.17	1.40
2. We were each open to the other's suggestions for resolving problems.	.68	3.30	1.24
3. We negotiated a solution to our conflict.	.74	2.81	1.28
4. I told my friend that there were problems in our friendship and suggested that we work them out.	.72	2.90	1.31
5. We talked openly and honestly about our differences in hopes of restoring the friendship.	.85	2.94	1.35
6. I made sure my friend realized that resolving our differences was important because I valued the friendship.	.69	3.35	1.21
7. We worked together to settle our differences.	.86	3.06	1.31
8. I told my friend what was bothering me and asked for his/her opinions on the matter.	.69	3.20	1.41
Loyalty (α = .84)			
1. I said nothing and waited for things to get better.	.73	3.16	1.45
2. I did not take things personally and just kept quiet so that things might improve.	.60	2.57	1.35
3. I hoped that the situation would resolve itself.	.62	3.45	1.29
4. I tried to pretend that the incident never occurred out of concern for the friendship.	.63	2.60	1.24
5. I allowed things to cool off rather than taking any action.	.64	3.33	1.16
6. I did nothing and remained loyal to the friendship.	.55	2.61	1.17
7. I said nothing and dealt with the situation by adopting a strategy of forgive and forget.	.71	2.75	1.21
8. I kept my concerns to myself to give my friend a chance to reconsider his/her actions.	.50	3.21	1.22

(continued)

TABLE 2.1
(continued)

Factor/Item	Loading	Mean	SD
Neglect (α = .78)			
1. I allowed my friendship to deteriorate.	.53	2.31	1.23
2. When my friend tried to discuss our problems, I refused to cooperate.	.56	1.62	.86
3. I said nasty things about my friend to other people.	.61	2.34	1.37
4. I ignored my friend for awhile.	.58	3.00	1.41
5. I said and did things out of anger to make my friend feel bad.	.58	2.20	1.28
6. While in the presence of my friend, I acted as though he/she did not even exist.	.70	2.08	1.26
7. I mentioned bad things that my friend did in the past to hurt and embarrass him/her.	.55	2.01	1.25
8. Out of anger, I said things to damage the reputation of my friend.	.59	1.81	1.16

that Rusbult's typology can be extended to friendship. These measures have obvious face validity and are internally consistent. The weakest scale appears to be the measure of neglect, and even this instrument had an adequate *alpha* reliability.

The correlations among the items are reported in Table 2.2. Use of exit was inversely related to voice for females, but unrelated to voice for males. There was no significant relationship between the use of exit and loyalty for females, but a slight inverse relationship between exit and loyalty for males. Very strong, positive relationships were obtained between exit and neglect for both genders. Voice was inversely related to loyalty and neglect for women and men. Finally, the extent to which loyalty and neglect were used was not significantly related for either gender. With the exception of the relationship of Exit to Neglect, it is clear from Table 2.2 that the use of one type of response tended to imply

TABLE 2.2
Correlations Among Measures for Females (Above Diagonal)
and Males (Below Diagonal)

	1	2	3	4
1 Exit	—	−.33***	−.08	.65***
2 Voice	−.09	—	−.39***	−.37***
3 Loyalty	−.20*	−.36***	—	.00
4 Neglect	.69***	−.26**	−.11	—

*p<.05; **p<.01; ***p<.001.

a lesser reliance on the other responses. This was especially true when voice was a respondent's primary response.

Assessing Collaboration.   In the rationale of this study, it was proposed that conflicting friends could collaborate in the presentation of their difficulties to others in at least two ways: by creating accounts that save face for both participants and by negotiating rules governing the manner in which they interact in future encounters. Recall that 10 items were written to represent the collaboration on accounts scale and the collaboration on future interaction measure, five for each instrument. Because one objective was to construct two unidimensional scales, one for each type of collaboration, an item analysis was initially conducted for each of the two sets of items. On the basis of these analyses, one collaboration on accounts item and one collaboration on future interaction item were rejected, reducing the two five-item scales to four items each.

Second, the factor structure of the eight collaboration items was examined via confirmatory factor analysis. Two models were examined. The first was a two-factor model in which the four remaining items written to assess collaboration on accounts were expected to load on one factor, whereas the four remaining items constructed to assess collaboration on future interaction were assigned to the second factor. For the second model, all eight items were represented by a single, more general factor called collaboration.

The test of the goodness of fit for the two-factor model was not promising: $\chi^2(19) = 105.36$, $p < .001$. With a χ^2/df ratio of 5.55, this model could not be accepted. The test for the more parsimonious one-factor model was encouraging: $\chi^2(20) = 75.30$, $p < .001$; χ^2/df ratio = 3.77. Furthermore, a direct comparison of the two models showed the one-factor model to be superior: $\chi^2_{diff} = 30.06$, $df = 1$, $p < .001$. No item had a loading below .54 on the factor. Thus, it was concluded that collaboration, as assessed here, is a unidimensional construct. The eight items originally written to assess collaboration on accounts and collaboration on future interaction were summed to create a single index of collaboration. Item factor loadings, means, and standard deviations for the measure are reported in Table 2.3.

Multidimensional Scaling of the Response Items

Although the results of the LISREL analyses appear to support the validity of Rusbult's typology, they do not necessarily provide evidence of the existence of the constructive/destructive and active/passive dimensions that presumably underlie it. To determine if the relationships

TABLE 2.3
Factor Loadings, Means, and Standard Deviations
for Collaboration Items

Item	Loading	Mean	SD
1. I discussed with my friend how we would describe our relationship to others given our problems.	.57	2.11	1.01
2. I talked with my friend about what had happened between us to create a story that would explain our troubles to mutual friends.	.54	1.92	1.08
3. I talked with my friend about how we would explain our conflict to other friends.	.80	1.80	0.88
4. I discussed with my friend ways to present our conflict to others so that we would not look bad in the eyes of other people.	.74	1.65	0.88
5. We agreed to pretend as though all was well in our friendship for the benefit of others.	.54	2.19	1.18
6. We identified those topics most likely to cause conflict and made it a point never to discuss them in public.	.58	2.00	1.02
7. To smooth things over, we discussed how to interact with each other when with other friends.	.69	2.05	1.09
8. We made an agreement to be polite to each other so that others would not feel uncomfortable when around us.	.58	1.95	1.08

among the items do conform to Rusbult's four-quadrant model depicted in Fig. 2.1, the 32 response items were subjected to a nonmetric multidimensional scaling using the ALSCAL program, as implemented on SPSS^X (SPSS Inc., 1986).

The input for the analysis was the 32 × 32 matrix of Euclidean Dissimilarity Coefficients, which assess the strength of association between all possible pairs of items. Stress values for the one- through six-dimensional solutions were as follows: .294, .108, .056, .039, .031, and .024. Stress is an index of "badness-of-fit," in that a high value indicates that the number of dimensions for which it was obtained cannot adequately reflect the relationships among variables. The three-dimensional solution provided a slightly better fit than did the two-dimensional solution, which was substantially better than the one-dimensional solution. Increases in dimensionality had little impact on stress beyond three dimensions. A comparison of the two- and three-dimensional solutions revealed no meaningful patterns in the three-dimensional stimulus configuration that were not observable in two dimensions. The more parsimonious two-dimensional solution was thus selected to represent relations among the items. The proportion of variance in the scaled data (disparities) accounted for by their corresponding distances in the configuration was $R^2 = .95$.

The two-dimensional stimulus configuration is reproduced in Fig. 2.2. The items in the two-space have been partitioned by the investigators in accordance with Rusbult's distinction between active and passive responses and constructive and destructive actions. Rusbult's distinction between the constructive responses of voice and loyalty and the destructive strategies of exit and neglect are very clear in the configuration. Furthermore, it appears that the strategies are ordered on a more precise continuum of constructiveness. Voice items and exit items occupy the polar extremes of the horizontal axis, whereas loyalty and neglect items hold intermediate positions in the space.

Rusbult's distinction between the active strategies of voice and exit and the passive strategies of loyalty and neglect is not well supported. The voice (active) and loyalty (passive) items are separated in the vertical dimension of the space, as should be expected by the model. However, neglect items, which are presumably passive, do not appear to be any more passive than exit items. Thus, the distinction between active and passive responses to dissatisfaction may be relevant only to the constructive responses. This result is in line with the finding of Rusbult and Zembrodt (1983) that the constructive/destructive dimension weighs more heavily on people's perception of strategy similarity than does the distinction between passive and active strategies.

This finding raises the question of whether there is such a thing as a passive, destructive strategy. Rusbult et al.'s definition of passivity as a response that does not directly address the problem at hand may be so subtle as to be meaningless to most people. Any response, including one that is not related to the issue of the conflict, may nonetheless be seen as action, not inaction. If, in fact, there is a passive, destructive counterpart to loyalty, such a response could be distinguished from loyalty only in terms of one's goals for the relationship. Whereas loyalty involves doing nothing in hopes that the problem resolves itself, a truly passive, destructive response ("disloyalty?") likely involves doing nothing in hopes that the relationship will fade away. Two implications follow. First, is it useful or even possible to make a distinction between "do nothing" responses that are motivated by good intentions and "do nothing" responses that are designed to damage the friendship? Behaviorally, both "responses" are identical. Second, this study suggests that neglect may be a weaker form, or perhaps a precursor, to exit; both may be active and destructive, but differ only in terms of their negativity and degree of destructiveness.

Investment Theory Predictions

The relationships between the response tendencies and the Investment Theory variables were examined via multiple regression analyses. Specifically, the variables satisfaction, alternative quality, and investment size were used as predictor variables, with exit, voice, loyalty, and neglect

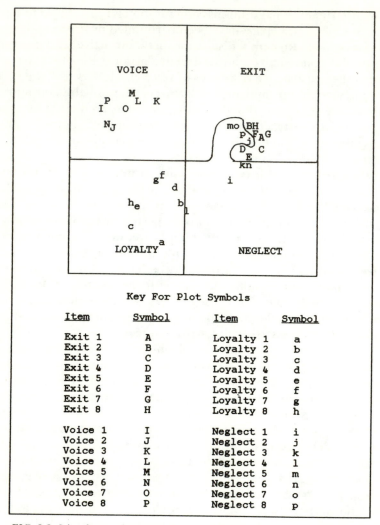

FIG. 2.2. Stimulus configuration from two-dimensional multidimensional scaling of proximities among 32 items in the Responses to Dissatisfaction in Friendship Instrument.

serving as dependent measures. Separate analyses were carried out for female and male subjects; thus, a total of eight analyses were conducted, the results of which are reported in Table 2.4. *Alpha* reliabilities for Investment Theory variables were .80 for satisfaction, .76 for alternative quality, and .65 for investment size. These reliabilities were considered acceptable for three-item scales.

It was expected that exit responses would be associated with low satis-

TABLE 2.4
Predicting Responses to Dissatisfaction with Investment
Theory Variables

Dependent measure	Beta			Adjusted R square
	Satisfaction	Alternatives	Investments	
Females (N=207)				
Exit	.065	.247***	−.246**	.12***
Voice	.199*	−.083	.285***	.21***
Loyalty	.006	−.124	−.229**	.04*
Neglect	−.117	.266***	−.131	.15***
Males (N=120)				
Exit	.074	.270**	.011	.05*
Voice	.076	−.253**	.051	.06*
Loyalty	−.162	−.098	−.141	.05*
Neglect	.065	.422***	−.056	.16***

*$p<.05$; **$p<.01$; ***$p<.001$.

faction, small investment size, and high alternative quality. For females, there was a significant positive beta weight for alternative quality and a significant negative weight for investment size. Satisfaction did not contribute significantly to the regression equation, however. For males, the only significant standardized regression coefficient was for alternative quality, with perceptions of alternatives being associated with exiting.

We expected voice to be most common when satisfaction, alternative quality, and investment size were all high. For females, the significant predictors were satisfaction and investment size; as expected, females were more likely to take a problem-solving approach in rewarding friendships in which many resources had been invested. For males, none of the predictions were supported. In fact, males were *less* likely to use voice when they had quality alternatives to the relationship. Perhaps they felt it easier to develop a promising new friendship than repair an old one.

It was predicted that loyalty would be greatest when satisfaction and investment size were high and alternative quality was low. None of these predictions were supported. In fact, for females the only significant predictor of loyalty was investment size, which was *inversely* related to such responses. For males, none of the three investment theory measures had significant beta weights in predicting loyalty, although they collectively produced a significant overall multiple correlation.

Neglect, as expected, was associated with high alternative quality for both sexes. Contrary to expectations, neglect responses were not predicted by low satisfaction or small investment size for either gender.

Taken together, these results were quite disappointing. Satisfaction, alternative quality, and investment size did not consistently relate to the response categories in ways that were suggested by Investment Theory. Furthermore, these variables accounted for very little of the variances in exit, voice, loyalty, and neglect. In part, these findings may reflect the modest reliabilities of the measures used in this investigation for assessing the three Investment Theory constructs. Males' responses were influenced almost exclusively by the availability of alternatives to the troubling friendship, whereas females' responses were shaped mostly by alternatives and investments. Satisfaction was a significant predictor in only one of the eight analyses.

Collaborating on Accounts and Rules of Future Interaction

It was uncommon for respondents to report having collaborated with the individual causing dissatisfaction for the purpose of constructing accounts and defining rules to guide subsequent interactions. The mean collaboration score was 15.63 (SD = 5.37; theoretical range: 8–40; actual range: 8–38). The tendency to collaborate was associated with the active response of exit (females: $r = .16$, $p < .02$; males: $r = .20$, $p < .02$) and voice (females: $r = .31$, $p < .001$; males: $r = .38$, $p < .001$). Collaboration was not related to loyalty for either females ($r = .07$, ns) or males ($r = -.12$, ns). Neglect correlated significantly with collaboration for males ($r = .17$, $p < .03$), but not for females ($r = .09$, ns). For females, exit and voice had a multiple correlation of .42 with collaboration [Adjusted $R^2 = .17$, $p < .001$; beta weights: .287 ($p < .001$) and .418 ($p < .001$), respectively]. For males, the significant predictors of collaboration in a multiple regression analysis were voice and neglect, with a multiple correlation of .46 [Adjusted $R^2 = .20$, $p < .001$; beta weights: .425 ($p < .001$) and .311 ($p<.001$), respectively]. The fact that collaboration most strongly co-occurred with voice was anticipated because both voice and collaboration involve efforts to resolve problems associated with the conflict through open discussion.

Preferred Responses of Men and Women

Table 2.5 reports the means and standard deviations for the four response scales and for collaboration, as well as tests of the significance of the difference in means for females and males. Only one significant difference was found; males were slightly more likely to report using the strategy of loyalty than were females. This result was opposite that found by Rusbult et al. (1986) for heterosexual romantic relationships, in which females reported a greater reliance on loyalty. No differences were found for exit, voice, neglect, or collaboration. Thus, there is little evidence that friends' responses to dissatisfaction are shaped in any significant way by their gender, a result that supports Pearson's contention (this volume)

TABLE 2.5
Gender Differences

Measure	Females		Males		t (df)	p
	Mean	SD	Mean	SD		
Exit	13.37	5.77	13.35	5.56	0.03(320)	.97
Voice	25.04	8.58	24.11	7.52	0.99(322)	.33
Loyalty	23.16	7.03	24.79	6.53	−2.05(321)	.04
Neglect	17.28	6.26	17.85	6.38	−0.78(319)	.44
Collaboration	15.22	5.50	16.33	5.08	−1.80(325)	.08

that sex differences in interpersonal conflict may not be as important as has often been assumed.

FUTURE DIRECTIONS

Despite notable exceptions, surprisingly little attention has been given to conflicts between friends. Our goal has been to improve on this situation by extending the thinking of Rusbult and her colleagues to the domain of friendship. Of course, the research reported here represents only a modest step in this direction. A variety of issues remain to be addressed. First, the measurement procedures developed here must be examined further for their reliability and validity. The results of the present study suggest that the exit, voice, loyalty, and neglect scales are reliable. In a subsequent investigation (chapter 6, this volume), we obtained alpha reliabilities that are comparable to those found here; the factor structure of the Responses to Dissatisfaction in Friendship Instrument was also replicated.

Although these findings indicate that the scales are internally consistent and empirically distinct, the validity of these self-reports requires additional investigation. First, the extent to which people are able to report their responses accurately needs study. Second, the possibility that respondents' reports are influenced by a need to place themselves in a socially desirable light must be considered. We attempted to overcome this potential problem by making respondents' reports of their actions anonymous. Nevertheless, social desirability needs may extend to people's perceptions of self. Third, self-reports of one's behaviors in conflict situations may reflect attributional biases (Sillars, 1985). A person may be more inclined to see his or her own behaviors as constructive responses to a relational problem than the behaviors of the friend. For instance, one's own silence might be thought of as loyalty, whereas the silence of the partner might be labeled *neglect*. It would be useful to examine the extent to which two friends' interpretations of their conflict differ and to attempt to account for these differing views in terms of varying attributions. Such differences should be treated as a phenomenon worthy of explication, not as measurement error.

We anticipate that most subsequent research, including our own, will focus on predictors of friends' responses to dissatisfaction. Toward this end, we examined the degree to which such responses are shaped by satisfaction with the relationship, irretrievable investments in it, and the availability of quality alternatives. The results were not promising. The weak association of these variables with exit, voice, loyalty, and neglect may be due to the brief measures used in the study. Longer, more reliable measures might produce results more in line with Investment Theory expectations. In addition to satisfaction, alternative quality, and investment size, it will be necessary to employ other predictors of responses to dissatisfaction. Potential predictors fall into four categories: characteristics of the conflict, the individual parties, the dyad, and the larger social context. Features of the *conflict* should affect one's response decisions in major ways. Most notably, the more serious a conflict, the more likely one should be to respond actively; that is, conflict seriousness should be positively related to the use of exit and voice. The extent to which one sees the conflict as resolvable should also influence his or her response. In particular, the use of voice should accompany perceptions that differences can be settled.

In attempting to account for individuals' selection of one response over others, characteristics of the *individuals* in conflict must also be examined. For instance, although we found gender to be relatively unimportant in influencing people's response tendencies, gender-role orientation may exert quite an influence. In romantic relationships, psychological femininity has been found to be associated with the use of voice and loyalty, whereas psychological masculinity has been linked to neglect (Rusbult, 1987). Other variables no doubt affect one's response. Poor social skills, for example, may constrain an individual's response options. The person who is assertive, especially when defending personal rights and privileges (Lorr & More, 1980), may be more inclined than an unassertive person to take action. Likewise, individuals armed with good argumentation skills may use voice more so than poor arguers (Infante & Rancer, 1982).

One's response may also be shaped by perceptions of the *friend's* personal features and social situation. For instance, beliefs that the other party is sensitive to rejection or is generally unwilling to consider other points of view may be a deterrent to confronting that person with one's grievances. The assumption that the friend cannot change those things about him or herself that are the source of conflict might also deter voice and encourage a response of exit (see Eidelson & Epstein, 1982). With regard to Investment Theory, it may also be fruitful to examine people's perceptions of their friend's level of satisfaction in the relationship, amount of irretrievable investments, and alternatives. For instance, one may be inclined to use Loyalty when one believes that the friend is not satisfied with the relationship, has alternatives to it, and would lose few resources by ending it.

In addition to satisfaction with one's friendship and investments in it, many other *dyadic-level* predictors merit attention. In particular, two friends' relational history—especially their history of conflict—will probably be considered when new interpersonal differences arise. For example, if one knows from past experience that his or her friend becomes verbally aggressive during conflicts, a passive response to new turmoils may be preferred. In contrast, voice may be the response of choice if past discussions on related points of disagreement have resulted in satisfactory resolution of conflicts.

Extra-dyadic factors may also have a potent effect on how an individual deals with conflict with a friend. This study shows that having alternatives to the friendship was associated with exit and neglect responses for both genders, and with the avoidance of voice for males. Other extra-dyadic constraints no doubt exist. We are presently examining the possibility that one's responses to dissatisfaction may be shaped by the extent to which the person causing dissatisfaction is a part of one's network. The basic hypothesis that we are exploring, which was derived from the theoretical essays of several relationship scholars (e.g., Duck, 1982; La Gaipa, 1982; McCall, 1982; McCarthy, 1986; Ridley & Avery, 1979), is that a person may have no choice but to stay in a friendship if the friend causing dissatisfaction is also a friend of one's other intimates. If this hypothesis is supported, it would suggest that friendship is not as much a voluntary relationship as has often been assumed (Wellman, 1982).

In addition to the effects of an antagonist's integration into one's network, responses to conflict may also be shaped by input from the network. In this study, we examined the degree to which two friends in conflict collaborate to construct a strategy for influencing other friends' perceptions of the situation. However, this influence process is probably mutual; the members of one's network may attempt to influence how one deals with another friend (Duck, 1982; La Gaipa, 1982). The network may give advice and offer to mediate differences. Sanctions may also be imposed if an individual takes actions that threaten the stability of the network. The degree to which a network intervenes in one's conflict with another friend is probably determined by the extent to which both parties are connected to it; the most intervention should be expected when the network is very dense—that is, when virtually all of its members have strong ties to each other (Salzinger, 1982).

In subsequent studies, it would also be useful to examine responses to dissatisfaction transactionally. The approach taken in this study has admittedly been static. First, it is not clear if our respondents' answers on the Responses to Dissatisfaction in Friendship Instrument should be read as a description of their most recent actions or as an inventory of all responses taken at one time or another during the course of the conflict. Presumably, an individual might employ several of the responses as his or her conflict develops. For instance, one might begin with loyalty in hopes that the conflict will resolve itself, turn to voice when it does not, engage in neglect when voice fails, and finally exit the relationship as a last resort. Second, the complexity of conflict will not be reflected in research until both parties' responses to relational upsets are examined in conjunction. The measures developed here can be used in longitudinal research designs to study conflicts between friends as a dynamic process involving mutual influence.

Finally, an important task of future research will be to examine the effects of one's responses to dissatisfaction on the resolution of the conflict and on the state of the relationship. It is probably tautological to observe that a constructive response should lead to more positive outcomes than a destructive one. However, there may be situations in which even neglect and threats of exit produce constructive outcomes. For instance, the friend whose behavior is unacceptable but who is not open to reason may make changes when coerced into doing so. In addition, the *quality* with which a particular response is enacted may exert as much of an impact on the outcomes of a conflict as the response itself. Voice, for instance, may be ineffective if one is weak at defining problems, has difficulty taking the perspective of others, or is quick to accept a compromise instead of working toward an integrative solution. One can even be inept at exiting. We know of an individual who has been attempting to walk away from a friendship for well over a year, but has been unable to leave permanently due to unassertiveness. We suspect that a person is best able to achieve desired outcomes when his or her repertoire of conflict-management tactics includes all categories of responses, and when he or she can adopt a line of action that meets the constraints imposed by the conflict, the parties' personalities, the relationship, and the larger social context.

REFERENCES

Argyle, M., & Henderson, M. (1984). The rules of friendship. *Journal of Social and Personal Relationships, 1*, 211–237.

Bailey, R. C., Finney, P., & Helm, B. (1975). Self-concept support and friendship duration. *Journal of Social Psychology, 96*, 237–243.

Baxter, L. (1982). Strategies for ending relationships: Two studies. *Western Journal of Speech Communication, 46*, 223–241.

Baxter, L. A. (1988). A dialectical perspective on communication strategies in relationship development. In S. Duck (Ed.), *Handbook of personal relationships* (pp. 257–273). Chichester: Wiley.

Berger, C. R. (1987). Communicating under uncertainty. In M. E. Roloff & G. R. Miller (Eds.), *Interpersonal process: New directions in communication research* (pp. 39–62). Newbury Park, CA: Sage.

Cahn, D. D., Jr. (1987). *Letting go: A practical theory of relationship disengagement and reengagement.* Albany, NY: State University of New York Press.

Cody, M. J. (1982). A typology of disengagement strategies and an examination of the role intimacy, reactions to inequity, and relational problems play in strategy selection. *Communication Monographs, 49,* 148–170.

Duck, S. (1982). A topography of relationship disengagement and dissolution. In S. Duck (Ed.), *Personal relationships. 4: Dissolving personal relationships* (pp. 1–30). London: Academic Press.

Eidelson, R. J., & Epstein, N. (1982). Cognition and relationship maladjustment: Development of a measure of dysfunctional relationship beliefs. *Journal of Counseling and Clinical Psychology, 50,* 715–720.

Infante, D. A., & Rancer, A. S. (1982). A conceptualization and measure of argumentativeness. *Journal of Personality Assessment, 46,* 72–80.

Johnson, M. P. (1982). Social and cognitive features of dissolving commitment to relationships. In S. Duck (Ed.), *Personal relationships. 4: Dissolving personal relationships* (pp. 51–73). London: Academic Press.

Jöreskog, K. G., & Sorbom, D. (1984). *LISREL VI: Analysis of linear structural relationships by the method of maximum likelihood.* Mooresville, IN: Scientific Software, Inc.

La Gaipa, J. J. (1982). Rules and rituals in disengagement from relationships. In S. Duck (Ed.), *Personal relationships 4: Dissolving personal relationships* (pp. 189–210). London: Academic Press.

Loehlin, J. C. (1987). *Latent variable models: An introduction to factor, path, and structural analysis.* Hillsdale, NJ: Lawrence Erlbaum Associates.

Lorr, M., & More, W. W. (1980). Four dimensions of assertiveness. *Multivariate Behavioral Research, 15,* 127–138.

McCall, G. (1982). Becoming unrelated: The management of bond dissolution. In S. Duck (Ed.), *Personal relationships. 4: Dissolving personal relationships* (pp. 211–231). London: Academic Press.

McCarthy, B. (1986). Dyads, cliques, and conspiracies: Friendship behaviors and perceptions within long-established social groups. In R. Gilmour & S. Duck (Eds.), *The emerging field of personal relationships* (pp. 77–89). Hillsdale, NJ: Lawrence Erlbaum Associates.

Miller, G. R., & Parks, M. R. (1982). Communication in dissolving relationships. In S. Duck (Ed.), *Personal relationships. 4: Dissolving personal relationships* (pp. 127–154). London: Academic Press.

Rawlins, W. K. (1983a). Negotiating close friendships: The dialectic of conjunctive freedoms. *Human Communication Research, 9,* 255–266.

Rawlins, W. K. (1983b). Openness as problematic in ongoing friendships: Two conversational dilemmas. *Communication Monographs, 50,* 1–13.

Ridley, C., & Avery, A. (1979). The influence of social networks on dyadic interaction. In R. L. Burgess & T. L. Huston (Eds.), *Social exchange and developing relationships* (pp. 223–246). New York: Academic.

Rose, S. M. (1984). How friendships end: Patterns among young adults. *Journal of Social and Personal Relationships, 1,* 267–277.

Rose, S. & Serafica, F. C. (1986). Keeping and ending casual, close, and best friendships. *Journal of Social and Personal Relationships, 3,* 275–288.

Rusbult, C. E. (1980a). Commitment and satisfaction in romantic associations: A test of the investment model. *Journal of Experimental Social Psychology, 16,* 172–186.

Rusbult, C. E. (1980b). Satisfaction and commitment in friendships. *Representative Research in Social Psychology, 11,* 96–105.

Rusbult, C. E. (1983). A longitudinal test of the investment model: The development (and deterioration) of satisfaction and commitment in heterosexual involvements. *Journal of Personality and Social Psychology, 45,* 101–117.

Rusbult, C. E. (1987). Responses to dissatisfaction in close relationships: The exit-voice-loyalty-neglect model. In D. Perlman & S. Duck (Eds.), *Intimate relationships: Development, dynamics, and deterioration* (pp. 209–237). Newbury Park, CA: Sage.

Rusbult, C. E., Johnson, D. J., & Morrow, G. D. (1986). Predicting satisfaction and commitment in adult romantic involvements: An assessment of the generalizability of the investment model. *Social Psychology Quarterly, 49,* 81–89.

Rusbult, C. E., & Zembrodt, I. M. (1983). Responses to dissatisfaction in romantic involvements: A multidimensional scaling analysis. *Journal of Experimental Social Psychology, 19,* 274–293.

Rusbult, C. E., Zembrodt, I. M., & Gunn, L. K. (1982). Exit, voice, loyalty, and neglect: Responses to dissatisfaction in romantic involvements. *Journal of Personality and Social Psychology, 43,* 1230–1242.

Salzinger, L. L. (1982). The ties that bind: The effects of clustering on dyadic relationships. *Social Networks, 4,* 117–145.

Sillars, A. L. (1985). Interpersonal perception in relationships. In W. Ickes (Ed.), *Compatible and incompatible relationships* (pp. 277–305). New York: Springer-Verlag.

SPSS, Inc. (1986). *SPSS^X users guide* (2nd ed.). Chicago: Author.

Stueve, C. A., & Gerson, K. (1977). Personal relations across the life-cycle. In C. S. Fischer (Ed.), *Networks and places: Social relations in the urban setting* (pp. 79–98). New York: The Free Press.

Thibaut, J. W., & Kelley, H. H. (1959). *The social psychology of groups.* New York: Wiley.

Wellman, B. (1982). Studying personal communities. In P. Marsden & N. Lin (Ed.), *Social structure and network analysis* (pp. 61–80). Beverly Hills, CA: Sage.

Wheaton, B., Muthen, B., Alwin, D., & Summers, G. (1977). Assessing reliability and stability in panel models. In D. R. Heise (Ed.), *Sociological methodology 1977* (pp. 84–136). San Francisco: Jossey-Bass.

The Chilling Effect in Interpersonal Relationships: The Reluctance to Speak One's Mind

Michael E. Roloff
Denise H. Cloven
Northwestern University

CONFLICT AVOIDANCE

Individuals in more intimate relationships such as marriage show indications of conflict avoidance. Birchler, Weiss, and Vincent (1975) discovered that over a 5-day period, spouses in nondistressed marriages reported their partner engaged in an average of 13 behaviors that were "displeasurable" to them but that they had only *one* argument during the same time frame. A similar ratio was observed in distressed marriages. Although it is possible that a given argument may focus on more than one "displeasurable" behavior, it is likely that some negative actions are never discussed. Indeed, Scanzoni (1978) found that 7% of a sample of wives said they were unable to confront their husbands about any of their undesirable traits.

Withholding grievances or irritations does not seem to be a functional way of dealing with interpersonal problems. Unless undesirable behavior is brought to the attention of transgressors, they have no basis on which to infer that a problem even exists. Indeed, relational partners who avoid conflicts have more difficulty resolving their disputes (e.g., Sillars, 1980).

A primary reason for withholding complaints may be fear of negative reactions from one's partner. Communicating grievances may lead to an argument, and such interactions are often loud, and stimulate criticism, disagreement, and sarcasm (Resick et al., 1981). Moreover, verbal attacks and criticisms aimed at intimates are frequently "things people wish they hadn't said" (Knapp, Stafford, & Daly, 1986). Hence, partners might fear that even raising certain issues might end or at least threaten the continuation of their relationship (cf. Baxter & Wilmot, 1985).

Withholding grievances could also indicate powerlessness. Fear of

49

negative relational consequences might inhibit the willingness to try to influence a partner's behavior. If true, then one partner might control the dynamics of a relationship without having to *overtly* exert influence; his or her behavior and proclivities are rarely, if ever, challenged. Hence, there is a chilling effect on the expression of grievances. This form of control may be the most efficient form of power. If a person is never confronted, then more overt and potentially costlier (cf. Folger & Poole, 1984) forms of control become unnecessary.

Although scholars have recognized the interrelationships among conflict, power, and communication (e.g., Folger & Poole, 1984), minimal research has been focused on the existence of a chilling effect within interpersonal relationships. Although the aforementioned studies imply its existence, none expressly examined the chilling effect. Moreover, prior research has not grounded avoidance behavior within any theoretical framework, let alone one based on power. This chapter adopts such a perspective and presents the results of a study testing hypotheses derived from it.

CONFLICT, POWER, AND THE CHILLING EFFECT

Our analysis is divided into three sections. First, we examine the chilling effect as a sign of powerlessness. Second, we focus on the effect of perceived relational alternatives on willingness to express interpersonal complaints, and finally, we explore the means by which perceptions of relational alternatives and ultimately, the chilling effect are created.

The Chilling Effect as a Sign of Powerlessness

Scholars have long recognized the inherent link between power and conflict. For example, Coser (1956) noted that "conflicts, as distinct from other forms of interactions, always involve power. . . . Whatever the goals of the conflicting parties, power (the chance to influence the behavior of others in accord with one's own wishes) is necessary for their accomplishment" (p. 134). However, scholarly attention has not focused on all manifestations of influence. Reviews of the family power literature indicate that prior research has been restricted to decision-making control and conversational influence (cf. Berger, 1980; Hocker & Wilmot, 1985). When studying control over decision making, relational partners are typically asked to self-report who ultimately decides or influences what should be done within a variety of domains (e.g., Blood & Wolfe, 1960; Grauerholz, 1987; Ting-Toomey, 1984), and indicators of conversational control include verbal manifestations of dominance and domineering-ness (cf. Millar & Rogers, 1987).

Although both forms of control have yielded useful insights, they mask the potential impact of the chilling effect. Decision making vested primarily in the hands of one relational partner could indicate an unwill-ingness to express disagreements, but might also result from a negotiated agreement, differential expertise, indifference, or even a biased set of decision-making domains (Heer, 1963). Conversational control is equally problematic. When examining interactions, one is inherently focused on enacted nonverbal behaviors and linguistic output. It is not possible to determine from these cues what relational partners might have wanted to say but did not. The absence of such information might provide inaccurate assessments of power. Hocker and Wilmot (1985) argued that often relational partners downgrade their requests *prior* to making them simply because they anticipate negative reactions from their more power-ful counterparts. The less powerful party may even enact more influence attempts during the interaction. To outside observers, the less powerful appears to be more influential and the more important covert process is missed.

Our notion of a chilling effect is similar to the covert process just described. However, we would go one step further; perhaps the less powerful parties are inhibited from even initiating influence attempts. Indeed, that would be the essence of the chilling effect.

The chilling effect has three characteristics. First, it is focused on those aspects of a relational partner (e.g., behaviors, personality, interpersonal network) that negatively impact (e.g., irritate, anger) his or her counter-part. In essence, these traits represent areas of incompatibility and are conflicts in and of themselves (Deutsch, 1973). Second, these conflicts remain ongoing (i.e., they are still irritating), but are withheld from the offending party. In some cases, they may be described to third parties such as friends (Blumberg, 1972), but the partner is not confronted. In that sense, they are *unexpressed* conflicts. Finally, the basis for not confronting the partner is fear that conflict escalation might damage the relationship. Whether this fear is an accurate assessment matters little; the individual believes it to be true and withholds the information.

Taken together, these characteristics imply that a relational partner has sacrificed a basic element of power: the ability to confront another with a grievance. By not communicating about the problem, the person may be forced to adapt to an ongoing, unpleasant circumstance with the possibility of growing resentment. Indeed, unresolved problems are a characteristic of distressed relationships (Birchler & Webb, 1977).

Such a sacrifice only occurs when certain circumstances are perceived. We believe the chilling effect stems from the perceived power of one's

partner. We describe the psychological factors leading to these perceptions in the next section.

Perceived Relational Alternatives and the Chilling Effect

It is unrealistic to assume that all people would believe that their relationship could not weather expressed conflict; only when individuals perceive
their relationship to be *tenuous* will they try to avoid disputes (Coser,
1956). If so, the chilling effect should occur when a person perceives that
his or her partner's alternative relationships are of higher quality (i.e.,
more rewarding) than their current one. Because the alternatives are
perceived to be superior to the extant relationship, the partner's perceived relational commitment is also believed to be lower. Indeed, there
is substantial evidence suggesting a negative correlation between the
quality of a person's relational alternatives and his or her commitment
to the current relationship (Rusbult, 1980, 1983; Rusbult, Johnson, &
Morrow, 1986b; Sprecher, 1988). Hence, the partner with superior alternatives might find leaving the relationship a viable and attractive response
to an argument. In such a case, that partner may be able to exert power
through issue control (cf. Folger & Poole, 1984), or the ability to prevent
grievances from being raised. If so, the following hypotheses should be
valid.

H1: The perceived quality of a relational partner's alternative rela-
     tionships should be positively correlated with the number of
     unexpressed conflicts reported by his or her counterpart in the
     relationship.

H2: The relationship between the perceived quality of a partner's
     alternative relationships and the number of unexpressed conflicts
     should be attenuated when controlling for the partner's per-
     ceived relational commitment.

However, this analysis ignores an important factor: the perceiver's
own relational alternatives. If a perceiver's alternatives are superior to
the current relationship, then he or she might be willing to run the
risks associated with a confrontation. Rusbult (1987) observed, "Good
alternatives (an alternative relationship, spending time with friends or
relatives, or solitude) provide the individual with the motivation to do
something (be active, voice or exit; "shape up or ship out") and give him
or her a source of power for effecting changes in the relationship" (p.
220). Consistent with Rusbult's analysis, having good relational alternatives is positively correlated with an expressed willingness to exit from a

relationship and to criticize one's partner, but negatively related to relational loyalty (Rusbult, Johnson, & Morrow, 1986a; Rusbult, Zembrodt, & Gunn, 1982).

This analysis suggests that the chilling effect may be produced by the joint influence of the partner's and one's own perceived relational alternatives. When the partner's alternatives are thought to be superior to the current relationship, a person may fear that relational termination may result from conflict. This fear may be enhanced if the person believes that his or her own alternatives are inferior to the extant relationship (i.e., the person is dependent on it). However, if the perceiver also has superior relational alternatives, concern about losing the relationship may lessen, and he or she may be more willing to express conflict. In essence, both parties now have equal but less commitment to and power in the relationship. A similar analysis might be applied to situations wherein a person perceives him or herself to be vulnerable because of inferior relational alternatives. The chilling effect should be especially likely when the partner's alternatives are also perceived to be superior, but should be less so when the partner's alternatives are thought to be equally inferior. In the latter case, both parties have equally high levels of relational commitment and power. Hence, the chilling effect should be more likely when there is a power deficit to one's disadvantage. If our analysis is correct, the following two hypotheses should be confirmed.

H3: When one's partner's perceived relational alternatives are superior to the current relationship, there should be a negative association between the perceived quality of one's own relational alternatives and the number of conflicts one has not expressed.

H4: When one's perceived relational alternatives are inferior to the current relationship, there should be a positive association between the perceived quality of one's partner's relational alternatives and the number of conflicts one has not expressed.

We have posited that the chilling effect is associated with perceptions of relational alternatives. The next section addresses how perceptions of relational alternatives are created.

The Creation of Perceived Relational Alternatives

Perceiving that one's partner has superior relational alternatives could result from a variety of factors. Individuals sometimes intentionally create the impression of superior relational alternatives as a means of exerting power. For example, White (1980) discovered that 24% of dating undergraduates sampled reported that they had deliberately attempted to induce jealousy by showing romantic interest toward others and their motives included making their partner's engage in more rewarding behaviors toward them. In other cases, the perception of quality alternatives may not be intentionally created, but simply occurs as an assessment by the perceiver. Regardless of intentionality, if one can identify the factors used to infer relational alternatives, we have additional variables from which to predict the chilling effect.

We posit that the perception of quality alternatives may emerge from a partner's involvement with others. For example, Hansen (1987) discovered that among a sample of dating undergraduates, 65% of the men and 39% of the women admitted having some form of extra-dyadic sexual contact, and over 40% of both sexes reported that they were at least fairly certain their dating partner knew about it. In fact, some individuals make sure that their partners know they are having extra-dyadic relations. In White's (1980) study, almost 24% of the individuals who reported trying to make their partners jealous did so by dating other people. The fact that someone has succeeded in forming an alternative relationship should be a sign of their inclination and ability to form new relationships. Hence, their partners might be reluctant to engage in behaviors, such as expressing grievances, that would prompt them to do so. We predict the following.

> H5: Relational partners who have extra-dyadic involvements will be perceived to have superior relational alternatives and will prompt a chilling effect to a greater extent than will relational partners who have no extra-dyadic involvements.

The quality of a person's alternatives may also be inferred from his or her willingness to actually leave the relationship. The aforementioned research by Rusbult and her colleagues indicates that the quality of one's alternatives is positively associated with threatening or actually exiting from a relationship. In a sense, this is the strongest indicator of one's alternatives because a current relationship is being jeopardized. As a result, such behaviors might inhibit the confrontative tendencies of another. We predict the following.

> H6: Individuals who have threatened to breakup a relationship or who actually have broken it up in the past will be perceived to have superior relational alternatives and will instill a chilling effect to a greater extent than will those who have not done so.

Thus, we believe that being influenced can be manifested in the unwillingness of a person to express conflicts. This reluctance stems from the perception that his or her partner has superior relational alternatives to the current relationship and is exacerbated when the perceiver's alternatives are inferior. The perceptions that one's partner has good relational alternatives stems from his or her extrarelational involvements and willingness to exit from the relationship. Here we report a study that tests these notions.

METHOD

Procedure and Sample

To test our hypotheses, we conducted a survey of individuals involved in a dating relationship.[1] Undergraduates enrolled at Northwestern University who were currently involved in what they defined as a "dating relationship" were solicited from introductory communication classes and from a sorority and a fraternity house. All questionnaires were completed in private and the participants were told that their answers would be held in strictest confidence. Each participant had the option of not continuing in the project, but none chose to drop out. After completing the questionnaire, respondents were told the nature of the study, and questions were answered.

Completing the survey were 104 undergraduates (66 females and 38 males).[2] Their ages ranged from 17 to 30, with a mean age of 20. Slightly

---

[1] Although researchers examining the effects of relational alternatives have utilized both experimental (e.g., Rusbult, 1980; Rusbult, Zembrodt, & Gunn, 1982) and survey designs (e.g., Rusbult, Johnson, & Morrow, 1986b; Rusbult, 1983), we felt that our initial attempt should be focused on determining the prevalence of the chilling effect within natural relationships before attempting to produce such effects through experimental manipulations. Our decision to focus on dating relationships rather than more intimate ones (e.g., marriage) stemmed from our desire to test our hypotheses in an environment in which perceived alternatives and commitment might operate relatively unencumbered by other constraints. For example, Johnson (1982) has noted that structural features of a person's environment might force an individual to continue with a course of action, such as remaining in a relationship, even though he or she is not personally committed to doing so. Johnson has noted that relative to marriage, fewer structural constraints are imposed on dating partners. In particular, undergraduates have easier access to large numbers of alternative dating partners and the costs of breaking up are less than for spouses. Hence, relational alternatives may have a more powerful and clearer effect in a dating population.

[2] Because of missing data, the number of subjects varied across some of the analyses. In addition to random mistakes and oversights by respondents, missing data resulted from a page that was inadvertently left off of 15 questionnaires. Fortunately, this oversight did not include any of the items measuring the predictor or dependent variables and hence, did not reduce the n for testing the hypotheses.

more than half were upperclassman (54% were juniors or seniors). The
length of involvement in their current dating relationship ranged from
1 week to 208 weeks, with a mean of 48 weeks. Respondents were asked
how frequently they see their partner on a 6-point scale ranging from
rarely (1) to daily (6). The mean response was 4.39, but the modal
response was 6 (39% of the sample). Only 6% reported rarely (1) seeing
their partner.

Predictor Variables

Four predictor variables were employed: relational alternatives, relational commitment, extra-dyadic involvement, and threats to terminate
the relationship. Subjects reported in counterbalanced sections their own
scores and their impression of their partner's scores on each of the
variables.

Relational Alternatives. This variable was operationalized by summing
responses to four items employed in prior research (Berg & McQuinn,
1986; Rusbult, 1983; Rusbult et al., 1986a, 1986b; Sprecher, 1988). Individuals responded to each of the following items on a 6-point Likert
scale: (a) "How does your relationship compare to those dating relationships your partner could have?" (1 = our relationship is a lot better; 6 =
our relationship is a lot worse); (b) "In general, how appealing are your
partner's alternatives (including dating other persons or being without
a romantic partner) to your dating relationship?" (1 = my partner's
alternatives are not appealing; 6 = my partner's alternatives are extremely appealing); (c) "All things considered, how do your partner's
alternatives compare to your dating relationship?" (1 = our current
relationship is much better; 6 = my partner's alternatives are much
better); (d) "If your dating relationship were to end today, how difficult
would it be for your partner to find a new one that was just as good or
better?" (1 = extremely difficult; 6 = extremely easy). Adequate reliability
was achieved for both the partner's perceived alternatives (α = .835) and
the respondent's own perceived alternatives (α = .814).

Relational Commitment. The measure of commitment was also derived
from prior research (Rusbult et al., 1986a, 1986b). On a 6-point Likert
scale, participants responded to each of the following four items: (a) "For
what length of time would your partner like this relationship to last?" (1
= a week or so; 6 = a lifetime); (b) "To what extent is your partner
attached to you?" (1 = not at all; 6 = extremely attached); (c) "To what
extent is your partner committed to the relationship?" (1 = not at all; 6

= extremely committed); (d) "How likely will your partner end your relationship in the near future?" (1 = not likely at all; 6 = extremely likely). The sum of the responses to these four items formed a highly reliable index for perceptions of the partner's commitment (α = .938) and the respondent's own commitment (α = .909).

Extra-Dyadic Involvement. This variable was assessed through two items. The first asked, "Is your partner currently going out with other people?" The second question asked respondents, "If your partner wants, how free is he or she to go out with other people?" Responses were indicated on a 6-point scale ranging from totally free (6) to not free at all (1). Although responses to these two items were significantly correlated for both the partner's perceived extradyadic involvement (point biserial r = .464, df = 100, p < .000) and the respondent's own (point biserial r = .419, df = 87, p < .000), the correlations were not of sufficient magnitude to justify combining them into a single index; hence, they were analyzed separately.[3]

Threats to Terminate the Relationship. This variable was operationalized through two items. One asked, "During an argument, has your partner ever threatened to breakup with you?" After the aforementioned question, respondents were asked, "Because of an argument, has your partner ever actually broken off the relationship?" There was no correlation between the partner's threatening to breakup and the partner actually terminating the relationship (ϕ = .054, df = 96, NSD), and although respondents who had threatened to breakup also had done so (ϕ = .254, df = 92, p < .007), the correlation is relatively low. Given the modest interrelationships, we chose to analyze each item separately.

Dependent Variable

Recall that we conceived of the chilling effect as the existence of unexpressed grievances or conflicts. We utilized a two-step process to operationalize this variable. First, respondents were asked to list things about their partner that irritated them. They were told these things could include both behaviors they wanted their partners to stop doing or acts they wanted their partners to start doing. Following that instruction were 10 sets (each set was numbered) of two lines on which 10 irritations

---

[3]In retrospect, there also seems to be good conceptual reason for doing so. The former assesses whether individuals are actually involved in extra-dyadic relations, whereas the latter indicates whether they have the potential to do so.

might be described. Second, on the following page, respondents read instructions that asked them to return to the list of irritations and circle each *one* that the respondents had *not* told their partners about. Our measure of the chilling effect was the number of irritations that were circled.[4]

Validity Check Measures

Because some of our measures are new, we included additional measures that might be used to assess validity. Four sets of the measures were employed: motives for not expressing conflict, types of conflicts, communication characteristics, and relational dynamics.

Motives for not Expressing Conflict. We argued that the chilling effect is motivated behavior; individuals are thought to withhold conflict because of fear that conflict escalation would threaten the relationship. Hence, we asked respondents who had at least one unexpressed conflict to write out why they had *not* told their partners about the irritations they had identified. These open-ended responses were then content analyzed for expressed motives. Two individuals independently coded each description for the presence or absence of a conflict avoidance justification (i.e., the person indicates that disclosure would result in a disagreement or endanger the relationship). Cohen's *Kappa* showed adequate intercoder reliability (.857). Disagreements were resolved through discussion.

Types of Conflicts. If valid, we felt that the partner's perceived alternatives should predict certain types of conflicts. Two individuals separately

---

[1]We felt this procedure afforded a number of advantages. First, individuals were allowed to generate their own list of problems rather than having one imposed by the researchers (cf. Buss, 1989). Hence, we should not have overlooked some problems because we could not anticipate their existence. Second, respondents generated irritations separately from judgments of whether they told their partners about them. Therefore, the judgment task was simplified as individuals focused on one aspect at a time. Third, we allowed respondents to judge the expression of each individual problem rather than make a general assessment of unexpressed conflict. Although the latter is of use as a validity check, we are more comfortable with a more individuated assessment. Fourth, by focusing on the number of unexpressed conflicts, we gain clearer insight into the extent of the phenomenon. Alternatively, we could have focused on the proportion of unexpressed conflict by dividing the total number of unexpressed conflicts by the total number of irritations. By doing so, respondents who have only one irritation which is unexpressed are treated as equivalent to those who have ten irritations of which none are expressed (both equal 1.00). We believe that the latter situation is a better indicator than the former and should be distinguished from it.

coded each of the 387 irritations into one of the following five content categories:

1. lack of affection (the respondent complains about the partner's unwillingness to express emotions or have sex; $\kappa = .696$);
2. independence (the respondent complains that the partner remains distant, won't let the respondent into his or her life, won't depend on the respondent; $\kappa = .800$);
3. lack of respect (respondent indicates that the partner is unappreciative, critical, insensitive to needs; $\kappa = .817$);
4. interest in other romantic partners (respondent complains that the partner flirts, goes out with others, talks about current or prior relationships; $\kappa = .966$); and
5. controlling behavior (respondent complains that the partner is too manipulative, and demanding; $\kappa = .692$).

A miscellaneous code was used, but not analyzed. Disagreements were resolved through discussion.

Communication Characteristics. Four items were included to determine the *nature* of *explicit* conflict occurring within the relationship. First, respondents were asked to indicate on a 6-point scale how assertive they were when arguing with their partners (1 = very unassertive; 6 = very assertive). The same item was reworded and used to determine the partner's perceived assertiveness. Second, individuals were asked how willing they were to tell their partner about his or her irritating behavior (1 = very unwilling; 6 = very willing). Third, respondents described the frequency with which they argue with their partners (1 = never; 6 = frequently). Finally, on a 7-point scale, individuals indicated how their arguments were usually settled (3 = I usually win, 0 = usually compromise, −3 = my partner usually wins).

Relational Benefits. We included two measures to assess the gratifications that might be associated with the dating relationship. First, a three-item index similar to that used by Rusbult (1983) was employed to measure relational satisfaction. Respondents responded to each of the following questions on 6-point scales: (a) "How satisfied are you with your relationship?" (1 = extremely dissatisfied; 6 = extremely satisfied); (b) "How happy are you with your relationship?" (1 = extremely unhappy; 6 = extremely happy); and (c) "To what extent are you attracted to your partner?" (1 = not at all; 6 = extremely attracted). These questions were reworded so that respondents could estimate their partner's satisfaction.

Item analysis indicated that the reliability of the index could be improved by deleting the third item. Hence, *alpha* for the two-item measure was .951 for the respondent's satisfaction and .888 for the partner's perceived satisfaction.

Second, a rewardingness index developed by Berg (1984) and also used by Berg and McQuinn (1986) was employed. This index essentially measures supportive behavior and was created by summing the responses to the following items: (a) "Rate the extent to which your partner has helped you with problems or projects." (1 = little help; 6 = great help), and (b) "Rate the extent to which your partner has done favors for you" (1 = few favors; 6 = many favors). The same items were reworded so as to assess how supportive the respondent thought he or she had been to the partner. The *alpha* for how supportive the partner has been was .843 and .859 for the supportiveness of the respondent.

RESULTS

Validity Checks

Before testing the hypotheses, we checked the validity of our operational-izations of the perceived quality of the partner's relational alternatives and the chilling effect. First, we verified the relational alternative measure by examining its association with types of irritations. We posited that a partner who is thought to have superior alternatives would engage in behaviors that signaled noninvolvement in the relationship and minimal concern for the respondent. Consistent with our expectations, the per-ceived quality of a partner's alternatives was positively correlated with the number of complaints about lack of affection ($r = .256$, $df = 97$, $p < .005$), the partner's excessive independence ($r = .203$, $df = 97$, $p < .022$), and the partner's interest in other romantic involvements ($r = .338$, $df = 97$, $p < .000$). Although a positive correlation was observed between the perceived quality of a partner's relational alternatives and the number of complaints about the partner's lack of respect, the relationship was not statistically significant ($r = .118$, $df = 97$, $p < .112$).

Of even greater interest, the same correlations were computed sepa-rately for the number of complaints that the partner had been told about and the number unexpressed. None of the correlations with expressed irritations were statistically significant; however, positive correlations were observed between the perceived quality of the partner's alternatives and unexpressed complaints about his or her lack of affection ($r = .408$, $df = 97$, $p < .000$), excessive independence ($r = .228$, $df = 97$, $p < .012$), lack of respect ($r = .220$, $df = 97$, $p < .014$), and interest in other romantic partners ($r = .415$, $df = 97$, $p < .000$). Hence the perceived quality of a partner's relational alternatives gives rise to certain types of conflicts and these irritations appear to go unexpressed.

Only one deviation was observed; none of the correlations between the perceived quality of the partner's relational alternatives and complaints about his or her controlling behavior (whether expressed or not) were significant, and all were of low magnitude (less than .06). This pattern was also evident in the absence of a correlation between the quality of the partner's alternatives and how assertive he or she was perceived to be when arguing. Apparently, the perceived quality of partner's alternatives is not associated with controlling or overtly dominating behavior.

Overall, we believe that our measure of relational alternatives is reasonably valid.[5] Recall that the chilling effect was assessed in two steps. First, respondents were asked to list things about their partners that were irritating. Two people indicated that they could not think of any complaints, but the average number of irritations listed was 3.706 ($SD = 2.132$). We reasoned that if this step was successful, the total number of irritations should be correlated with measures of relational difficulties. Consistent with this expectation, the total number of conflicts listed was negatively correlated with the respondent's relational satisfaction ($r = -.391$, $df = 99$, $p < .000$), and was positively correlated with the frequency of arguments ($r = .197$, $df = 100$, $p < .023$) and the respondent having threatened to terminate the relationship (point biserial $r = .253$, $df = 98$, $p < .006$).

Given prior research that indicates that females express more reasons for ending a relationship than do males (Baxter, 1986; Hill, Rubin, & Peplau, 1976), we expected that females might list more irritations than

---

[5]We also attempted to replicate prior findings with our measures of relational alternatives. For example, higher quality relational alternatives are associated with lower levels of relational satisfaction (Berg, 1984; Sprecher, 1988) and less perceived supportiveness from one's partner (Berg, 1984). Similarly, our data set indicates that the quality of one's own relational alternatives is negatively correlated with own relational satisfaction ($r = -.688$, $df = 101$, $p < .000$) and with the amount of perceived support received from one's partner ($r = -.629$, $df = 101$, $p < .000$). Because the quality of one's alternatives is a comparison of the benefits derived from the current relationship relative to possible others, it is not surprising that deficient benefits would be associated with judgments of better alternatives. Given these patterns, we expected that the perceptions of the quality of a partner's alternatives would show similar associations with his or her perceived satisfaction and the amount of support received from the respondent. Indeed, the perceived quality of the partner's relational alternatives was negatively correlated with the partner's relational satisfaction ($r = -.527$, $df = 99$, $p<.000$) and the amount of support the respondent said he or she gave to the partner ($r = -.482$, $df = 99$, $p<.000$).

males. Indeed, there was a significant negative correlation between our dummy-coded gender variable (1 = male; 0 = female) and the total number of complaints ($r = -.163$, $df = 100$, $p < .05$).

The second step required the respondent to identify each listed conflict that he or she had *not* expressed to the partner. On the average, individuals had not expressed 1.55 irritations ($SD = 1.872$) and the average proportion of unexpressed conflicts was .401 ($SD = .380$). If valid, this measure should be negatively correlated with other measures that imply assertive behavior. Consistent with this analysis, the number of unexpressed conflicts was negatively correlated with the number of conflicts the respondent had told the partner about ($r = -.376$, $df = 98$, $p < .000$), the self- reported willingness to tell the partner about irritating behavior ($r = -.468$, $df = 98$, $p < .000$), the respondent winning arguments ($r = -.227$, $df = 93$, $p < .013$), and the respondent's assertiveness during arguments ($r = -.349$, $df = 96$, $p < .000$). Although the frequency of arguments was also negatively correlated with the number of unexpressed irritations, it was not statistically significant ($r = -.113$, $df = 98$, $p < .131$). We also anticipated that the number of unexpressed conflicts would be related to relational problems and accordingly, it was negatively correlated with the respondent's relational satisfaction ($r = -.393$, $df = 97$, $p < .000$) and the partner's supportiveness ($r = -.315$, $df = 98$, $p < .001$).[6]

We argue that the chilling effect arises from fear that conflict escalation might damage the relationship. Hence, we correlated the number unexpressed conflicts with the various reasons given by the respondents for withholding complaints. As expected, the number of unexpressed irritations was positively correlated with conflict avoidance (point biserial $r = .346$, $df = 98$, $p < .000$).[7]

---

[6]Although unanticipated, we found a negative correlation between our dummy-coded gender variable and the number of unexpressed conflicts ($r = -.239$, $df = 98$, $p < .016$, two-tailed). Apparently, females have larger numbers of unexpressed conflicts than do males.

[7]Our perusal of the written descriptions yielded several other motives of which we had the two coders assess the presence or absence: (a) low importance (the person says that the problem is not of sufficient magnitude to argue about; $\kappa = .960$); (b) negative image (the person indicates that complaining might make him or her appear to be jealous, possessive, coercive, or a nag; $\kappa = .880$); (c) futility of arguing (the person indicates that the partner won't change; $\kappa = .839$); and (d) nonintimacy (the person says that the relationship is not of sufficient intimacy to warrant or justify complaining; $\kappa = 1.00$). Disagreements were resolved through discussion. Although we did not anticipate other motivations, we examined the correlations between unexpressed conflict and the four other coded motivations and evaluated them with two-tailed significance tests. The number of unexpressed conflicts was positively correlated with the fear of creating a negative image (e.g., jealous, nag) with

Although the magnitude of some of the correlations is small, our measures evidence sufficient validity.

Hypothesis 1

H1, which predicted that a positive correlation should exist between the perceived quality of the partner's relational alternatives and the number of unexpressed conflicts, was supported ($r = .314$, $df = 95$, $p < .005$).[8] Moreover, the perceived quality of the partner's alternatives was *negatively* correlated with the respondent's willingness to tell the partner about irritations ($r = -.295$, $df = 98$, $p < .001$) and the number of irritations expressed to the partner ($r = -.254$, $df = 95$, $p < .006$), but *positively* correlated with withholding grievances because of conflict avoidance (point biserial $r = .207$, $df = 94$, $p < .021$).

Hypothesis 2

H2 predicted that the relationship between the perceived quality of a partner's relational alternatives and the number of unexpressed conflicts will be attenuated when controlling for the partner's perceived level of relational commitment. This hypothesis was predicated on the notion that when the partner is perceived to have superior alternatives, his or her relational commitment will be perceived to be lower and withholding complaints will result. Based on zero-order correlations, there is support for this notion. The quality of the partner's alternatives is *negatively* correlated with the partner's perceived commitment ($r = -.655$, $df = 99$, $p < .000$) and the partner's perceived commitment is *negatively* correlated with the number of unexpressed conflicts ($r = -.409$, $df = 97$, $p < .000$).

To more fully test the hypotheses, we utilized a three-step, hierarchical

---

the partner ($r = .352$, $df = 98$, $p < .01$) and being unable to motivate the partner to change ($r = .256$, $df = 98$, $p < .01$). Although not expressing conflict avoidance per se, the former motive implies a fear of driving the partner away and the latter implies a sense of powerlessness. The correlation between unexpressed conflict and having a relationship of insufficient intimacy to allow grievances to be aired only approached significance ($r = .189$, $df = 98$, $p < .06$), and the number of unexpressed irritations was not significantly related to the lack of importance of the listed problems ($r = .015$, $df = 98$, NSD).

[8]One might speculate that this relationship is an artifact created by a relationship between the total number of irritations identified and the perceived quality of the partner's relational alternatives. To test this possibility, we examined the correlation between the total number of complaints about the partner and the perceived quality of the partner's alternatives. This relationship was trivial ($r = .098$, $df = 97$, NSD).

regression technique (cf. Cohen & Cohen, 1975). On the first step, the number of unexpressed conflicts was regressed on perceived partner's commitment, and on the second, the perceived quality of the partner's alternatives was entered. On the third step, we added an interaction term formed by multiplying the partner's commitment by his or her relational alternatives (cf. Cohen & Cohen, 1975). This step was necessary to establish that the effect of either commitment or alternatives was not contingent on the value of the other (cf. Cohen & Cohen, 1975). If H2 is valid then the quality of perceived partner's alternatives should not be able to account for significant variance beyond that accounted for by perceived commitment, and the interaction should not account for significant additional variance. The results are presented in Table 3.1.

Consistent with H2, the partner's alternatives could not account for significant additional variance after commitment had been entered on the first step. Despite the aforementioned significant zero-order correlation between the partner's alternatives and the number of unexpressed conflicts, the unstandardized regression weight between those two variables is not significant when the partner's commitment is also in the regression equation. However, this analysis is compromised because the interaction term accounts for significant variance beyond that accounted for by the additive effects of perceptions of the partner's commitment and alternatives. Hence, there is a contingent association between the two predictor variables.

To assess the nature of that contingent association, we followed a technique suggested by Cohen and Cohen (1975) that is also presented in Table 3.1. Their approach involves reordering the unstandardized regression weights or slopes associated with the two predictor variables, the interaction term, and the Y intercept to examine the regression of unexpressed conflict on one predictor variable within various levels of the other predictor.

The clearest picture of the interaction emerges from examining the regression of the number of unexpressed conflicts on perceived partner commitment within low and high levels of the perceived partner's alternatives (formed respectively by one standard deviation below and above the mean level of partner's alternatives). The values of the Y intercepts of the two regressions indicate that more irritations are withheld at low levels of commitment when the partner's alternatives are thought to be superior (4.944) rather than inferior (.925). Given the unstandardized regression weight associated with the partner's alternatives was statistically significant and positive (slope = .443, $p < .005$) on the third step of the hierarchical regression, the increasing pattern reflected by these intercepts is significant (Cohen & Cohen, 1975).

TABLE 3.1

Hierarchical Regression of the Number of Unexpressed Conflicts
on the Perceived Quality of the Partner's Relational Alternatives,
the Partner's Perceived Commitment, and Their Interaction.

Step 1:	
Partner's commitment	−.152***
Y Intercept	4.473
R	.404***
Change in R^2	.163***
Step 2:	
Partner's commitment	−.132**
Partner's alternatives	.034
Y Intercept	3.746
R	.409**
Change in R^2	.004
Step 3:	
Partner's commitment	.127
Partner's alternatives	.443**
Interaction	−.021**
Y Intercept	−1.501
R	.481**
Change in R^2	.064**

Regression of the Number of Unexpressed Conflict
on Perceived Partner's Commitment Within Inferior and
Superior Partner Alternatives

Inferior partner alternatives (1 standard deviation below the mean=5.474)	$\hat{Y} = (.012)$ commitment + .925
Superior partner alternatives (1 standard deviation above the mean = 14.546)	$\hat{Y} = (−.178)$ commitment + 4.944

Unstandardized regression weights (slopes) are reported.
*=$p<.05$; **=$p<.01$; ***=$p<.001$.

Moreover, when the partner's alternatives are thought to be good, there is a negative unstandardized regression weight between the perceived partner's commitment and the number of unexpressed conflicts (slope = −.178). This implies that individuals will be motivated to withhold grievances whenever their partners are perceived to have superior relational alternatives *and* their partners' projected relational commitment is of insufficient magnitude to restrain them from pursuing those options. In comparison, the regression of the number of unexpressed conflicts on partner commitment within low levels of alternatives is positive and of lower magnitude (slope = .012). Indeed, the absence of a significant unstandardized regression weight (slope = .127, NSD) for partner's commitment on the third step of the hierarchical regression suggests these differences are statistically trivial.

Thus, the combination of a partner's low commitment and good alternatives evidence a greater chilling effect on expressing conflict than do other combinations.

Hypotheses 3 and 4

H3 and H4 are both evidenced in the interaction of the quality of the partner's alternatives and one's own alternatives. To test them, we employed a hierarchical regression approach similar to that used to examine H2. On the first step, the number of unexpressed conflicts was regressed on both the partner's and the respondent's alternatives. On the second step, the interaction of the two alternative measures (formed by multiplying the two variables) was entered. As an initial test of the two hypotheses, we expected the interaction term would account for significant additional variance. The results are presented in Table 3.2.

As predicted, the interaction term accounted for significant additional variance. In order to determine the shape of the interaction, we examined the regression of the number of unexpressed conflicts on the partner's commitment within levels of low and high partner alternatives (defined respectively as 1 standard deviation below and above the alternative mean). These regressions are also included in Table 3.2.

H3 posited that when the partner's alternatives are perceived to be better than the current relationship, there should be a negative association between the quality of one's own alternatives and the number of unexpressed conflicts. Consistent with this expectation, there is a modest negative unstandardized regression weight (slope = $-.053$) between the perceived quality of the respondent's alternatives and the number of unexpressed conflicts when the partner's alternatives are thought to be superior to the current relationship.

H4 predicted that when one's own alternatives are perceived to be more inferior than the current relationship, there should be a positive association between the quality of the partner's perceived relational alternatives and the number of unexpressed conflicts. By examining the Y intercepts of the two regression equations, one can determine the relationship between the partner's perceived alternatives and unexpressed conflict when one's alternatives are low (cf. Cohen & Cohen, 1975). Consistent with H4, when the partner's alternatives are perceived to be high, the intercept is of greater magnitude (2.834) relative to low partner alternatives ($-.392$). Because the unstandardized regression

TABLE 3.2

Hierarchical Regression of the Number of Unexpressed Conflicts
on the Perceived Quality of the Partner's Relational Alternatives,
the Quality of the Respondent's Own Relational Alternatives,
and their Interaction

Step 1:	
Respondent's alternatives	.059
Partner's alternatives	.121**
Y Intercept	−.294
R	.392***
Change in R^2	.154***
Step 2:	
Respondent's alternatives	.282**
Partner's alternatives	.357**
Interaction	−.023*
Y Intercept	−2.375
R	.444**
Change in R^2	.043*

Regression of the Number of Unexpressed Conflict on Quality
of Respondent's Own Relational Alternatives Within Inferior
and Superior Partner Alternatives

Inferior partner alternatives (1 standard deviation below the mean = 5.813)	$\hat{Y}$ = (.154) resp. alt. −.392
Superior partner alternatives (1 standard deviation above the mean = 14.563)	$\hat{Y}$ = (−.053) resp. alt. + 2.834

Unstandardized regression weights (slopes) are reported.
*=$p<.05$; **=$p<.01$; ***=$p<.001$.

weight for the partner's alternatives in the hierarchical regression is statistically significant and positive (slope = .357, $p < .002$), the increasing pattern evidenced by the intercepts is significant.

Although the two hypotheses are confirmed, one unanticipated pattern was detected. Because our analysis of the chilling effect is focused on power deficits, we did not advance a hypothesis about situations in which the respondent is at a relative power advantage. When one examines the regression of unexpressed conflict on the respondent's own alternatives when the partner's alternatives are low, one finds such a test. That regression yielded a positive unstandardized regression weight between the partner's alternatives and unexpressed conflict (slope = .154). This implies that when the partner has low alternatives, there is greater unexpressed conflicts at higher levels of respondent alternatives. In essence, when the respondent had a power advantage, he or she withheld more irritations than when both the partner and respondent had equal but low alternatives. We elaborate on this in the discussion section of the chapter.

Hypothesis 5

H5 posited that partners who are dating others will be perceived to have better relational alternatives and will prompt a chilling effect to a greater extent than those who are not dating others. Recall that we had two separate indicators of extra-dyadic activity. The first focused on the degree to which the partner is free to see other people. Consistent with H5, the partner's freedom to date others was positively correlated with the quality of his or her relational alternatives ($r = .436$, $df = 95$, $p <$ .000) and the number of unexpressed conflicts ($r = .312$, $df = 95$, $p <$ .001).

To determine whether the partner's alternatives could account for any variance in the chilling effect beyond that of his or her freedom to date others, we employed the same three-step hierarchical regression used to test H2. On the first step, the number of unexpressed conflicts was regressed on the freedom to see others, and on the second step the perceived quality of the partner's alternatives was entered. The interaction of the two predictor variables was entered on the final step. The results are presented in Table 3.3.

The regression indicates that the partner's alternatives can still account for significant additional variance beyond that accounted for by the freedom to see others. Moreover, when the partner's alternatives criterion is entered on the second step, the unstandardized regression weight for the freedom to date is no longer statistically significant. This is not to say that the freedom to see others has no impact at all on the relationship between the quality of the partner's alternatives and unexpressed conflict. The partial correlation between the partner's alternatives and unexpressed conflict controlling for the freedom to date others is lower ($r = .219$) than is the zero-order correlation ($r = .312$). Thus, the freedom to see others somewhat attenuates the association, but cannot reduce it below levels of statistical significance.

H5 is also supported when examining the influence of the partner actually dating others. For these tests, a dummy-coded variable was created in which partners who were going out with someone else were assigned a code of 1 and those not seeing others were coded 0. As expected, partners dating others were perceived to have better relational alternatives than those who were not (point biserial $r = .318$, $df = 94$, p < .001), and respondents involved with partners who were seeing others

TABLE 3.3
Hierarchical Regression of the Number of Unexpressed Conflicts
on the Perceived Quality of the Partner's Relational Alternatives,
the Partner's Freedom to Date Others, and Their Interaction.

Step 1:	
Partner's freedom	.277**
Y Intercept	.529
R	.282**
Change in R^2	.079**
Step 2:	
Partner's freedom	.177
Partner's alternatives	.097*
Y Intercept	−.062
R	.409**
Change in R^2	.044*
Step 3:	
Partner's freedom	.197
Partner's alternatives	.107
Interaction	−.002
Y Intercept	−.141
R	.351**
Change in R^2	.000

Unstandardized regression weights (slopes) are reported.
$* = p<.05; ** = p < .01; ***p < .001$.

have greater numbers of unexpressed conflicts (point biserial $r = .318$, $df = 94, p < .001$).

To determine whether dating others might attenuate the association between the partner's alternatives and unexpressed conflicts, we employed the same three-step hierarchical procedure used earlier. The results are presented in Table 3.4.

Rather than attenuate the association, the regressions uncovered an interaction between dating others and the quality of the partner's alternatives. The form of the interaction was clearest when examining the relationship between dating others and unexpressed conflicts within conditions of low and high partner alternatives (formed by 1 standard deviation below and above the mean level of alternatives). These two regression are included in Table 3.4. As can be seen, when the partner's alternatives are perceived to be superior to the existing relationship, dating others yields higher levels of unexpressed conflict than not seeing others (slope = 1.818). This pattern suggests that respondents held back conflicts when their partners were dating others and those alternative relationships were perceived to be of higher quality. However, when the partner's alternatives are thought to be inferior, dating others is associated with fewer unexpressed conflicts than not seeing others (slope =

TABLE 3.4

Hierarchical Regression of the Number of Unexpressed Conflicts
on the Perceived Quality of the Partner's Relational Alternatives,
the Partner's Extradyadic Dating Activity, and Their Interaction.

Step 1:	
Partner's extradyadic dating	1.504**
Y intercept	1.286
R	.318**
Change in R^2	.101***
Step 2:	
Partner's extradyadic dating	1.511*
Partner's alternatives	.098*
Y intercept	.379
R	.388**
Change in R^2	.049*
Step 3:	
Partner's extradyadic dating	−2.195
Partner's alternatives	.039
Interaction	.278**
Y intercept	.926
R	.465**
Change in R^2	.066**

Regression of the Number of Unexpressed Conflict on Partner's Extradyadic Dating
Within Inferior and Superior Partner Alternatives

Inferior partner Alternatives (1 standard deviation below the mean = 5.428)	$\hat{Y} = (-.691)$ dating + 1.138
Superior partner alternatives (1 standard deviation above the mean = 14.488)	$\hat{Y} = (1.818)$ dating + 1.491

Unstandardized regression weights (slopes) are reported.
* = $p < .05$;   ** = $p < .01$;   *** = $p < .001$.

−.691). Because the unstandardized regression weight for dating others
in the hierarchical regression was not statistically significant, this association may not be meaningful.

Hypothesis 6

H6 posited that partners who had threatened to break up the relationship
would be perceived to have superior relational alternatives and would
instill a chilling effect to a greater extent than those who had not. Recall
that we asked respondents if their partner had ever threatened to terminate the relationship and if they had actually done so. Answers to these

questions were dummy coded 1 if yes and 0 if no and correlated with the perceived quality of the partner's alternatives and the number of unexpressed conflicts. No support is found for H6. No significant correlations were observed between either measure of relational termination and the partner's alternative or the number of unexpressed conflicts.

DISCUSSION

Although some of our preliminary ideas clearly require revision, two fundamental expectations were confirmed. There is evidence of a chilling effect, and that phenomenon is positively correlated with perceiving that one's partner has superior relational alternatives to the extant relationship (H1).

Our results also provide intriguing insights into other phenomena related to the chilling effect. We discovered that controlling for the partner's perceived commitment substantially attenuates the association between the partner's alternatives and the number of unexpressed complaints (H2), but we also uncovered an unanticipated interaction between perceptions of the partner's alternatives and commitment. The form of the interaction suggests that when the partner's alternatives are thought to be superior, the number of unexpressed irritations is greater when the partner is perceived to be relatively uncommitted to the relationship. When the partner is perceived to have inferior alternatives, the level of his or her commitment has minimal impact on the chilling effect. Perhaps then, the partner appears to be "trapped" regardless of his or her desire to remain in the relationship and conflict avoidance is less necessary.

The confirmation of H3 and H4 suggests that the chilling effect is associated with power deficits arising from dependency (own alternatives are inferior, whereas the partner's are thought to be superior). However, we also found an unanticipated relationship involving *power advantages* (own alternatives are superior, whereas the partner's are believed to be inferior). When the partner's alternatives are thought to be inferior, more withholding occurs when the respondent's own alternatives are thought to be superior rather than inferior. Although speculative, perhaps individuals who perceive they are in an advantageous power position have little motivation to try to change the partner's behavior by telling him or her about their relational problems. After all, why bother when one has better alternatives? If substantiated in future investigations, this would imply that individuals in relative power positions may withhold grievances for different reasons than those at a power disadvantage. The former simply do not care enough to fight.

The results suggest that having access to other dating partners is also related to the chilling effect (H5). When the partner is free to date others, he or she is perceived to have better relational alternatives and more complaints are withheld. We found that controlling for their perceived freedom somewhat attenuates the association between partner's alternatives and unexpressed conflict, but not substantially. However, an unanticipated interaction was uncovered between the partner's alternatives and whether he or she is actually going out with others. Apparently, when the partner's alternatives are superior and he or she is taking advantage of them by dating others, the chilling effect is maximized. After all, the partner might not come back to the respondent if angered. When the partner's alternatives are inferior, extra-dyadic activity has minimal impact. Perhaps, the threat that the partner will stay with one of the inferior alternatives is sufficiently low so as to not to warrant conflict avoidance.

Finally, we found no evidence that partners who threaten to or actually do terminate the relationship are perceived to have greater relational alternatives or instill a chilling effect. Moreover, our validity checks found no evidence that partners who are perceived to have superior relational alternatives are perceived to be more assertive in arguments, nor are they the subject of complaints about their controlling behavior. This pattern suggests that having superior alternatives may not lead to *overt* attempts to control or dominate their counterpart. Perhaps partners with superior alternatives exert control through their indifference (e.g., lack of affection, excessive independence, minimal respect, and interest in other romantic involvements), rather than through more direct or even indirect power tactics (cf. Folger & Poole, 1984). If their superior perceived alternatives lead to a chilling effect, they do not have to act in a controlling fashion. Their relational counterparts have persuaded themselves.

Although the associations uncovered in this data set are important, its limitations suggest important future research directions. First, the cross-sectional nature of the study makes it difficult to unambiguously specify the direction of the effect. Hence, individuals who have substantial numbers of unexpressed irritations might come to perceive their partners have superior alternatives in conjunction with low commitment, that their partner's alternatives are good and their own are inferior, and perhaps, that their partners are dating others and those alternative are superior. Although we have no statistical basis from which to rule out these self-perception effects (i.e., because of their conflict avoidance behavior, they attribute certain traits to self and partner), we do not think they are likely. Research that has manipulated the quality of one's own alternatives suggests the causal direction is from alternatives to conflict behavior (cf. Rusbult, 1987). It is plausible that such a direction would also be uncovered for the partner's alternatives.

Second, we did not interview both relational partners to determine mutual perceptions of the key variables. One intriguing question is whether the partner is aware of the unexpressed grievances directed toward his or her behavior, and if so, how did this awareness occur? It is possible that the undisclosive person communicates these grievances in an indirect fashion (cf. Sillars, 1980). The person may hint about desired changes, try to set a good example through his or her own behavior, criticize third parties for similar undesirable behaviors, or show nonverbal signs of disapproval. If such actions are undertaken, the next question becomes: Are they perceived by the partner and is corrective action undertaken? It seems reasonable that unless complaints are "placed on the floor," little may be done to alter the situation.

Third, our findings may be limited to dating populations. Hence, it is important to determine whether similar associations can be uncovered in more constrained relationships such as marriage (Johnson, 1982). For example, Udry (1981) discovered that economic (income, employment) as well as relational alternatives play a role in marriage. It seems unlikely that such economic factors are as important in dating as in marriage. Hence, within marital relationships, being economically dependent on the spouse might induce the chilling effect, rather than merely perceiving inadequate relational alternatives.

Finally, we focused on the chilling effect as a phenomena that occurs prior to an interaction and ignored its influence within conversational interchanges. Sillars, Coletti, Parry, and Rogers (1982) have developed a coding scheme for interaction behaviors that suggests that conflict avoidance can occur within a communication interchange. If so, we might find that individuals who wish to withhold grievances but are forced to discuss them may engage in such avoidance acts to disengage from the conversation, and for some couples, such behavior might even be functional (cf. Rands, Levinger, & Mellinger, 1981; Sillars, Pike, Jones, & Redmon, 1983).

Under other conditions the chilling effect might lead to more explosive interactions. If a relational partner is accumulating grievances against his or her counterpart, but not expressing them, a severe argument may occur when disclosure is finally forced. This outcome is similar to what others have referred to as "gunnysacking" (e.g., Galvin & Brommel, 1986; Wilmot & Wilmot, 1978) or the silent, simmering accumulation of issues until a critical incident forces all of the grievances to be "dumped" on the transgressor.

Overall, we believe the chilling effect is an important phenomena that warrants further research.

ACKNOWLEDGMENTS

The authors wish to express their gratitude to Tracy L. Meisinger and Katherine L. Scoulas for their invaluable assistance at a variety of points in this research. Also, we acknowledge the useful feedback received on earlier versions from Professors Robert Bell and Dudley D. Cahn. An earlier version of this paper was presented at the annual meeting of the International Communication Association, Dublin, 1990.

REFERENCES

Baxter, L.A. (1986). Gender differences in the hetero-sexual relationship rules embedded in break-up accounts. *Journal of Social and Personal Relationships, 3*, 289–306.

Baxter, L.A., & Wilmot, W.W. (1985). Taboo topics in close relationships. *Journal of Social and Personal Relationships, 2*, 253–269.

Berg, J.H. (1984). Development of friendship between roommates. *Journal of Personality and Social Psychology, 46*, 346–356.

Berg, J.H., & McQuinn, R.D. (1986). Attraction and exchange in continuing and noncontinuing dating relationships. *Journal of Personality and Social Psychology, 50*, 942–952.

Berger, C.R. (1980). Power and the family. In M.E. Roloff & G.R. Miller (Eds.), *Persuasion: New directions in theory and research* (pp. 197–224). Newbury Park, CA: Sage.

Birchler, G.R., & Webb, L.J. (1977). Discriminating interaction behaviors in happy and unhappy marriages. *Journal of Consulting and Clinical Psychology, 45*, 494–495.

Birchler, G.R., Weiss, R.L., & Vincent, J.P. (1975). Multimethod analysis of social reinforcement exchange between maritally distressed and nondistressed spouse and stranger dyads. *Journal of Personality and Social Psychology, 31*, 349–360.

Blood, R.O., & Wolf, D.M. (1960). *Husbands and wives.* New York: The Free Press.

Blumberg, H.H. (1972). Communication of interpersonal evaluations. *Journal of Personality and Social Psychology, 23*, 157–162.

Buss, D.M. (1989). Conflict between the sexes: Strategic interferences and the evocation of anger and upset. *Journal of Personality and Social Psychology, 56*, 735–747.

Cohen, J., & Cohen, P. (1975). *Applied multiple regression/correlation analysis for the behavioral sciences.* Hillsdale, NJ; Lawrence Erlbaum Associates.

Coser, L. (1956). *The functions of social conflict.* New York: The Free Press.

Deutsch, M. (1973). *The resolution of conflict: Constructive and destructive processes.* New Haven, CT: Yale University Press.

Folger, J.P., & Poole, M.S. (1984). *Working through conflict: A communication perspective.* Glenview, IL: Scott, Foresman.

Galvin, K.M., & Brommel, B.J. (1986). *Family communication: Cohesion and change* (2nd ed.). Glenview, IL: Scott, Foresman.

Grauerholz, E. (1987). Balancing the power in dating relationships. *Sex Roles, 17*, 563–571.

Hansen, G.L. (1987). Extradyadic relations during courtship. *Journal of Sex Research, 23*, 382–390.

Heer, D.M. (1963). The measurement and bases of family power: An overview. *Marriage and Family Living, 25,* 133–139.

Hill, C.T., Rubin, Z., & Peplau, L.A. (1976). Breakups before marriage: The end of 103 affairs. *Journal of Social Issues, 32,* 147–168.

Hocker, J.L., & Wilmot, W.W. (1985). *Interpersonal conflict* (2nd ed.). Dubuque, IA: Wm. C. Brown.

Johnson, M. (1982). Social and cognitive features of the dissolution of commitment to relationships. In S. Duck (Ed.), *Personal relationships.* Vol *4: Dissolving personal relationships* (pp. 51–74). New York: Academic Press.

Knapp, M.L., Stafford, L., & Daly, J.A. (1986). Regrettable messages: Things people wish they hadn't said. *Journal of Communication, 36,* 40–58.

Millar, F.E., & Rogers, L.E. (1987). Relational dimensions of interpersonal dynamics. In M.E. Roloff & G.R. Miller (Eds.), *Interpersonal processes: New directions in communication research* (pp. 117–139). Newbury Park, CA: Sage.

Rands, M., Levinger, G. & Mellinger, G.D. (1981). Patterns of conflict resolution and marital satisfaction. *Journal of Family Issues, 2,* 297–321.

Resick, P.A., Barr, P.K., Sweet, J.J., Kieffer, D.M., Ruby, N.L., & Spiegel, D.K. (1981). Perceived and actual discriminators of conflict from accord in marital communication. *The American Journal of Family Therapy, 9,* 58–68.

Rusbult, C.E. (1980). Commitment and satisfaction in romantic associations: A test of the investment model. *Journal of Experimental Social Psychology, 16,* 172–186.

Rusbult, C.E. (1983). A longitudinal test of the investment model: The development (and deterioration) of satisfaction and commitment in heterosexual involvements. *Journal of Personality and Social Psychology, 45,* 101–117.

Rusbult, C.E. (1987). Responses to dissatisfaction in close relationships: The exit-voice-loyalty-neglect model. In D. Perlman & S. Duck (Eds.), *Intimate relationships: Developmental dynamics and deterioration* (pp. 209–237). Newbury Park, CA: Sage.

Rusbult, C.E., Johnson, D.J., & Morrow, G.D. (1986a). Determinants and consequences of exit, voice, loyalty, and neglect: Responses to dissatisfaction in adult romantic involvements. *Human Relations, 39,* 45–63.

Rusbult, C.E., Johnson, D.J., & Morrow, G.D. (1986b). Predicting satisfaction and commitment in adult romantic involvements: An assessment of the generalizability of the investment model. *Social Psychology Quarterly, 49,* 81–89.

Rusbult, C.E., Zembrodt, I.M., & Gunn, L.K. (1982). Exit, voice, loyalty, and neglect: Responses to dissatisfaction in romantic involvements. *Journal of Personality and Social Psychology, 43,* 1230–1242.

Scanzoni, J. (1978). *Sex roles, women's work, and marital conflict.* Lexington, MA: Lexington Books.

Sillars, A.L. (1980). Attributions and communication in roommate conflicts. *Communication Monographs, 47,* 180–200.

Sillars, A.L., Coletti, S.F., Parry, D., & Rogers, M.A. (1982). Coding verbal conflict tactics: Nonverbal and perceptual correlates of the "avoidance-distributive-integrative" distinction. *Human Communication Research, 9,* 83–95.

Sillars, A.L., Pike, G.R., Jones, T.S., & Redmon, K. (1983). Communication and conflict in marriage. In R. Bostrom (Ed.), *Communication yearbook 7* (pp. 414–429). Newbury Park, CA: Sage.

Sprecher, S. (1988). Investment model, equity, and social support determinants of relationship commitment. *Social Psychology Quarterly, 51,* 318–328.

Ting-Toomey, S. (1984). Perceived decision-making power and marital adjustment. *Communication Research Reports, 1,* 15–20.

Udry, J.R. (1981). Marital alternatives and marital disruption. *Journal of Marriage and the Family, 43,* 889–897.

White, G.L. (1980). Inducing jealousy: A power perspective. *Personality and Social Psychology Bulletin, 6,* 222–227.

Wilmot, J.H., & Wilmot, W.W. (1978). *Interpersonal conflict.* Dubuque, IA: Wm. C. Brown.

Nonverbal Conflict Behaviors:
Functions, Strategies, and Tactics

Deborah A. Newton
Judee K. Burgoon
University of Arizona

Relationship conflict typically occurs because at least one party perceives a violation or threat to relationship rules, themes, beliefs, or boundaries (Galvin & Brommel, 1986). Conflict becomes a suasory process as partners tacitly or overtly attempt to negotiate these violations or threats. Thus, conflict necessarily involves interpersonal influence, or the use of verbal and nonverbal strategies to establish, reinforce, and alter others' cognitions, emotions, and behaviors (Seibold, Cantrill, & Meyers, 1985).

Heretofore, most studies of conflict behavior have focused almost exclusively on verbal channels and ignored the nonverbal cues used in place of, or in conjunction with, verbal messages. Yet it is evident that a complete account of conflict requires examining both. Berger (1985) argued that failure to account for the nonverbal communication used in the influence process is to "doom oneself to study the tip of a very large iceberg" (p. 483). Millar, Rogers, and Bavelas (1984) concurred that in order to fully understand what leads relational partners to constructive and destructive outcomes, researchers must identify and distinguish which nonverbal behaviors constitute "one-up" or "one-down" messages.

This chapter offers a starting point in addressing such matters. It deals with those amorphous signals—the exasperated sigh, the disapproving grunt, the prolonged stare, the upturned lip, the harsh voice, the ignored comment—that convey potent messages and turn simple discussions into hostile arguments. As Galvin and Brommel (1986) noted, "If you closely monitor any developing conflict, usually nonverbal cues of conflict appear before verbal ones" (p. 170). The focus here is on nonverbal behaviors manifested by relational partners as they attempt to influence one another during conflict. As such, it serves as a companion to our previous work (Newton & Burgoon, in press) on the verbal strategies used by relational partners during disagreements. By examining what nonverbal behaviors accompany those verbal strategies, we hope to contribute to the ultimate development of a strategy and tactic taxonomy that weds verbal and nonverbal behaviors and forms message composites. Toward that end, we consider what nonverbal behaviors are likely components of conflict displays. We then present the results of an exploratory investigation that identifies some of the nonverbal behaviors exhibited during couples' disagreements and the extent to which those differ by gender. This parallels the descriptive profiles of verbal strategy use presented in Newton and Burgoon (in press). We conclude by analyzing how those behaviors relate to the concomitant verbal strategies in use and how, together, the verbal and nonverbal strategies affect the interaction outcomes of persuasiveness, satisfaction, and perceived relational communication. Linking combined verbal and nonverbal strategies to interaction consequences serves to reveal which strategies are the most and least efficacious and can eventually translate into behavioral recommendations for promoting conflict resolution and relational satisfaction.

FUNCTIONS SERVED BY COMMUNICATION DURING CONFLICT

Clark and Delia (1979) argued that regardless of the specific goals individuals may have in interpersonal interactions, communication serves three general functional objectives. At the broadest level, communication addresses *instrumental objectives,* which pertain to the content of the interaction, *interpersonal objectives,* which involve establishing and maintaining the relationship, and *identity objectives,* which relate to the management of a desired self-image and maintaining a particular identity. These objectives frame influence behavior as partners attempt to negotiate mutually agreed upon definitions and understandings. Accomplishment of these objectives is not necessarily a conscious process (see Berger, 1985; Berger & Douglas, 1982; Lewis, 1969; Miller, Boster, Roloff, & Seibold, 1987; Roloff, 1980). Quite likely, relationship partners cycle between highly conscious or mindful states and nonreflective, adaptive states as they try simultaneously to accomplish instrumental, relationship-, and identity-management goals during interactions.

Nonverbal behaviors can be analyzed according to how they fulfill these functions. Although numerous functional analyses of nonverbal behavior have been forwarded (e.g., Argyle, 1972; Eisenberg & Smith, 1971; Ekman & Friesen, 1969; Harrison, 1974; Higginbotham & Yoder, 1982, Kendon, 1967; Scheflen, 1967, 1974), those advanced by Burgoon

(1980, 1985; Burgoon, Buller, & Woodall, 1989; Burgoon & Saine, 1978) and Patterson (1982, 1983, 1985) are the most comprehensive. For comparison and contrast, their functional classifications are summarized in Table 4.1, where their relationship to the three broader classes of instrumental, interpersonal, and identity objectives are proposed. Although Patterson's system focuses specifically on nonverbal involvement, it should be apparent that there are many similarities between the two systems.

Our concern here is with those functions that are particularly relevant to conflict between intimate partners. The most pertinent functions appear to be:

1. identification/information,
2. expressive communication/affect management,
3. impression formation and management/presentational management,
4. relational communication/intimacy,
5. mixed messages/deception,
6. structuring and regulating interaction, and
7. social influence/social control.

The extensiveness of this list reveals that numerous nonverbal cues are potentially implicated. It also suggests the enormity of the task of handling conflict, if one is simultaneously to protect one's ego, manage emotional outbursts, project a particular image, send messages regarding the current state of the relationship, keep the conversation going, and persuade another to his or her point of view.

In serving these functions, nonverbal cues may be used deliberately. For example, one might decrease gaze, turn away, and increase movement and gestural activity when feeling strong negative affect; one might initiate touch when communicating support; or one might move closer, increase gaze, and use appropriate paralinguistic emphasis when making an accusation designed to win a concession. Nonverbal cues may also be communicated unintentionally for expressive or cathartic purposes; they may perform the adaptive, partially nonreflective functions of influence. Moreover, a functional view of nonverbal communication implies that different behaviors may serve the same function. A wife may derogate her husband's comment by responding with an exasperated look or a sarcastic vocal pattern. Or the same behavior may serve different functions. Forward lean may communicate both involvement and a desire to influence. In sum, many nonverbal behaviors can be used interchange-

TABLE 4.1
Two Functional Classification Systems for Nonverbal Communication

---

Burgoon's Classification System

Identity Functions:
1. *Identification:* Nonverbal behaviors project self-identities through cues revealing one's culture, gender, race, personality, and the like.
2. *Expressive communication:* Nonverbal behavior is the primary vehicle for emotive messages, which include intentional affect displays and unintentional, carthartic ones.
3. *Impression formation and management:* Nonverbal cues are used to foster and manage certain impressions.

Relationship Functions:
4. *Relational communication:* Nonverbal cues signal interactional partners' definitions of their relationship, such as degree of intimacy, involvement, and dominance.
5. *Mixed messages and deception:* Nonverbal cues are used to create incongruity among messages and send mixed signals that may be used to mislead someone about the true state of affairs.
6. *Structuring and managing interaction:* Nonverbal behaviors define the situation and influence the progression and patterning of conversation.

Instrumental Functions:
7. *Social influence:* Nonverbal behaviors are used to alter attitudes and overt behaviors of message recipients.
8. *Message production, processing and comprehension:* Nonverbal signals are central to cognitive processing of social information and facilitate or impede the learning of new concepts and behaviors.

Patterson's Functional Classification System

Identity Functions:
1. *Informational function:* Nonverbal behaviors supply a wide range of information from which observers can make attributions about the actor.
2. *Affect management:* Individuals regulate the experience and nonverbal display of affect, and with it, the consequences of emotional displays.
3. *Presentational function:* Nonverbal involvement behaviors are used to present or enhance an identity or image at the individual or relationship level.

Relationship Functions:
4. *Expressing intimacy:* Nonverbal involvement behaviors signal differential intimacy levels between partners.
5. *Interaction regulation:* Nonverbal behaviors control the flow of interaction and the degree of involvement that is expressed.

Instrumental Functions:
6. *Social control:* Nonverbal involvement may be managed to influence another person's perceptions or behavior.
7. *Service-task function:* Nonverbal involvement behaviors may be used in achieving service and task goals, such as touch during a physical examination.

---

ably to serve a variety of functions, including revealing the intensity of psychological and emotional states, defining the nature of the relationship between interacting parties, and influencing the way a conversation is progressing.

In assessing nonverbal behavior, it is important to remember that a communicator's purpose is likely to be achieved by coordinating multiple nonverbal behaviors with one another and with the verbal channel (Burgoon, 1985). Several behaviors may operate simultaneously to facilitate, qualify, or contradict the interpretation of verbal messages. In turn, verbal content frames the interpretation of nonverbal signals. The inextricable intertwining of behaviors among and between the nonverbal and verbal channels reinforces the necessity of examining them in combination to derive the total meaning of an exchange.

PREVIOUS MEASUREMENT OF CONFLICT STRATEGIES AND TACTICS

A primary research thrust has been to associate conflict behavior directly or indirectly with some other construct of interest such as *communication competence* (Canary & Cupach, 1988; Canary & Spitzberg, 1987, 1989), *relationship type* (Fitzpatrick, 1988; Fitzpatrick, Fallis, & Vance, 1982; Sillars, Pike, Jones, & Redmon, 1983), *relational satisfaction* (Cupach, 1982; Gottman, 1979; Koren, Carlton, & Shaw, 1980; Pike & Sillars, 1985; Sillars, 1980a), *nonverbal encoding and decoding accuracy* (Noller, 1984; Noller & Gallois, in press), and *communicator gender* (Falbo & Peplau, 1980; Kimmel, Pruitt, Mageneau, Konar-Goldband, & Carnevale, 1980; Shokley-Zalabak & Morley, 1984). In such cases, only inferences are made about how nonverbal behaviors function during conflict, or a limited set of nonverbal cues that supplement verbal messages is assessed. As a result, questions remain about how nonverbal behaviors may be used as tactics to enact strategies and how complexes of nonverbal signals combine to produce meaning. The relevant research is reviewed briefly to determine how verbal and nonverbal tactics might combine to form conflict strategies.

The Verbal Channel

Depending on how broadly or narrowly one defines conflict, a number of coding schemes and taxonomies have been advanced for assessing verbal behavior related to conflict (e.g., Brown & Levinson, 1978; Cupach, 1980; Falbo, 1977; Falbo & Peplau, 1980; Fitzpatrick et al., 1982;

Fitzpatrick & Winke, 1979; Hall, 1969; Hawkins, Weisberg, & Ray, 1977; Kilmann & Thomas, 1977; Kipnis, 1976; Lawrence & Lorsch, 1967; Millar et al., 1984; Peterson, 1983; Pruitt & Rubin, 1986; Putnam & Wilson, 1982; Rands, Levinger, & Mellinger, 1981; Rausch, Barry, Hertel, & Swain, 1974; Roloff, 1976; Ross & DeWine, 1982; Sillars, 1980b; Walton & McKersie, 1965; Ware, 1980; Weiss & Summers, 1983).

The majority of these schemes are based on results of factor analyses that categorize verbal messages. For example, Putnam and Wilson (1982) delineated three communicative strategies used in conflict situations: *nonconfrontational* (avoidance, smoothing, withdrawing, and indirectness); *solution-orientation* (direct confrontation, discussion of alternatives, and acceptances of compromises), and *control* (direct confrontation that leads to persistent argument). Roloff (1976) identified five modes of conflict resolution including revenge, regression, verbal aggression, physical aggression, and prosocial strategies. Hawkins et al. (1977) and Rands et al. (1981) each distinguished four communication styles or patterns used by conflicting couples.

One of the criticisms of such research is that little attention is paid to *how* strategies are enacted behaviorally at the tactical level (Berger, 1985; Clark, 1979; Cody, McLaughlin, & Jordon, 1980; Roloff, 1980). To clarify, we are referring to *strategies* as broad, overarching objectives and *tactics* as lower level behavioral routines used to actualize strategies (Berger, 1985). On self-report measures, most strategies are described at a relatively high degree of abstraction (Roloff, 1980), making it difficult for respondents to visualize exactly how a strategy is enacted. Without specification of lower level behavioral tactics instantiated to carry out higher level strategies, measurement is imprecise.

In response to this shortcoming, Newton (1988) developed a system of strategies and tactics revolving around instrumental, relationship-management, and identity-management objectives. Her categorical system, which classifies influence attempts during disagreements, analyzes strategies at three levels. At the *content level,* strategies are used to validate or invalidate issues in order to accomplish task-related objectives; claims, warrants, and data are accepted or rejected for their truth value or accuracy. At the *relationship level,* positive and negative relational-management strategies are used to validate and confirm, or invalidate and disconfirm, the other so that at the end of an interaction a specifiable relationship is obtained. At the *identity-management level,* assertive and defensive strategies are used to manage one's identity so that a particular image is fostered. The following six strategies are identified as serving these functions: content-validation, content-invalidation, other-support, other-accusations, self-assertions, and self-defense. These strategies are, in turn, "fleshed out" at the tactical level with 36 *verbal* tactics. Newton and Burgoon (in press) provide a complete description of this category system, including how strategies and tactics serve overarching functions.

The Nonverbal Channel

Despite the recognized importance of nonverbal messages in conflictual situations, research to date has been conducted on an extremely limited set of nonverbal behaviors (e.g., eye gaze, voice tone, and immediacy cues). For example, Gottman, Markman, and Notarius (1977) examined both the verbal and nonverbal behaviors of conflicting marital partners, yet only coded facial affect, vocalic affect, or body position and movement as positive, negative, or neutral. Sillars, Coletti, Parry, and Rogers (1982) studied only seven nonverbal behaviors associated with the 27 conflict tactics in Sillars' interpersonal conflict coding system. Noller and Gallois (in press) assessed the presence or absence of nine facial behaviors to determine whether there were differences related to gender, marital adjustment level, or encoding ability. Fitzpatrick (1988) indexed partners' nonverbal responsiveness by evaluating six cues that express intimacy— touch, lean, body orientation, gaze, smiling, and laughter. Although focus on a small number of nonverbal cues is more manageable for the researcher, problematic is the incomplete representation they provide of the large behavioral repertoires communicators typically exhibit in interactions, as well as the inability to assess the interrelationships among variables in accomplishing various functions.

Departing from the typical tradition is the recent work by Burgoon and associates (Burgoon, Kelley, Newton, & Keeley-Dyerson, 1989; Coker & Burgoon, 1987) on the nonverbal indicants of arousal and conversational involvement. In the two studies combined, 59 nonverbal behaviors aggregated into 21 composite or individual measures were linked to arousal and involvement. Because of the conceptual relevance of arousal and involvement to conflict behavior and the multifunctional nature of the nonverbal indices included in those studies, the same behaviors were selected for examination in the current investigation. Although this represents a relatively comprehensive look at nonverbal behavior, it should be recognized at the outset that it is not exhaustive but merely a first step toward profiling nonverbal conflict strategies and tactics.

LINKING NONVERBAL AND VERBAL
BEHAVIORS DURING CONFLICT

A general argument can be made that conflict between relational partners should produce high levels of conversational involvement and moderate to high levels of physiological and/or psychological arousal. *Conversational involvement* refers to the degree to which communicators are cognitively or behaviorally engaged in the topic, relationship, and/or situation (Coker & Burgoon, 1987). During a conflict, participants are likely to be highly involved, a state that Cegala, Savage, Brunner, and Conrad (1982) described as an integration of feelings, thoughts, and experiences with the ongoing interaction. *Arousal* refers to states of cognitive activation, attention, or alertness in response to sensory stimuli (for a thorough discussion, see Burgoon et al., 1989). Although the compresence of individuals or processing of novel or complex information are arousal producing, the adversarial nature of conflict further increases the probability of an orienting reflex.

The nonverbal indicants of arousal and involvement may be triggered as a relationship partner simultaneously engages attack–defense mechanisms and protects salient values or self-interests. Threats or challenges to deep-seated beliefs, anticipated evaluative or negative responses from another, and discrepancies between the expected and actual behavior of another are potential activators of arousal and involvement. The intensity of arousal or degree of involvement may range from low to high as one experiences physiological, cognitive, or behavioral activation during conflict; the interpretation placed on the experience of arousal, or arousal valence, may range from pleasant to unpleasant.

The two aforementioned investigations examined how involvement is encoded nonverbally and what nonverbal indices are associated with arousal. Coker and Burgoon (1987) found the following dimensions and behaviors associated with involvement: *immediacy* (e.g., body orientation, body lean, nodding), *expressiveness* (e.g., facial animation, loudness, speaking tempo, pitch), *altercentrism* (e.g., kinesic, proxemic, and vocal attentiveness), *interaction management* (e.g., silences, coordinated movement), and *social anxiety* (e.g., adaptor behaviors, random movement). Although high involvement in this relatively nonthreatening situation was enacted via high immediacy, expressiveness, and altercentrism, smooth interaction management, and a lack of social anxiety, it seems likely that during conflict, some of these patterns would change. The same dimensions should be maintained, but conflict might instead prompt egocentrism, awkward interaction, and high anxiety.

Burgoon et al. (1989) analyzed what behaviors are associated with the two dimensions of arousal intensity and valence. Intensity was found to be signalled by curvilinear changes in attentiveness (which is akin to altercentrism), performance coordination (which is similar to interaction management), and stress (which is isomorphic with social anxiety); linear decreases in activation and expressiveness; and decreased immediacy. Heightened, negative arousal was indexed by decreased attentiveness, decreased body coordination, less fluency, moderate postural tension, less vocal relaxation, more frequent self-adaptors and random movement, moderate gestural activity, and indirect orientation and gaze, while positive arousal was associated with greater stillness (reduced activation) and greater fluency.

If one attempts to tie these dimensions to the verbal strategies advanced by Newton and Burgoon (in press), several correspondences suggest themselves. First, the more positively oriented verbal strategies of *content-validation* and *other-support* should be associated with nonverbal indicants of *altercentrism, immediacy, positive arousal valence,* and *moderate arousal intensity.* The strategies of content-validation and other-support involve tactics that reinforce or confirm the other's position (e.g., agreement on issue, positive information seeking) and self or relationship (e.g., compliments, concessions, emphasizing commonalities). Altercentrism or other orientation is the tendency to be interested in, attentive to, and adaptive to another in a conversation (Spitzberg & Cupach, 1984). Cognitive orienting toward the other should produce overall kinesic and proxemic patterns that create gestalt perceptions of interest, attention, focus, alertness, and overall involvement and vocal behaviors that create impressions of warmth, appeal, interest, involvement, pleasantness, and friendliness (Bell, 1985; Norton, 1978; Norton & Pettegrew, 1979; Robinson & Price, 1980).

Second, the more negatively oriented strategies of *content-invalidation* and *other-accusations* are likely to be associated with *nonimmediacy, high arousal intensity/expressiveness, negative arousal valence,* and *stress/social anxiety.* Behaviors such as disagreeing, correcting the other, accusing, and blaming are likely to carry with them nonverbal cues of negative affect and rejection and to be delivered under greater stress than positive, accepting statements. High levels of arousal might also be experienced when one uses self-assertions and self-defense strategies. It is unclear how interaction management and performance coordination are likely to differ when using more positively oriented versus negatively oriented verbal strategies.

AN EMPIRICAL INVESTIGATION

Given the scarcity of previous research associating nonverbal cues and verbal strategies and tactics, an exploratory effort was made to validate the kinesic, proxemic, and vocalic cues that combine with verbal messages to form composites of conflict behavior. To adequately account for conflict behavior in close relationships, a study of actual interaction behavior is required. As Canary and Cupach (1988) argued, "Researchers have yet to sort the differences between self-reported and observed communication behavior. It is important to determine if observed communication tactics are associated with relational features in the same manner as self-reported tactics" (pp. 322–323). Burgoon (1985) similarly claimed that to better understand the influence of partners' behaviors on each other and the interplay between nonverbal signals and verbal utterances, messages must be embedded in naturally occurring interactions.

Overview

The investigation focused on disagreement behavior. Disagreements, a subset of conflictual behavior, typically involve partners' deep-seated latent differences (Putnam & Wilson, 1982) and threats or challenges to individuals' salient values or self-interests (Waln, 1984). Discrepant attitudes or values frequently give rise to what Lloyd and Cate (1985) refer to as recurrent conflicts or discussions about issues to which partners have given careful consideration but on which they disagree. The consequences of ongoing disagreements may be severe. Duck (1988) noted that in recurrent conflicts not only do partners feel badly about not being able to reach an agreement, they develop questions about the other's reasonableness, they become further entrenched in their own position, they become dissatisfied with the other, and they may eventually disengage. Clearly, disagreements offer fertile ground for assessing the communication strategies and tactics partners use to influence one another.

A complete description of the methods and procedures of this investigation may be found in Newton and Burgoon (in press). In brief, married or cohabitating couples (N = 50 dyads) were recruited from a large southwestern metropolitan area and told they would be participating in a 15-minute, videotaped discussion with their partner. Upon arrival at a communication research laboratory, couples were given a list of 18 common areas of disagreement in relationships derived from Roach's Marriage Problem Checklist (Bowden, 1977). They were asked to select a few areas that reflect recurring, unresolved issues in their relationship and were requested to enact a disagreement in as "typical" a manner possible for 15 minutes. After the disagreement, partners were separated and completed outcome measures indexing their responses to one another. These measures indexed: (a) how effective partners were at persuading one another, (b) how satisfied they were with the communication event, and (c) how partners interpreted one another's relational messages. After the experiment, videotapes of the disagreements were analyzed by judges who assessed verbal and nonverbal strategic and tactical behavior.

Measurement of Verbal Behavior

Newton and Burgoon (in press) reported procedures for measuring the verbal influence strategies participants employed. Briefly, judges were trained to categorize utterances at the tactical level then to code behavior into one of the six strategic categories. Ratings were made for each utterance during the 15-minute exchange. Frequency counts for individual strategies were summed, then percentages were derived for each strategy in relation to the total number of strategies used during the disagreement. Four judges rated the strategic behavior of male participants and four judges rated the behavior of female participants.

Measurement of Nonverbal Behavior

An index of kinesic, proxemic, and vocalic behavior was derived from assessment of 56 variables that are common in dyadic, seated interactions and amenable to coding from videotapes. Variables were measured as seven-interval rating scales that were taken or modified from measures previously used by Baglan and Nelson (1982); Burgoon, Birk, and Pfau (in press); Burgoon and Aho (1982); Burgoon et al. (1989); Burgoon and Koper (1984); Burgoon, Pfau, Birk, and Manusov (1987); Coker and Burgoon (1987); McCroskey and Wright (1971); Monti, Kolko, Fingeret, and Zwick (1984); and Scherer (1982).

Assessing this large number of nonverbal cues provides maximum information about the nonverbal behaviors used during influence. However, with such a large variable pool, if each variable is analyzed independently, the possibility of Type I error is increased. To reduce the risks associated with the number of statistical tests being conducted and to reduce multicollinearity, the majority of cues were reduced to dimensions. This effort was guided by results of previous studies (Burgoon et al., 1989; Coker & Burgoon, 1987) in which the same nonverbal indices were assessed and a principal components factor analysis with varimax rotation was used to create composite behaviors. Alpha coefficients were quite high across the resultant behavioral composites. The composites, their constituent items, coefficient alphas, and interrater reliabilities appear in Table 4.2.

Nonverbal Behavior Ratings. Judges of nonverbal behavior were eight (four pairs) undergraduate students who received 30 hours of training over a 5-week period. Instruction included conceptual and operational definitions of behaviors, review of samples of specific cues, practice coding of behaviors, and assessments and corrections of rater inconsistencies. Dyadic partners were coded separately in the following manner: two

TABLE 4.2
Nonverbal Behaviors: Dimensions, Item Constituents, Coefficient Alphas, and Interrater Reliabilities for Male and Female Participants

Dimensions	Alpha coeffs	Rater coeffs (males)	Rater coeffs (females)	Items	Continuum (1–7)
			Proxemics/Kinesics		
Orientation	.93	.96	.89	Body orientation	indirect–direct
				Face orientation	indirect–direct
				Gaze	averted–direct
Gesturing	.94	.96	.91	Gestures	none–frequent
				Gestures	impassive–animated
Expressiveness/ animation	.89	.87	.89	Facial expression	unpleasant–pleasant
				Facial animation	impassive–animated
				Smiling	none–frequent
				Concern	indifferent–concerned
				Nodding	none–frequent
				Laughter	none–frequent
Random movement	.43	.63	.77	Trunk/limb movement	none–frequent
					none–frequent
				Rocking/twisting	none–frequent
				Head movement	
Relaxation	.75	.86	.71	Cool	nervous–cool
				Relaxed	tense–relaxed
				Loose	rigid–loose
				Slumped	erect–slumped
Physical involvement	.94	.90	.90	Involved	uninvolved–involved
				Interested	uninterested–interested
				Open	closed–open
				Active	passive–active
				Concerned	apathetic–concerned
				Warm	cold–warm
				Receptive	unreceptive–receptive
Physical cooperation	.88	.62	.73	Cooperative	uncooperative–cooperative
				Equal	unequal–equal
				Supportive	competitive–supportive
				Similar	dissimilar–similar
Proxemics/lean	—*	.80	.50	Body lean	backward–forward
Head-shaking (side-to-side)	—*	.86	.63	Head shaking	none–frequent
Self-adaptors	—*	.88	.82	Self-adaptors	none–frequent
Object-adaptors	—*	.86	.82	Object-adaptors	none–frequent

				Vocalics	
Vocal loudness	.81	.83	.83	Loudness Sharpness	loud–soft sharp–mellow
Vocal rate/ Pitch variety	.67	.70	.79	Rate/tempo Pitch	slow–fast monotone–varied
Fluency	.89	.76	.78	Articulation Fluency Rhythm	unclear–clear nonfluent–fluent jerky–rhythmic
Vocal involvement	.94	.89	.93	Warm Involved Interested Receptive Concerned Pleasant Kind Friendly Cooperative Patient	cold–warm uninvolved–involved uninterested–interested unreceptive–receptive apathetic–concerned unpleasant–pleasant unkind–kind unfriendly–friendly uncooperative–cooperative impatient–patient
Vocal dominance	.86	.84	.87	Control Dominance Condescending Competitive Unequal	yielding–controlling submissive–dominant respectful–condescending supportive–competitive equal–unequal
Pitch	—*	.72	.58	Pitch	high–low/deep

*These items were treated as individual scales rather than as composites.

judges rated male participants' kinesic/proxemic behavior; two judges rated male vocalic behavior; two judges rated female participants' kinesic/proxemic behavior; and two judges rates female vocalic behavior. Kinesic/proxemic judges observed the video-only portion of the discussion; vocalic judges listened to the audio portion only. Judges worked separately to ensure independent ratings.

The judges observed 10 minutes of behavior per subject to achieve representative samples of behavior. Ratings were made at the end of 2-minute intervals after judges observed or listened to minutes 2–3, 5–6, 9–10, and 13–14. Two approaches were taken to measurement, which provided mid-level ratings of nonverbal behavior (see Boice & Monti, 1982). Wish, D'Andrade, and Goodnow (1980) substantiated the utility of an intermediate- as opposed to micro-level analysis for assessment of multiple behaviors. Results of their investigation strongly support the argument that dyadic behavior can be measured efficaciously at intermediate levels of analysis. Using mid-level measurement was likely to reflect the level of awareness and observation of partners and the evaluations they might make about one another's nonverbal behavior; it also maximized efficiency.

Judges initially rated distal indicator cues that measured specific externalized behaviors (such as forward lean or pitch variety). Twenty-two proxemic and kinesic behaviors and 8 vocalic behaviors were rated in this manner. Judges then rated proximal percepts (see Scherer, 1982), or the impressions these behaviors foster (such as receptivity or competitiveness). Eleven proxemic and kinesic behaviors and 15 vocalic behaviors were rated in this subjective manner. After each time period, 33 ratings were made by proxemic/kinesic judges; 23 assessments were made by vocalic judges. Judges were instructed to proceed slowly and deliberately through the analysis. Although large numbers of judgments were made, the exploratory nature of this effort justified exchanging precision for greater exhaustivity.

Measurement of Outcomes and Relationship Satisfaction

The *consequences* of strategy usage were measured by three instruments that participants completed. First, the degree to which communicators were successful in influencing their partners was indexed with 10 seven-interval, Likert-type items related to persuasiveness. The coefficient alpha reliability of this scale was .84. Second, satisfaction with communication during the disagreement was assessed by a slightly modified version of Hecht's (1978) Interpersonal Communication Satisfaction Inventory ($r = .91$). Third, as a measure of the level of satisfaction partners generally experience in their intimate relationship, participants responded to a 17-item questionnaire prior to their scheduled laboratory interaction. This questionnaire involved 10 behavioral satisfaction subscales obtained from Spanier (1976), 2 global satisfaction subscales from the Marital-Adjustment Test (Locke & Wallace, 1959), and 5 additional global items developed by Kelley (1988). Treated as a composite, the scale produced an alpha coefficient of .90. Finally, assessment of relational message interpretation was made by having participants rate their partners on the seven relational messages themes developed by Burgoon and Hale (1987). Reliabilities were: immediacy/affection, .84; depth/similarity, .54; equality, .80; dominance, .47, informality, .41; receptivity/trust, .81; and composure, .76. Combined, these measures were used to determine the effects of partners' verbal and nonverbal messages.

CONFLICT STRATEGY PROFILES

Enactment of Verbal Strategies

Results of the relative frequency of strategy usage across all participants showed the most likely verbal strategies partners employed during the disagreement were: *content-validation* (e.g., agreement, description of issue, problem solving; $M = 31\%$), *self-assertions* (e.g., self-promotion, ex-emplification; $M = 26\%$), and *other-accusations* (e.g., blaming, criticizing, threatening; $M = 21\%$). Partners were less likely to rely on verbal strate-gies of *content-invalidation* (e.g., disagreement, exaggeration, abstraction; $M = 10.9\%$), *self-defense* (e.g., justifications, excuses, denials; $M = 5\%$) and *other-support* (e.g., reinforcement, concessions; $M = 4\%$).

Enactment of Nonverbal Behaviors

The mean frequency of behaviors exhibited across participants on the 12 nonverbal composites and 5 individual behaviors is presented in Fig. 4.1. A cursory examination of this figure reveals that during the disagree-ments, participants were directly oriented, physically involved, and re-laxed, used moderate forward lean, and physically expressed a coopera-tive rather than competitive attitude. They also engaged in moderately frequent and animated gesturing, random movement, and self-adaptors but exhibited relatively few object adaptors and minimal head-shaking. Participants spoke moderately quickly, loudly, and sharply, and were rated relatively highly on fluency and vocal involvement.

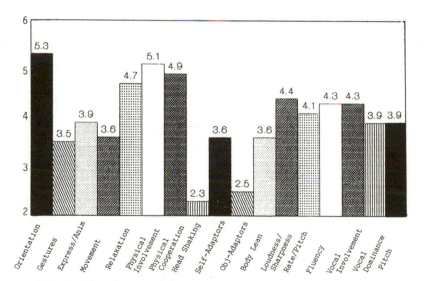

FIG. 4.1. Mean frequency of nonverbal behaviors present during disagree-ments. High means reflect direct orientation; frequent/animated gestures; more facial expressiveness/animation, random movement, postural relax-ation, physical involvement, and physical cooperation; frequent head-shaking, self- and object-adaptors; forward body lean; louder/sharper vocal tone; faster vocal rate and more pitch variety; more fluency, vocal involvement, and vocal dominance; and lower/deeper pitch.

Gender Differences in Nonverbal Behavior. Post-hoc analyses using *t* tests were conducted to assess gender differences. Analyses revealed 10 significant behavioral differences at the .008 Bonferroni corrected alpha level; another three significant differences were found at the more liberal .05 level (see Table 4.3). Males were rated as engaging in more random movement, showing more relaxation, using a louder and sharper speaking voice, and using a deeper pitch than females. Females were rated higher than males on frequency and animation of gestures, facial expressiveness/animation, physical involvement, physical cooperation, head shaking, forward lean, fluency, vocal involvement, and vocal dominance.

Combining Verbal and Nonverbal Behaviors

To determine which nonverbal cues were most closely associated with verbal strategies, profiles were created by correlating the 6 verbal strategies with the 12 nonverbal composites and 5 individual behaviors. Table 4.4 presents the significant correlations and resultant strategy profiles.

Some general commonalities are noteworthy across the three strategies of content-invalidation, other-accusations, and self-assertions. Taken together, these strategies may be associated with high levels of activation, involvement, and/or intense affect, which was manifested in frequent

TABLE 4.3
Gender Differences in Nonverbal Behavior Used During Influence

	Males		Females			
Nonverbal Behavior	M	SD	M	SD	*t*	*p*
Orientation	5.33	.85	5.16	.74	1.07	.285
Gestures	3.21	1.25	3.72	1.08	− 2.17	.032
Expressiveness/animation	3.58	.54	4.28	.61	− 6.03	.001
Movement	3.77	.57	3.49	.69	2.27	.026
Relaxation	4.79	.40	4.55	.35	3.19	.002
Physical involvement	4.83	.42	5.43	.47	− 6.72	.001
Physical cooperation	4.72	.36	5.01	.54	− 3.25	.002
Head-shaking	1.86	.73	2.64	.79	− 5.04	.001
Self-adaptors	3.44	.95	3.75	.97	− 1.57	.119
Object-adaptors	2.28	.92	2.64	1.12	− 1.78	.078
Lean	3.20	.45	4.01	.32	−10.35	.001
Vocal loudness/sharpness	4.47	.41	4.24	.63	2.14	.036
Vocal rate/pitch variety	4.00	.26	4.06	.42	− .93	.357
Fluency	4.02	.25	4.59	.32	−10.09	.001
Vocal involvement	4.02	.27	4.63	.28	−11.10	.001
Vocal dominance	3.74	.27	4.15	.37	− 6.30	.001
Pitch	4.28	.39	3.64	.59	6.35	.001

TABLE 4.4

Strategy Profiles Based on Significant Correlations Between Verbal
and Nonverbal Behaviors

Strategy	Verbal Tactics*	Nonverbal Behaviors	r	p
Content-validation	agreement on issue	postural relaxation	.30	.001
	description of issue	frequent self adaptors	.29	.002
	explanation of issue	soft/mellow vocal tone	.30	.001
	summarizing issue	slow vocal rate/monotone	.16	.050
	problem solving	lack of fluency	.22	.010
	positive info-seeking	lower/deeper pitch	.21	.020
Content-invalidation	disagreement on issue	frequent/animated gestures	.26	.005
	correcting other	random movement	.21	.020
	exaggeration	lack of postural relaxation	.16	.050
	pseudo-accommodation	forward lean	.20	.020
	abstraction	head shaking	.34	.001
		loud/sharp vocal tone	.40	.001
		fast vocal rate/varied pitch	.28	.002
		verbal fluency	.17	.050
		high pitch	.31	.001
Other-support	reinforcement of other	direct orientation	.22	.010
	support of other/relatn	expressiveness/animation	.31	.001
	emphasize commonalities	physical involvement	.29	.002
	accepting responsibility	physical cooperation	.28	.002
	concessions to other	vocal involvement	.20	.020
	complements	vocal submissiveness	.17	.040
Other-accusations	accusations/blaming	indirect orientation	.18	.030
	implied accusations	frequent/animated gestures	.27	.003
	criticism of other	random movement	.16	.050
	superiority over other	head shaking	.35	.001
	poking fun at other	loud/sharp vocal tone	.37	.001
	advice giving to other	fast vocal rate/varied pitch	.21	.020
	threats	verbal fluency	.18	.030
	neg information-seeking	vocal dominance	.21	.020
		high pitch	.22	.010
Self-assertions	assertions	frequent/animated gestures	.24	.008
	self-promotion	random movement	.32	.001
	exemplification	infrequent self-adaptors	.17	.040
	stubbornness	frequent object-adaptors	.27	.003
	disclosure	loud/sharp vocal tone	.22	.010
	wish statements	lack of vocal involvement	.19	.030
	wants/needs statements	vocal dominance	.20	.020
Self-defense	justifications	random movement	.20	.020
	excuses			
	denials			
	self-inquiry			

*Verbal tactics were included in strategies by definition.

and animated gestures, random movement, head-shaking, a loud/sharp vocal tone, fast rate, verbal fluency, high pitch, and a dominant vocal style. This generalization is supported by the previously cited findings that several cues (frequent gesturing, loud vocal tone, faster rate, and fluency) are indicants of high conversational involvement; random movement is associated with greater activation, expressiveness, and negatively valenced arousal.

By contrast, the nonverbal behaviors associated with content-validation (the most frequently used strategy) showed lower levels of overall activation. Cues associated with content-validation were postural relaxation, soft-mellow tone, slow rate, monotone pitch, and lower/deeper pitch. An interpretation that these behaviors are stabilizing forces during much of the interaction is tempered by the presence of frequent self-adaptors and lack of fluency. The co-presence of cues indicative of only moderate intensity and involvement, and behaviors potentially expressing anxiety, indicate a complex relationship between the nonverbal behaviors associated with content-validation that must be addressed in future research.

Other-support strategies were associated with nonverbal behaviors that have been empirically linked to expressions of altercentrism (Coker & Burgoon, 1987; Norton & Pettegrew, 1979; Spitzberg & Cupach, 1984). Moderately strong to strong relationships were found between other-support and direct orientation, facial expressiveness and animation, physical involvement, and vocal involvement.

CONSEQUENCES OF STRATEGY USAGE

To determine how nonverbal behaviors combine with verbal strategies to predict outcome and global measures, multiple regression analyses regressed the dependent measures of persuasiveness, satisfaction, and relational message perceptions on the 6 verbal strategies and 17 nonverbal composites/behaviors (see Table 4.5). Given the high multicollinearity among many of the verbal and nonverbal variables, this analysis must be regarded as merely exploratory. However, it does provide some indication of which combinations of variables are most strongly related to outcome measures.

The *persuasion* analysis produced two predictors accounting for 18% of the variance: verbal content-invalidation and fluency. Fluent communication that eschewed content-invalidation was more persuasive. Partner's *communication satisfaction* was most strongly predicted by the other's physical involvement (e.g., appearing warm, receptive, interested, concerned) and a lack of verbal accusations, which together accounted for

TABLE 4.5
Multiple Regression Analyses on Verbal and Nonverbal Behaviors
Predicting Persuasiveness, Communication Satisfaction, Relational
Messages, and Relationship Satisfaction

Outcome measures	Order of entry of variables	r	b	Beta	RSQ	RSQ change	F ratio change	p
Persuasiveness	v Content-invalidation	−.32	− .06	− .39	.10	.10	11.32	.001
	nv Fluency	.19	.71	.29	*.18*	.08	9.17	.003
Communication Satisfaction								
	nv Physical involvement	.34	.63	.34	.12	.12	13.04	.001
	v Other accusations	−.29	− .02	− .28	*.20*	.08	9.79	.002
Relationship Satisfaction								
	nv Physical cooperation	.32	.47	.29	.11	.11	11.60	.001
	nv Self-adaptors	.23	.15	.19	.15	.04	4.60	.030
	nv Gestures	.24	.12	.20	.18	.03	4.10	.040
	v Other-support	.23	.04	.20	.22	.03	4.28	.040
	nv Relaxation	−.09	− .37	− .20	*.25*	.04	4.56	.030
Relational Message Interpretation								
Immediacy	nv Physical involvement	.35	.39	.19	.13	.13	14.12	.001
	v Other-accusations	−.21	− .07	− .76	.17	.04	5.17	.020
	v Self-assertions	−.08	− .06	− .54	.21	.04	5.42	.020
	nv Gestures	.25	.23	.25	.27	.05	6.68	.010
	v Content-validation	.10	− .03	− .33	*.30*	.03	4.83	.030
Similarity	nv Physical-cooperation	.86	1.51	1.26	.74	.74	274.57	.001
	nv Physical-involvement	.37	− .56	− .52	.84	.10	66.22	.001
	nv Vocal-involvement	.13	− .15	− .11	.85	.01	9.73	.002
	nv Gestures	.02	.05	.11	.86	.01	5.55	.020
	v Other-accusations	−.16	−.01	− .11	.87	.01	5.26	.020
	nv Vocal loudness	−.14	.10	.10	*.88*	.01	4.63	.030
Equality	v Other-accusations	−.37	− .04	− .35	.14	.14	15.35	.001
	nv Self-adaptors	.28	.31	.24	.20	.06	7.67	.007
	nv Physical involvement	.22	.49	.21	*.24*	.04	5.47	.020
Dominance	nv Head-shaking	.37	.48	.33	.15	.15	16.84	.001
	v Other-accusations	.29	.02	.20	*.19*	.04	4.68	.030
Informality	nv Physical involvement	.28	.53	.28	*.08*	.08	8.26	.005
Receptivity	nv Vocal involvement	.85	1.09	.85	*.72*	.72	259.40	.001
Composure	nv Physical cooperation	.58	.35	.30	.34	.34	50.33	.001
	nv Fluency	.51	.47	.34	.47	.13	23.87	.001
	nv Gestures	.00	− .14	− .30	.50	.03	6.83	.010
	nv Physical involvement	.58	.33	.31	*.53*	.03	5.35	.020

*Note:*v = Verbal Strategies (content-validation, content-invalidation, other-support, other-accusations, self-assertions, self-defense); nv = Nonverbal Behaviors (orientation, gestures, expressiveness/animation, random movement, relaxation, physical involvement, physical cooperation, head shaking, self-adaptors, object-adaptors, lean, vocal loudness, vocal rate/pitch, fluency, vocal involvement, vocal dominance, pitch)

20% of the variability in satisfaction with the actual interaction. Four variables accounting for 25% of the variance predicted *relationship satisfaction:* physical cooperation, self-adaptors, gestures, other support, and a lack of relaxation.

The majority of predictors of relational message interpretations were nonverbal. Five significant predictors of *immediacy* emerged: physical involvement, the lack of verbal accusations and self-assertions, frequent and animated gestures, and content-validation. While the beta weight for content-validation showed a negative relationship with immediacy, this is probably a case of classical suppression (with content-validation suppressing irrelevant variance in other-accusations and gestures), given that the simple correlation coefficient indicated a weak but positive relationship.

The variance accounted for in *similarity* was greatly improved by allowing nonverbal behaviors to enter the regression equation (88% as compared to no variance accounted for by verbal strategies alone). Indicants of similarity were: physical cooperation, physical involvement, vocal involvement, gestures, the absence of other accusations, and a soft/mellow vocal tone. Although the *b*-weights for physical involvement and vocal involvement showed negative relationships with similarity, this was due to net suppression between physical involvement and physical cooperation, which were highly correlated ($r = .70$), and vocal involvement and physical cooperation, which were moderately correlated ($r = .44$). The suppression of irrelevant variance in these variables resulted in a stronger relationship between similarity and physical cooperation (as evidenced by the large *B*) than was reflected in the zero-order correlations (see Cohen & Cohen, 1975). Vocal loudness may also have acted as a net suppressor of physical involvement. Although a weak zero-order correlation existed between vocal loudness and physical involvement ($r = .21$), the change in sign from the zero-order correlation to the standardized *B* suggests that vocal loudness was serving to increase the variance accounted for in similarity by physical involvement. To summarize, caution should be exercised when interpreting the relative predictive contributions of both physical cooperation and physical involvement to relational interpretations of similarity.

Other accusations, self-adaptors, and physical involvement accounted for 24% of the variance in *equality*. More perceived equality was associated with the lack of accusations, the presence of adaptors, and high involvement. *Dominance* was primarily indicated by head-shaking and other accusations ($R^2 = .19$). *Informality* was predicted by the other's physical involvement during the interaction ($R^2 = .08$) and *receptivity* by the other's vocal involvement ($R^2 = .72$). *Composure* was conveyed most by physical cooperation, fluency, minimal gestures, and physical involvement ($R^2 =$

.53). The inflated *b*-weight associated with gestures again indicates a case of classical suppression. The zero-order correlations between the independent variables showed a moderately high relationship between gestures and physical involvement ($r = .49$), suggesting that gestures suppressed some of the irrelevant variance in physical involvement. The lack of relationship between gestures and composure ($r = .00$) renders the relative contribution of gestures to the equation uninterpretable.

DISCUSSION

More than any other type of communication, conflict has been said to test the integrity of a relationship (Canary & Cupach, 1988). The crux of the argument presented in this chapter is that adequate assessment of conflict behavior between intimate partners must involve both verbal and nonverbal behaviors. In the past, critical nonverbal cues either have been totally ignored or relegated to secondary status. The current investigation was intended as a starting point toward analyzing how verbal and nonverbal behaviors are combined to form conflict strategies, and with what success.

The composite picture that emerges here is one of most partners relying on verbal content-validation and self-assertions (with some other-accusations thrown in) while nonverbally displaying moderate involvement and immediacy and minimal anxiety. This picture may be overly rosy in that participants may have been more restrained and pleasant while being observed and while recreating their disagreements than they would be in private and in the midst of an actual conflict. However, their own ratings of the typicality of these disagreements (see Newton & Burgoon, in press) offers some assurance that these discussions approximated their normal styles.

This general picture must also be qualified on the nonverbal side by the substantial differences in patterns due to gender. Females used more verbal content-invalidation and other-accusations reflective of an offensive, rather than defensive, orientation. This assertive or domineering verbal style was nonverbally supplemented by a dominant vocal style (e.g., a controlling, competitive, and condescending tone). However, these findings are tempered when additional nonverbal behaviors are taken into consideration. It appears that females may be compensating for their verbal and vocal assertiveness/aggressiveness by exhibiting supportive nonverbal cues and high involvement in the discussion. Females significantly differed from males in their use of frequent/animated gesturing, facial animation and expressiveness, and forward lean. Females were also rated by judges as more physically and vocally involved in relation to their partners than were males; that is, females fostered impressions of greater interest, involvement, openness, concern, warmth, cooperation, receptivity, similarity, and equality than did males.

Verbally, males used more self-assertions than did females, which may be interpreted as indicative of a general instrumental or distributive orientation. The manner in which this verbal pattern was executed is interesting as males, in comparison to females, were less physically and vocally involved in the discussion. Males also engaged in more random movement, were more posturally relaxed, used a louder/sharper tone, and had a lower/deeper pitch than females. Further research is necessary to determine whether or not during disagreements the relative lack of male involvement in comparison to females conforms to the general profile found in previous research that males opt for strategies of nonnegotiation (Fitzpatrick & Winke, 1979) and avoid high levels of emotional involvement in situations involving conflict (Kelley et al., 1978).

As for the relationship between verbal strategies and nonverbal behaviors, several intriguing patterns emerged. Content-validation is generally accompanied by a relatively relaxed postural and vocal pattern, but with some hints of anxiety in the form of nonfluencies and self-adaptors. Alternatively, these latter two cues may be indicative of more cognitive effort as one attempts to phrase one's position in more diplomatic and nonconfrontive terms. The other more positively oriented strategy of other-support is accompanied by displays conveying immediacy, expressiveness, cooperativeness, and submissiveness.

By contrast, the more negative verbal strategies of content-invalidation, other-accusations, and self-assertions are accompanied by much more activation (in the form of frequent gesturing, random movement, object-adaptors, head shaking, and rapid speaking tempo), more dominance and aggressiveness (e.g., forward lean, loud/sharp voice), and more tension and negative arousal (e.g., postural tension, high pitch). (Self-defense cannot be described accurately because of its infrequency of occurrence). Thus one's verbal content finds parallels and complements in one's nonverbal demeanor. Ignoring these nonverbal concomitants is likely to produce serious misestimates of the valence and intensity of verbal strategies.

Recognition of the nonverbal behaviors used by partners during disagreements adds to an understanding of how conflict strategies affect outcomes and how they are interpreted as relational messages. Although conclusions must remain tentative, given the exploratory and incomplete nature of this assessment of nonverbal behaviors, the significant increases in variance accounted for by the inclusion of the nonverbal variables in the regression analyses strongly suggests that they are at least as important as the verbal behaviors. Whereas persuasiveness was most influenced by verbal content-invalidation, followed by nonverbal fluency, satisfaction with the discussion was most influenced by nonverbal physical involvement, followed by the verbal strategy of other-accusations. Thus nonverbal behaviors played a key role in each of these outcomes. Moreover, relationship satisfaction was far more strongly associated with nonverbal demeanor than verbal strategies; four nonverbal behaviors predicted satisfaction, compared to only one verbal behavior. Finally, relational interpretations were heavily loaded toward nonverbal cues, indicating that the relational import of conflict behaviors resides less in *what* is said than *how* it is said.

Again, it must be emphasized that these results are merely suggestive of the role nonverbal behaviors play during conflict. Future research should examine additional nonverbal variables, as well as analyze concomitant verbal and nonverbal behaviors more microscopically so that co-occurring behaviors may be matched within each time period. In this manner, a more precise estimate can be gained of which nonverbal tactics accompany which verbal ones. Ultimately, it should be possible to describe conflict strategies that are integrated composites of verbal and nonverbal behaviors and to analyze more fully the efficacy of each.

ACKNOWLEDGMENT

The authors express their appreciation to Krystyna Strzyzewski for her assistance in coder training and data collection.

REFERENCES

Argyle, M. (1972). Non-verbal communication in human social interaction. In R. A. Hinde (Ed.), *Nonverbal communication* (pp. 243–268). Cambridge: Cambridge University Press.

Baglan, T., & Nelson, D. J. (1982). A comparison of the effects of sex and status on the perceived appropriateness of nonverbal behaviors. *Women's Studies in Communication, 5,* 29–38.

Bell, R. A. (1985). Conversational involvement and loneliness. *Communication Monographs, 52,* 218–235.

Berger, C. R. (1985). Social power and interpersonal communication. In M. L. Knapp & G. R. Miller (Eds.), *Handbook of interpersonal communication* (pp. 439–499). Beverly Hills, CA: Sage.

Berger, C. R., & Douglas, W. (1982). Thought and talk: "Excuse me, but have I been talking to myself?" In F. E. X. Dance (Ed.), *Human communication theory* (pp. 42–60). New York: Harper & Row.

Boice, R., & Monti, P. M. (1982). Specification of nonverbal behaviors for clinical assessment. *Journal of Nonverbal Behavior, 7,* 79–94.

Bowden, S. R. (1977). *An assessment of the validity of the marital satisfaction inventory.* Unpublished doctoral dissertation, Texas A & M University, College Station, TX.

Brown, P., & Levinson, S. (1978). Universals in language use: Politeness phenomena. In E. Goody (Ed.), *Questions and politeness: Strategies in social interaction* (pp. 256–289). New York: Cambridge University Press.

Burgoon, J. K. (1980). Nonverbal communication research in the 1970s. In D. Nimmo (Ed), *Communication yearbook 4* (pp. 179–197). New Brunswick: Transaction Books.

Burgoon, J. K. (1985). Nonverbal signals. In M. L. Knapp & G. R. Miller (Eds.), *Handbook of interpersonal communication* (pp. 344–390). Beverly Hills, CA: Sage.

Burgoon, J. K., & Aho, L. (1982). Three field experiments on the effects of violations of conversational distance. *Communication Monographs, 49,* 71–88.

Burgoon, J. K., Birk, T., & Pfau, M. (in press). Nonverbal behavior, persuasion, and credibility. *Human Communication Research.*

Burgoon, J. K., Buller, D. B., & Woodall, W. G. (1989). *Nonverbal communication: The unspoken dialogue.* New York: Harper & Row.

Burgoon, J. K., & Hale, J. L. (1987). Validation and measurement of the fundamental themes of relational communication. *Communication Monographs, 54,* 19–41.

Burgoon, J. K., Kelley, D. L., Newton, D. A., & Keeley-Dyerson, M. P. (1989). The nature of arousal and nonverbal indices. *Human Communication Research, 16,* 217–255.

Burgoon, J. K., & Koper, R. J. (1984). Nonverbal and relational communication associated with reticence. *Human Communication Research, 10,* 601–626.

Burgoon, J. K., Pfau, M., Birk, T., & Manusov, V. (1987). Nonverbal communication performance and perceptions associated with reticence: Replications and classroom implications. *Communication Education, 36,* 119–130.

Burgoon, J. K., & Saine, T. (1978). *The unspoken dialogue.* Boston: Houghton-Mifflin.

Canary, D. J., & Cupach, W. R. (1988). Relational and episodic characteristics associated with conflict tactics. *Journal of Social and Personal Relationships, 5,* 305–325.

Canary, D. J., & Spitzberg, B. H. (1987). Appropriateness and effectiveness perceptions of conflict strategies. *Human Communication Research, 14,* 93–118.

Canary, D. J., & Spitzberg, B. H. (1989). A model of the perceived competence of conflict strategies. *Human Communication Research, 15,* 630–649.

Cegala, D. J., Savage, G. T., Brunner, C. C., & Conrad, A. B. (1982). An elaboration of the meaning of interaction involvement: Toward the development of a theoretical concept. *Communication Monographs, 49,* 229–248.

Clark, R. A. (1979). The impact of self interest and desire for liking on the selection of communicative strategies. *Communication Monographs, 46,* 257–273.

Clark, R. A., & Delia, J. (1979). Topoi and rhetorical competence. *Quarterly Journal of Speech, 65,* 187–206.

Cody, M. J., McLaughlin, M. L., & Jordon, W. J. (1980). A multidimensional scaling of three sets of compliance-gaining strategies. *Communication Quarterly, 28*, 34–46.

Cohen, J., & Cohen, P. (1975). *Applied multiple regression/correlation analysis for the behavioral sciences.* Hillsdale, NJ: Lawrence Erlbaum Associates.

Coker, D. A., & Burgoon, J. K. (1987). The nature of conversational involvement and nonverbal encoding patterns. *Human Communication Research, 13*, 463–494.

Cupach, W. R. (1980, November). *Interpersonal conflict: Relational strategies and intimacy.* Paper presented at the annual Speech Communication convention, New York.

Cupach, W. R. (1982, May). *Communication satisfaction and interpersonal solidarity as outcomes of conflict message strategy use.* Paper presented at the annual International Communication Association convention, Boston.

Duck, S. W. (1988). *Relating to others.* Chicago: Dorsey.

Eisenberg, A. M., & Smith, R. R., Jr. (1971). *Nonverbal communication.* Indianapolis: Bobbs-Merrill.

Ekman, P., & Friesen, W. V. (1969). The repertoire of nonverbal behavior: Categories, origins, usage, and coding. *Semiotica, 1*, 49–98.

Falbo, T. (1977). A multidimensional scaling of power strategies. *Journal of Personality and Social Psychology, 35*, 537–547.

Falbo, T., & Peplau, L. A. (1980). Power strategies in intimate relationships. *Journal of Personality and Social Psychology, 38*, 618–628.

Fitzpatrick, M. A. (1988). *Between husbands and wives: Communication in marriage.* Beverly Hills, CA: Sage.

Fitzpatrick, M. A., Fallis, S., & Vance, L. (1982). Multifunctional coding of conflict resolution strategies in marital dyads. *Family Relations, 31*, 611–670.

Fitzpatrick, M. A., & Winke, J. (1979). You always hurt the one you love: Strategies and tactics in interpersonal conflict. *Communication Quarterly, 27*, 3–11.

Galvin, K. M., & Brommel, B. J. (1986). *Family communication: Cohesion and change* (2nd ed.). Glenview, IL: Scott, Foresman.

Gottman, J. M. (1979). *Marital interaction: Experimental investigations.* New York: Academic Press.

Gottman, J., Markman, H., Notarius, C. (1977). The typology of marital conflict: A sequential analysis of verbal and nonverbal behavior. *Journal of Marriage and the Family, 39*, 461–477.

Hall, J. (1969). *Conflict management survey.* Conroe, TX: Teleometrics.

Harrison, R. P. (1974). *Beyond words: An introduction to nonverbal communication.* Englewood Cliffs, NJ: Prentice-Hall.

Hawkins, J. L., Weisberg, C., & Ray, D. L. (1977). Perception of behavioral conformity, imputation of consensus, and marital satisfaction. *Journal of Marriage and the Family, 39*, 479–490.

Hecht, M. L. (1978). The conceptualization and measurement of interpersonal communication satisfaction. *Human Communication Research, 4*, 253–264.

Higginbotham, D. J., & Yoder, D. E. (1982). Communication within natural conversational interaction: Implications for severe communicatively impaired persons. *Topics in Language Disorders, 2*, 1–19.

Kelley, D. L. (1988). *Understanding relational expectations and perceptions of relational satisfaction in marital relationships.* Unpublished doctoral dissertation, University of Arizona, Tucson, AZ.

Kelley, H. H., Cunningham, J. D., Grisham, J. A., Lefebvre, L. M., Roberts Sink, C., & Yablon, G. (1978). Sex differences in comments made during conflict with close heterosexual pairs. *Sex Roles, 4,* 473–492.

Kendon, A. (1967). Some functions of gaze-direction in social interaction. *Acta Psychologica, 26,* 22–63.

Kilmann, R. H., & Thomas, K. W. (1977). Developing a forced-choice measure of conflict-handling behavior: The "MODE" instrument. *Educational and Psychological Measurement, 37,* 309–325.

Kimmel, M. J., Pruitt, D. G., Mageneau, J. M., Konar-Goldband, E., & Carnevale, P. J. D. (1980). Effects of trust, aspiration, and gender on negotiation tactics. *Journal of Personality and Social Psychology, 38,* 9–22.

Kipnis, D. (1976). *The powerholders.* Chicago: University Press.

Koren, P., Carlton, K., & Shaw, D. (1980). Marital conflict: Relations among behaviors, outcomes, and distress. *Journal of Consulting and Clinical Psychology, 48,* 460–468.

Lawrence, P. R., & Lorsch, J. W. (1967). *Organization and environment.* Homewood, IL: Irwin.

Lewis, D. K. (1969). *Convention: A philosophical study.* Cambridge, MA: Harvard University Press.

Lloyd, S. A., & Cate, R. M. (1985). The developmental course of conflict in premarital relationship dissolution. *Journal of Social and Personal Relationships, 2,* 179–194.

Locke, H. J., & Wallace, K. M. (1959). Short marital adjustment and prediction tests: Their reliability and validity. *Marriage and Family Living, 2,* 251–255.

McCroskey, J. C., & Wright, D. W. (1971). The development of an instrument for measuring interaction behavior in small groups. *Speech Monographs, 38,* 335–349.

Millar, F. E., Rogers, L. E., & Bavelas, J. B. (1984). Identifying patterns of verbal conflict in interpersonal dynamics. *Western Journal of Speech Communication, 48,* 231–246.

Miller, G. R., Boster, F., Roloff, M., Seibold, D. R. (1987). MBRS rekindled: Some thoughts on compliance gaining in interpersonal settings. In M. E. Roloff & G. R. Miller (Eds.), *Interpersonal processes: New directions in communication research* (pp. 89–116). Beverly Hills, CA: Sage.

Monti, P. M., Kolko, D. J., Fingeret, A. L., & Zwick, W. R. (1984). Three levels of measurement of social skill and social anxiety. *Journal of Nonverbal Behavior, 8,* 187–194.

Newton, D. A. (1988). *Influence strategies used by relational patterns during disagreements.* Unpublished doctoral dissertation, University of Arizona, Tucson, AZ.

Newton, D. A., & Burgoon, J. K. (in press). Influence strategies used by relational partners during disagreements. *Human Communication Research.*

Noller, P. (1984). *Nonverbal communication in marital interaction.* New York: Pergamon.

Noller, P., & Gallois, C. (in press). Nonverbal behaviors in the marital situation. *British Journal of Social Psychology.*

Norton, R. W. (1978). Foundations of a communicator style construct. *Human Communication Research, 4,* 99–112.

Norton, R. W., & Pettegrew, L. S. (1979). Attentiveness as a style of communication. A structural analysis. *Communication Monographs, 46,* 13–26.

Patterson, M. L. (1982). A sequential function model of nonverbal exchange. *Psychological Review, 89,* 231–249.

Patterson, M. L. (1983). *Nonverbal behavior: A functional perspective.* New York: Springer-Verlag.

Patterson, M. L. (1985). Presentational and affect-management functions of nonverbal involvement. *Journal of Nonverbal Behavior, 11,* 110–122.

Peterson, D. R. (1983). Conflict. In H. H. Kelley, E. Berscheid, A. Christensen, J. H. Harvey, T. L. Huston, G. Levinger, E. McClintock, L. A. Peplau, & D. R. Peterson (Eds.), *Close relationships* (pp. 360–396). New York: Freeman.

Pike, G. R., & Sillars, A. L. (1985). Reciprocity of marital communication. *Journal of Social and Personal Relationships, 2,* 303–324.

Pruitt, D. G., & Rubin, J. Z. (1986). *Social conflict: Escalation, schemes, and settlement.* New York: Random House.

Putnam, L. L., & Wilson, C. E. (1982). Communicative strategies in organizational conflicts: Reliability and validity of a measurement scale. In M. Burgoon (Ed.), *Communication yearbook 6* (pp. 629–652). Beverly Hills, CA: Sage.

Rands, M., Levinger, G., & Mellinger, G. (1981). Patterns of conflict resolution and marital satisfaction. *Journal of Family Issues, 2,* 297–321.

Rausch, H., Barry, W., Hertel, R., & Swain, M. (1974). *Communication, conflict and marriages.* San Francisco: Jossey-Bass.

Robinson, E. A., & Price, M. G. (1980). Pleasurable behavior in marital interaction: An observational study. *Journal of Consulting and Clinical Psychology, 48,* 117–118.

Roloff, M. E. (1976). Communication strategies, relationships, and relational change. In G. R. Miller (Ed.), *Explorations in interpersonal communication* (pp. 173–195). Beverly Hills, CA: Sage.

Roloff, M. E. (1980). Self-awareness and the persuasion process: Do we really *know* what we're doing? In M. E. Roloff & G. R. Miller (Eds.), *Persuasion: New directions in theory and research* (pp. 29–66). Beverly Hills, CA: Sage.

Ross, R., & DeWine, S. (1982, November). *Interpersonal conflict: Measurement and validation.* Paper presented at the annual Speech Communication Association convention. Louisville, KY.

Scheflen, A. E. (1967). On the structuring of human communication. *American Behavioral Scientist, 10,* 8–12.

Scheflen, A. E. (1974). *How behavior means.* Garden City, NJ: Anchor.

Scherer, K. R. (1982). Methods of research on vocal communication: Paradigms and parameters. In K. R. Scherer & P. Ekman (Eds.), *Handbook of methods in nonverbal behavior research* (pp. 136–189). New York: Cambridge University Press.

Seibold, D. R., Cantrill, J. G., & Meyers, R. A. (1985). Communication and interpersonal influence. In M. L. Knapp & G. R. Miller (Eds.), *Handbook of interpersonal communication* (pp. 551–611). Beverly Hills, CA: Sage.

Shokley-Zalabak, P. S., & Morley, D. D. (1984). Sex differences in conflict style preferences. *Communication Research Reports, 1,* 28–32.

Sillars, A. L. (1980a). The sequential and distributional structure of conflict interactions as a function of attributions concerning the locus of responsibility and stability of conflicts. In D. Nimmo (Ed.), *Communication yearbook 4,* (pp. 217–235). New Brunswick, NJ: Transaction.

Sillars, A. L. (1980b). Attributions and communication in roommate conflicts. *Communication Monographs, 47,* 180–200.

Sillars, A. L., Coletti, S. F., Parry, D., & Rogers, M. A. (1982). Coding verbal conflict tactics: Nonverbal and perceptual correlates of the "Avoidance-distributive-integrative" distinction. *Human Communication Research, 9,* 83–95.

Sillars, A. L., Pike, G. R., Jones, T. S., & Redmon, K. (1983). Communication and conflict in marriage. In R. Bostrom (Ed.), *Communication yearbook 7* (pp. 414–429). Beverly Hills, CA: Sage.

Spanier, G. B. (1976). Measuring dyadic adjustment: New scales for assessing the quality of marriage and similar dyads. *Journal of Marriage and the Family, 38,* 15–28.

Spitzberg, B. H., & Cupach, W. R. (1984). *Interpersonal communication competence.* Newbury Park, CA: Sage.

Waln, V. G. (1984). Questions in interpersonal conflict: Participant and observer perceptions. *Southern Speech Communication Journal, 49,* 277–288.

Walton, R. E., & McKersie, R. B. (1965). *A behavioral theory of labor negotiations: An analysis of a social system.* New York: McGraw-Hill.

Ware, J. P. (1980). *Bargaining strategies: Collaborative versus competitive approaches.* HBS case 9–480–055. Cambridge, MA: HBS Case Services.

Weiss, R. L., & Summers, K. J. (1983). Marital interaction coding system-III. In E. E. Filsinger (Ed.), *Marriage and family assessment* (pp. 85–115). Beverly Hills, CA: Sage.

Wish, M., D'Andrade, R. G., & Goodnow II, J. E. (1980). Dimensions of interpersonal communication: Correspondence between structure for speech acts and bipolar scales. *Journal of Personality and Social Psychology, 34,* 848–860.

The Use of Humor in Managing Couples' Conflict Interactions

Janet K. Alberts
Arizona State University

The importance of conflict processes to both individuals and organizations is reflected in the variety of scholars who choose to examine them. Conflict has been studied by those interested in rhetorical communication (Di Mare, 1987), small groups (Bateman, 1980; Rabbie & Huygen, 1974), organizations (Brett, 1984; Freedman, 1981; Stern, 1971), and personal relationships (Billings, 1979; Canary & Cupach, 1988; Gottman, 1979; Sillars, 1980). This attention to conflict has prompted Fisher and Ury (1981) to refer to *conflict* as a "growth industry." Although it is unlikely that people are more contentious now than in decades past, certainly there has been increased focus by both scholars and popular writers on the causes and consequences of conflict. And of the areas that have served as the focus for this interest, there is perhaps no arena in which the study of conflict can have more impact than the marital dyad.

CONFLICT RESOLUTION VERSUS CONFLICT MANAGEMENT

Traditionally, couples' conflict studies have focused on conflict resolution. As Hawes and Smith (1973) stated, the view has been that "the only good conflict is a resolved conflict" (p. 424). Specifically, it has been claimed that the greater the unresolved relational conflicts, the greater the likelihood that a current disagreement will be perceived as important (Roloff, 1987), and Duck (1988) suggested that, although not all conflicts are "bad," unresolved conflicts put couples "on a collision course" (p. 111). Lloyd and Cate (1985) argued that when couples are unable to resolve conflict they feel badly about the issues and begin to develop doubts about each other that then set in motion a series of activities that can lead ultimately to a "strong falling out."

Because of the belief that ending conflict is important and a failure to resolve conflict will have negative consequences for relationships, much of conflict research has focused on conflict resolution (Billings, 1979; Chafetz, 1980; Filley, 1975; Fitzpatrick, 1988; Pruitt & Rubins, 1986). This model of conflict tends to view conflict as episodic, occurring as a disruption to the "normal" state of affairs. In this view, conflict disruption has a "beginning, in all likelihood a cause, and is terminated allowing a return to a state which, although possibly altered by the conflict, will remain stable until the next episode of disruption" (Hawes & Smith, 1973, p. 425). Following this model, then, the purpose of conflict research would be to determine effective strategies for ending the disruption and allowing a return to the normal state of affairs with as little harm done to the parties and their relationship as possible. Thus, a primary goal of such research would be to explicate effective strategies for resolving conflict.

Models for conflict resolution propose that during conflict each party develops a distinct set of moves, or ways of pursuing the conflict in order to settle it. A series of moves, or tactics, make up a strategy of conflict resolution (Fitzpatrick, 1988). These strategies can be classified along two major dimensions: assertiveness (which satisfies one's own concerns) and cooperativeness (which satisfies the partner's concerns) (Blake & Mouton, 1964; Kilmann & Thomas, 1977; Putnam & Wilson, 1982). As Hawes and Smith (1973) pointed out, effective strategies for a conflict resolution model would necessarily stress "procedures for compromise, resolving differences, mediation and conciliation. . . ." (p. 424).

A diverse set of research projects have been conducted using these "normative" (Hawes & Smith, 1973) theories of conflict. For example, Ting-Toomey (1983a) analyzed couples' conflict interactions to determine how differentially satisfied couples resolved their differences. She coded for 12 different conflict strategies and found that highly satisfied couples tend to use coaxing, confirming, socioemotional questions, and task-oriented statements during conflict interactions. Fitzpatrick (1988) analyzed couples' interactions for examples of conflict avoidance, accommodating, collaborating, and competing strategies during conflict resolution; she found that traditional couples are cooperative and conciliatory and engage in avoidance more than they recognize, independents tend to be confrontive, and separates are more likely to engage in hostile acts and avoidance.

Gottman (1979) studied satisfied and dissatisfied couples' conflict behavior and determined that unhappy couples were more likely to use cross-complaining sequences and less likely to engage in validation sequences (complaint–agreement). <u>Rausch, Barry, Hertel, and Swain</u> (1974) found husbands in discordant marriages used more coercive strategies (power plays, guilt induction, and disparagement) and fewer emotionally reconciling acts in response to coercive or resolving acts. Billings (1979) also found that distressed couples tend to be more coercive and less cognitive in their conflict discussions. Much of this literature, then, suggests that unhappy couples are more likely to escalate conflicts, and nondistressed couples are more likely to seek resolution of conflicts (Pike & Sillars, 1985).

In the process of conducting this research, however, several scholars (Fitzpatrick, 1988; Rausch et al., 1974; Pike & Sillars, 1985) discovered, unexpectedly, that avoidance strategies were associated with satisfied and nondistressed couples. For example, Pike and Sillars (1985) found in their study of couples' conflict behavior that more satisfied couples used conflict avoidance to a greater extent than the dissatisfied couples, and Fitzpatrick (1988) also discovered that satisfied couples engaged in avoidance tactics.

Traditionally, the skills approach treated avoidance as dysfunctional, primarily because it does not lead to resolution. The implicit assumption of models that treat avoidance as an antisocial tactic (Bochner, 1983; Roloff, 1976) is that the individual who avoids conflict is more constricted, less capable of solving problems, and more likely to be unhappy. However, Pike and Sillars (1985), Fitzpatrick's (1988), and Rausch et al.'s (1974) findings seem to contradict this notion.

Fitzpatrick (1988) concluded that avoiding the discussion of conflict issues does not, then, appear to always have negative consequences for a marriage. Bach and Wyden (1968) had suggested that couples postpone or avoid the discussions of serious conflict until they have time and energy to handle them. However, not only short-term avoidance but also long-term avoidance may be functional for certain couples. As Fitzpatrick (1988) stated,

> When the issue is essentially unresolvable, functional approaches to communication suggest that the issue be avoided and the discussion channeled into more agreeable topics. In sum, the nature of the issue under discussion, the timing of the conversation, and specific communication tactics suggest that conflict avoidance can be either a pro-social or an antisocial strategy. (p. 144)

Most conflict theorists have viewed the establishment of lines of communication as a necessary condition for effective conflict resolution; avoidance violated this condition. However, Krauss and Deutsch (1966) have pointed out that under certain conditions, communication may serve to intensify conflict instead of reduce it, and Hawes and Smith (1973) state that the assumption that increased communication leads to a greater likelihood of conflict resolution is flawed. They do not see the role of communication in conflict as "simple and direct" as such an assumption would presume.

Thus, it appears that conflict resolution models do not provide sufficient guidance for couples in handling their conflict interactions. Consequently, a number of scholars have begun to focus on and suggest the importance of conflict management strategies. Hawes and Smith (1973) argued for an approach to studying conflict that stresses maintenance and management rather than resolution. Such an approach views conflict not as a disruption but rather as an on-going process. If conflict is viewed as continuous and the normal state of affairs (Coser, 1956; Simmel, 1964; Sprey, 1969), then attention must be paid to managing conflict and maintaining relationships in the face of it.

Boulding (1968) argued for a management model when he stated that

> The distinction between constructive and destructive conflicts is not necessarily the same as the distinction between those which are resolved and those which are not . . . Sometimes there is a need for protracting conflict and for keeping it unresolved perhaps by diminishing its intensity and increasing its duration. (p. 410)

Betcher (1988) offered additional support for this view when he argued that in some situations one's partner or oneself cannot or should not change, and some way must be found for tolerating these differences. Therefore, because some issues cannot productively be resolved, some times are bad, and some relationships not sufficiently stable to handle conflict resolution, conflict management skills are necessary for the functionality of long-term relationships.

Despite the need for conflict management skills in enduring relationships, relatively few studies have focused on management strategies; avoidance has only reluctantly been admitted as a possible strategy for managing conflict. Consequently, there is a need for other strategies to be delineated and examined in the context of couples' conflict. One such strategy that has been alluded to, although more often as an antisocial than a pro-social strategy, is the use of humor during conflict interactions.

In her discussions of conflict avoidance, Fitzpatrick (1988) delineated a number of communication acts that are designed to move the discussion away from the matter at hand; among these she listed making jokes. Cupach (1982) noted that tactics such as teasing the other person constitute forms of avoidance, and Zietlow and Sillars (1988) listed hostile jokes (along with criticism and rejection) as a form of confrontative remarks.

However, not all discussions of humor and conflict suggest that humor is antisocial or inhibits conflict management. Ting-Toomey's (1983b) Intimate Negotiation Coding System (INCS) lists humor and jokes as a form of integrative behavior; Jacobs (1985) stated that some forms of humor are indicative of and conducive to healthy relationships, and Wuerffel (1986) found that healthier families used humor more frequently than did less healthy ones.

However, most of these studies focused not on humor as a conflict strategy but on broader or related issues, and two studies that have focused on humor (Jacobs, 1985; Wuerffel, 1986) relied on self-report data for their analyses. Consequently, it seems that humor has potential as a conflict management strategy, but little is known about how it functions, both positively and negatively, as such in natural conversation.

THE FUNCTIONS OF HUMOR

In order to analyze the uses of humor during couples' conflict discussions, it is necessary to understand the nature and functions of humor. One of the two most common models for humor conceptualize it as a method for expressing unacceptable emotions (Fine, 1983). A major theme in anthropological theories is that expressions of humor are the result of attempting to resolve ambivalence in social situations, roles, status, cultural values, and ideologies; humor may provide relief from this ambivalence (Apte, 1983). Psychoanalysts have long recognized that humor expresses underlying issues that cannot be expressed directly. In doing this, it provides a sense of social control for the participants when handling threatening or embarrassing topics (Fine, 1983).

Although many functions of humor might be suggested, three general functions are recognized by most researchers of humor (Fine, 1983; Martineau, 1972; Stephenson, 1951). Humor has been shown to function to promote consensus, provide social control, and provoke conflict.

Teasing and humor can function to establish consensus, that is, to create a more unified couple. More specifically, it can serve to promote solidarity, establish intimacy, and excuse a slight. Teasing and humor can establish intimacy and comraderie, or it can hallmark that such a relationship has been achieved. It serves to create and remind the partners of their bonding. It can also serve to create consensus when it is used to cover up or excuse a slight, whether the slight was intentional or inadvertent. To say "Oh I'm sorry, I was only teasing" is a form of apology to right a wrong and reinstate consensus. The implication is that what was said or done was not meant to be taken as truth or aggression (Alberts, 1982).

As a means of social control, teasing and humor may act to express approval or disapproval of social forms and actions, or it can express collective approbation of actions not explicitly condoned (Stephenson, 1951). The control function of humor can be aggressive (Lumley, 1925); it differs, however, in that it does not divide or separate couples or groups. Rather, it attempts to make the participants accept group norms. The kidding that occurs among intimates may well be an example of this kind of humor. Although overtly nonpunitive, it reveals the expectations that intimates have for one another (Fine, 1983).

Finally, humor can also serve a conflict function. The particular adaptability of humor as a conflict tool stems from the fact that humor may conceal malice or allow malice without the consequences of overt behavior (Stephenson, 1951). Fine stated that the potential conflict function of humor may be very serious indeed. Although humor by its nature is supposed to be "unserious," and by definition is so, there are some cases in which the conflictual elements of humor are so evident that they are taken seriously. The ambiguity in the function of humor is also related to the way in which it is interpreted. When humor is viewed positively, it may control or solidify; when it is defined as an affront it can cause conflict or demoralization (Fine, 1983).

Although scholars from anthropology, sociology, and psychology have examined the multiple functions that humor may serve, most of this research has focused at the level of the culture (Radcliffe-Brown, 1940) or the group (Coser, 1956; Fine, 1980, 1981; Martineau, 1972; Stephenson, 1951). The functioning of humor within close relationships, particularly couples, has received less attention.

Betcher (1981, 1988) provided a general analysis of the uses of play and humor in couples' relationships. He suggested that play can serve adaptive purposes in imtimate relationships, that it can enhance communication and social bonding while reducing conflict. He added that play can allow the expression of aggression between couples without induly threatening intimacy or provoking withdrawal. He cited behavior such as wrestling and "poking fun at one another" as types of play that may do this. He further suggested that tongue-in-cheek humor, logical paradox, and absurd exaggeration of an individual's problematic behavior are ways of modulating aggression and inducing behavioral flexibility.

Several studies have either specifically or tangentially examined the relationship between humor and relational quality. Wuerffel (1986) examined the use of humor in the family. Using an inventory of family humor and one for family strength, he determined that stronger families used humor more often than weaker families to maintain a positive outlook on life, for entertainment, to reduce tension, to express warmth, and to help cope with difficult situations. Putdowns were used less by stronger than weaker families, and stronger families reported negative effects when humor was used as a putdown.

Ting-Toomey's (1983a) examination of the communication patterns of differentially satisfied marital couples determined that highly satisfied couples tended to inject a sense of humor into their interaction with "teasing" and "sweet talking" behavior, whereas low satisfied couples did not. Farley and Peterson (1979) examined the interactions of distressed and nondistressed couples to determine if naive judges could identify couple type by the couples' interactions patterns. It was found that the patterns that differentiated couples were talk-time imbalance, attention, humor, laughter, positive physical contact, and agreement. The analysis pointed to laughter and attention as the primary interaction cues to marital satisfaction.

The most comprehensive study of couples' use of humor is Jacobs' (1985) *The Functions of Humor in Marital Adjustment.* Although she focused on a variety of functions for humor, the conflict function was examined at length. Jacobs asserted that humor can serve a variety of purposes in marital discord, from keeping the lines of communication open to attack and escalation. In terms of positive functions, humor can serve to dispel anger, allow a safe approach to sensitive topics, and aid couples in altering their perspective on their problems, thereby improving problem solving.

Joking may be an attempt to dissipate anger or tension (felt on the part of either the joking party or the partner). Complaints can be offered as teases that allows relief for the complainer while permitting the recipient to accept the criticism more easily. Humor can also function as an indirect request for a cessation of hostilities, or a signal that the intimate relationship continues despite the conflict. However, humor can also be a medium for expressing hostile and/or ambivalent messages. It can be a means of attack when the negative aspect of the message dominates the humorous one, and it may not be accepted as a joke (Jacobs, 1985, p. 30).

The purpose of Jacobs' research was to examine the relationship between marital adjustment and the various functions of humor. Unsurprisingly, she determined that marital adjustment was associated to a greater degree with positive humor use and that there was an association between less successful marital adjustment and negative humor use.

Although Jacobs' study provides an important initial investigation of couples' uses of humor, it did not analyze actual discourse. Couples' reports of their humor usage do offer salient information about how couples perceive their relationship and interactional patterns, but they do not reveal what couples actually do, nor how often they do it. The following discussion attempts to provide some of this information through a preliminary analysis of couples' use of humor during conflict conversations.

A PRELIMINARY ANALYSIS

Method. The data for this analysis was acquired from 40 heterosexual couples' conflict interactions. All of the couples had been married or living together for a minimum of 6 months. The individuals ranged from 19 to 71 years old, and a diversity of socioeconomic backgrounds was represented. The 40 couples represented a range that could be divided into the subgroups of adjusted and maladjusted. Twenty couples were chosen who fell into each category based on Spanier's (1976) Dyadic Adjustment Scale (DAS). Because these couples represented "normal relationships" and not clinical ones, it was decided to place all couples in the category of maladjusted in which one member had a score of 100 or less. The adjusted couples had a mean DAS score of 242.5, whereas the maladjusted couples had a mean score of 195.5. The obtained alpha reliability estimate for the Dyadic Adjustment Scale was .90. A t test was conducted on the DAS scores for the two groups; the two groups were significantly different [$t(38) = 7.49, p < .001$].

Participants were informed that the experimenter was interested in learning how couples discuss issues on which they disagree. First, each member of the couple filled out Spanier's (1976) DAS privately. Once the DAS was completed, each member was given a modified version of Strodtbeck's (1951) Revealed Differences Form. In addition to the 20 items on the revealed differences form, each member of the couple was asked to write a scene that described a problem area or area of disagreement in the relationship.

After the participants completed the forms, the investigator circled all items on the revealed differences form on which the couple disagreed. The couple was then instructed to discuss these items while a tape recorder recorded the interaction. The couples were encouraged to strive for agreement, but, if that was not possible, they were allowed to "agree to disagree." They also were asked to discuss the items each had written. The couples were encouraged to talk for 30–60 minutes.

The 40 tapes yielded 19 hours and 43 minutes of interaction. The length of the tapes ranged from 15 minutes to 1 hour. Of the approximately 20 hours of tape, 47% (9 hours, 16 minutes) was produced by adjusted couples and 53% (10 hours, 27 minutes) was produced by maladjusted couples.

Once the data were collected, each tape was transcribed. These transcriptions were typed in script form and attempted to capture both overlapping speech and laughter as well as the actual words spoken. These transcripts were then used for the descriptive analysis provided here. The data were analyzed for number of couples who used humor as a conflict management tool; number of humorous interactions; types of humor; frequency of humor acceptance/reciprocation; and number of times the humorous comment(s) terminated the interaction. These analyses were conducted in order to extend previous research findings based on interviews and written self-report measures.

Analysis. Although humor may be an important management technique, it likely does not arise in every, or even most, conflict interactions. Of the 40 couples interactions examined, 15 (38%) revealed instances in which humor was used to manage interpersonal conflict. Although there were instances where the couples used humor as they talked, only those interactions in which couples specifically used humor as they engaged in conflictual communication were examined.

The analysis revealed that 7 of the 20 dissatisfied couples used joking and teasing whereas 8 of the satisfied couples used humor. In the 15 interactions there were 22 humorous interactions during the couples' talk.

Analysis of the types of humor the couples used in this study revealed that five categories of humor were used. Specifically, there were jokes about the partner, jokes about the self, jokes about the relationship, jokes about outside events/people, and sarcasm. Jokes about the partner included those comments that made fun of or playfully threatened the partner. For example, one couple disagreed at length about the drinking and replacement of orange juice in the refrigerator. The female complained that she bought the juice for herself but that her partner repeatedly drank it and failed to replace it. After almost 10 minutes of discussion on the issue, the male joked to his partner, "I think you're (ha) just capitalizing on this situation to get some juice." When another wife refused to agree with her husband he called her "a stubborn wench."

Jokes about the self, then, were comments that made fun of the speaker. In the disagreement over orange juice, the man joked (about his failure to replenish the juice) "I'm sorry. I was gonna go buy some, then I got off on this really lofty thought, (ha ha)." There were also jokes about the couple as a dyad. During one couple's disagreement about the husband's slowness, the couple was unable to reach agreement about who was at fault or what should be done. Toward the end of the interaction, the wife began to laugh about their inability to resolve the issue and said, "No (ha ha) . . . Now we're just gonna hafta go beat each other up, (.) no I'm just kidding."

There were also jokes about people and events connected to the relationship. After extended, unresolved disagreement about where they should vacation, one husband laughingly remarked "Well, gee, this was fun, let's do this again." (referring to the taped disagreement). Finally, there were instances of sarcasm or hostile humor. During one couple's discussion of the husband's tendency to visit bars after work rather than come home, his wife stated that she wanted him to come home when she needed him. He replied, "Well, I usually do." She then laughed unhappily and replied with sarcasm "Yeah, u-usually!"

The 22 instances of humor in the transcripts fell into the five categories as listed in Table 5.1.

For purposes of analysis, the types of humor were placed into the dichotomous categories of "benign" and "hostile." Benign humor included jokes about the self, about the relationship, or about the partner in a gentle manner. Hostile humor was defined as humor that joked about the partner in a negative way, particularly with sarcasm.

A variety of sources characterize sarcasm as negative or hostile humor. Farrelly and Brandsma (1974) defined *sarcasm* as cutting, hostile, contemptuous or caustic remarks. Wuerffel (1986) referred to *putdowns* as a particularly negative (and harmful) form of humor used in the family. And Ting-Toomey (1983a), citing the INCS coding categories, listed sarcasm under the category of direct rejection (a form of disintegrative behavior).

Table 5.2 shows what was revealed by coding for type of humor.

Chi-square analysis established there was a significant difference in the couples' use of humor ($p < .01$), with adjusted couples more likely to use benign humor and maladjusted couples more likely to use hostile.

Individuals' responses to their partners' humor attempts were also analyzed. Response was considered because it strongly influences how an interaction will unfold. Research on persistence and change conducted by Watzlawick, Weakland, and Fisch (1974) indicates that sequencing is an important factor in relational communication. Their research indicates that negative spirals often develop during relational conflict. These spiral are generally composed of accusations that lead to unacceptable denials that lead to further accusations that lead to more unacceptable denials, and so forth. This pattern leads to less and less satisfying communication that ultimately results in a less satisfying relationship. In this context, humor can be seen as one attempt to arrest this cycle and to

TABLE 5.1
Types of Humor in Conflict Interactions

	Adjusted	Maladjusted
Jokes about partner	8	3
Jokes about self	3	0
Jokes about relationship	1	2
Jokes about others	1	0
Sarcasm	0	4

TABLE 5.2
Type of Humor

	Benign	Hostile
Adjusted	13	0
Maladjusted	5	4

provide an exit from this spiral. However, the success of this attempt is strongly dependent on the partner's response. If the humor is met with acceptance then the spiral is more likely to be arrested, but if it is rejected, then it is more likely the cycle will continue.

In analyzing the interactions, the partners' responses to the humor attempts were coded into the categories of acceptance and rejection. Those responses that included laughter and returned humor were placed in the acceptance category. For example, after one couple engaged in extensive disagreement about spending habits, the husband joked "Noooo. When's the divorce, when's the divorce . . ." His wife laughed and replied "Yeah, we are getting divorced see, all this has caused a divorce." Those responses that were placed in the category of rejection primarily included instances of the recipient ignoring the humor attempt. In these cases, after the joke, the partner refused to laugh, failed to acknowledge the humor attempt, and generally returned to the issue under discussion.

Using these two categories the 22 responses to humor attempts were coded as shown in Table 5.3. The chi-square analysis of these differences did not achieve significance ($p < .12$).

The final chi-square analysis was conducted on whether the humor attempt did or did not terminate the conflictual interaction for each couple type. I have suggested that humor, when used successfully, should be useful in managing conflict that cannot be resolved. Also, if effective humor functions to terminate negative spirals, as I propose, then there should be some differences between satisfied and dissatisfied couples in how successful the humor attempts are in terminating the disagreements. The data were coded and Table 5.4 shows what was determined:

The analysis revealed that there was a significant difference between the couple types in the likelihood that humor would bring the conflict to

TABLE 5.3
Response to Humor Attempts

	Accepted	Rejected
Adjusted	10	3
Maladjusted	4	5

TABLE 5.4
Humor Attempts Ending the Interaction

	Yes	No
Adjusted	10	3
Maladjusted	3	6

a close ($p < .04$), with adjusted couples' humor more likely to terminate an interaction than maladjusted couples'.

DISCUSSION

The analysis indicates that for these 40 couples humor was a mode of conflict management, although this management technique may be somewhat underrepresented with this sample. It is possible that the elicitation device, the conscious focus on conflict, and the explicit suggestion that the conflict be "resolved" may all have contributed to more restricted interaction than may be typical. It is likely that during couples' normal, day-to-day interaction humor plays a more significant role in managing the irritations, complaints, and conflicts that are an attendant part of couples' lives together. Thus, these data suggest that there is an untapped potential for analyzing an important tool that intimates may use for managing conflict.

Wuerffel (1986) suggested that weaker families used putdowns more frequently and that their humor had more negative effects than stronger families. Jacobs also suggested that dissatisfied couples reported using more negative humor overall in their interactions. These data support the overall claim that negative humor use and dysfunctional relationships are connected. The maladjusted couples in this study were significantly more likely to use negative humor, particularly sarcasm, in their attempts to manage conflict. All of these studies suggest, then, that humor itself does not effectively manage conflict. Rather, it appears that the nature of the couples' relationship influences the type of humor used, that in turn influences how effectively the conflict is managed. It will require a more extensive study to determine if it is the couples' relational type, the type of humor used, or a combination of the two that ultimately influences the effectiveness of humor in conflict interactions.

As was suggested earlier, it is likely that a partner's response to a humor attempt is equally if not more important than the attempt itself. Canary and Spitzberg (1989) supported this claim when they argued that "the relational impact of conflict may be determined less by its occurrence, and more by its form and the evaluations its form evokes" (p. 632).

If a relationship is not strong and/or is dysfunctional, it could be that any humor attempt may be interpreted and responded to negatively. Given that humor generally contains both playfulness and aggression (Alberts, 1982; Jacobs, 1985), in dysfunctional relationships the aggressive element may be perceived more readily than the playful. In this study, maladjusted couples more often ignored or failed to respond to the attempt with laughter, although the difference was not statistically significant.

Finally, it is important to note whether humor is effective in managing, at least temporarily, the conflict interaction. These data indicate that for adjusted couples humor was a precipitating factor in the termination of disagreement episodes. This does not provide any assurance that the conflict was resolved, but at least for this conversational interaction, the conflict was brought to an end, and generally on a playful note. Unfortunately for the maladjusted couples, the interaction was less often brought to a close. For these couples the interaction continued until one or both parties tired of the interaction. It appeared that the failure of the humor to achieve a positive response from the partner was linked to the failure of the humor to help manage the conflict.

Thus far, studies of humor and conflict suggest that certain types of humor could be a useful tool for some couples in handling persistent problems in the relationship. Folger and Poole (1984) argued that it is not so much the strategy as the "inflexibility" of the parties that lock them into escalation or avoidance cycles. Humor is one strategy that can be used in a repertoire that might also include avoidance and direct confrontation.

This study is but an initial foray into the study of conflict management strategies and humor as a particular strategy. The small sample size (both in number of couples and examples) necessarily limits the claims that may be offered. However, this initial analysis of couples' discourse does offer support for the claims made by Jacobs (1985) and Wuerffel (1986) about couples' and families' reports of their humor interactions. It also suggests that humor may be a productive conflict management tool and that this avenue of research is worth pursuing. Future studies needs to address these issues with a larger sample of subjects and perhaps under even more natural conditions.

REFERENCES

Alberts, J. K. (1982, May). *A conversational analysis of teasing.* Paper presented at the International Communication Association convention, Dallas, TX.
Apte, M. L. (1983). Humor research, methodology, and theory in anthropology.

In P. E. McGhee & J. H. Goldstein (Eds.), *Handbook of humor research* (pp. 184–212). New York: Springer-Verlag.

Bach, W., & Wyden, P. (1968). *The intimate enemy.* New York: William Morrow.

Bateman, T. S. (1980). Contingent concession strategies in dyadic bargaining. *Organizational Behavior and Human Performance, 26,* 212–221.

Betcher, W. (1981). Intimate play and marital adaptation. *Psychiatry, 44,* 13–33.

Betcher, W. (1988). *Intimate play.* New York: Penguin.

Billings, A. (1979). Conflict resolution in distressed and nondistressed married couples. *Journal of Consulting and Clinical Psychology, 47,* 368–376.

Blake, R. R. & Mouton, J. S. (1964). *The managerial grid.* Houston, TX: Gulf.

Bochner, A. P. (1983). The functions of human communication in interpersonal bonding. In C. C. Arnold & J. W. Bowers (Eds.), *Handbook of rhetorical and communication theory* (pp. 544–621). Boston: Allyn & Bacon.

Boulding, K. E. (1968). Preface to a special issue. *The Journal of Conflict Resolution, 12,* 409–411.

Brett, J. M. (1984). Managing organizational conflict. *Professional Psychology and Research Practice, 15,* 664–678.

Canary, D. J., & Cupach, W. R. (1988). Relational and episodic characteristics associated with conflict tactics. *Journal of Social and Personal Relationships, 5,* 305–325.

Canary, D. J., & Spitzberg, B. H. (1989). A model of the perceived competence of conflict strategies. *Human Communication Research, 15,* 630–649.

Chafetz, J. S. (1980). Conflict resolution in marriage: Toward a theory of spousal strategies and marital dissolution rates. *Journal of Family Issues, 1,* 397–421.

Coser, L. A. (1956). *The functions of social conflict.* New York: The Free Press.

Cupach, W. R. (1982, May). *Communication satisfaction and interpersonal solidarity as outcomes of conflict message strategy use.* Paper presented at the International Communication Association convention, Dallas, TX.

Di Mare, L. A. (1987). Functionalizing conflict: Jesse Jackson's rhetorical strategy at the 1984 democratic national convention. *Western Journal of Speech Communication, 51,* 218–226.

Duck, S. (1988). *Relating to others.* Chicago: Dorsey.

Farley, F. H., & Peterson, J. M. (1979). Identifying a distressed marriage from the interactions between spouses: A structural analysis. *Family Therapy, 6*(3), 119–122.

Farrelly, F., & Brandsma, J. (1974). *Provocative therapy.* Eagle River, WI: Shields.

Filley, A. C. (1975). *Interpersonal conflict resolution.* Glenview IL: Scott, Foresman.

Fine, G. A. (1980). The natural history of preadolescent male friendship groups. In H. C. Foot, A. J. Chapman, & J. R. Smith (Eds.), *Friendship and social relations in children* (pp. 293–320). Chichester: Wiley.

Fine, G. A. (1981). Impression management and preadolescent behavior. In S. R. Asher & J. M. Gottman (Eds.), *The development of children's friendships* (pp. 23–41). Cambridge: Cambridge University Press.

Fine, G. A. (1983). Sociological approaches to the study of humor. In P. E. McGhee & J. H. Goldstein (Eds.). *Handbook of humor research* (pp. 159–183). New York: Springer-Verlag.

Fisher, E., & Ury, W. (1981). *Getting to yes: Negotiating agreement without giving in.* Boston: Houghton Mifflin.

Fitzpatrick, M. A. (1988). *Between husbands and wives: Communication in marriage.* Beverly Hills, Ca: Sage.

Folger, J. P., & Poole, M. S. (1984). *Working through conflict: A communication perspective.* Glenview, IL: Scott, Foresman.

Freedman, S. C. (1981). Threats, promises, and coalitions. A study of compliance and relations in a simulated organizational setting. *Journal of Applied Social Psychology, 11,* 114–136.

Gottman, J. M. (1979). *Marital interaction: Experimental investigations.* New York: Academic Press.

Hawes, L. C., & Smith, D. H. (1973). A critique of assumptions underlying the study of communication in conflict. *Quarterly Journal of Speech, 62,* 423–435.

Jacobs, E. C. (1985). *The functions of humor in marital adjustment.* Unpublished doctoral dissertation, The New School for Social Research, New York.

Kilmann, R. H., & Thomas, K. W. (1977). Developing a forced choice measure of conflict-building behavior: The "MODE" instrument. *Educational and Psychological Measurement, 37,* 309–325.

Krauss, R. M., & Deutsch, M. (1966). Communication in interpersonal bargaining. *Journal of Personality and Social Psychology, 4,* 572–577.

Lloyd, S. A., & Cate, R. M. (1985). The developmental course of conflict in premarital relationship dissolution. *Journal of Social and Personal Relationships, 2,* 3–23.

Lumley, F. E. (1925). *Means of social control.* New York: Century.

Martineau, W. H. (1972). A model of the social functions of humor. In J. H. Goldstein & P. E. McGhee (Eds.), *The psychology of humor.* New York: Academic Press.

Pike, G. R., & Sillars, A. L. (1985). Reciprocity of marital communication. *Journal of Social and Personal Relationships, 2,* 303–324.

Pruitt, D. G., & Rubins, J. Z. (1986). *Social conflict: Escalation, stalemate and settlement.* New York: Random House.

Putnam, L. L., & Wilson, C. E. (1982). Communicative strategies in organizational conflicts: Reliability and validity of a measurement scale. In M. Burgoon (Ed.), *Communication Yearbook 6* (pp. 629–652). Newbury Park, CA: Sage.

Rabbie, J. M., & Huygen, K. (1974). Internal disagreements and their effects on attitudes toward in and outgroups. *International Journal of Group Tensions, 4,* 222–245.

Radcliffe-Brown, A. R. (1940). On joking relationships. *Africa, 13,* 195–210.

Rausch, H. L., Barry, W. A., Hertel, R. K., & Swain, M. A. (1974). *Communication, conflict and marriage.* San Francisco, CA: Jossey Bass.

Roloff, M. E. (1976). Communication strategies, relationships, and relational change. In G. R. Miller (Ed.), *Explorations in interpersonal communication* (pp. 173–195). Beverly Hills, CA: Sage.

Roloff, M. E. (1987). Communication and conflict. In C. R. Berger & S. H. Chaffee (Eds.), *Handbook of communication science* (pp. 484–553). Beverly Hills, CA: Sage.

Sillars, A. L. (1980). Attributions and communication in roommate conflicts. *Communication Monographs, 47,* 180–200.

Simmel, G. (1964). *Conflict and the web of group-affiliations.* K. H. Wolff & R. Bendix, Trans.) New York: The Free Press.

Spanier, G. B. (1976). Measuring dyadic adjustment: New scales for assessing the quality of marriage and similar dyads. *Journal of Marriage and the Family, 38,* 15–28.

Sprey, J. (1969). Conflict theory and the study of marriage and the family. In W. L. Burr, R. Hill, F. D. Nye, & I. L. Reiss (Eds.), *Contemporary theories about the family, 2* (pp. 130–159). New York: The Free Press.

Stephenson, R. M. (1951). Conflict and control functions of humor. *American Journal of Sociology, 56,* 569–574.

Stern, L. W. (1971). Potential conflict management mechanisms in distribution channels: An interorganizational analysis. In D. N. Thompson (Ed.), *Contractual marketing systems* (pp. 111–145). Boston: Heath-Lexington Books.

Strodtbeck, F. L. (1951). Husband-wife interactions over revealed differences. *American Sociological Review, 17,* 468–473.

Ting-Toomey, S. (1983a). An analysis of verbal communication patterns in high and low marital adjustment groups. *Human Communication Research, 9,* 306–319.

Ting-Toomey, S. (1983b). Coding conversations between intimates: A validation study of the intimate negotiation coding system (INCS). *Communication Quarterly, 31,* 69–77.

Watzlawick, P., Weakland, J. H., & Fisch, R. (1974). *Change.* New York: Norton.

Wuerffel, J. L. (1986). *The relationship between humor and family strengths.* Unpublished doctoral dissertation, University of Nebraska–Lincoln, Lincoln, NE.

Zietlow, P. M. & Sillars, A. L. (1988). Life-stage differences in communication during marital conflicts. *Journal of Social and Personal Relationships, 5*(2), 223–245.

Effects of Social Networks on Individuals' Responses to Conflicts in Friendship

Jonathan G. Healey
University of Southern California

Robert A. Bell
University of California, Davis

Many students of intimate relationships have become interested in describing the interface between dyadic relationships and the social networks in which they are embedded (Bott, 1971; Duck, 1982; Hinde, 1981; La Gaipa, 1981; Milardo, 1983, 1986, 1987; Ridley & Avery, 1979). The potential impact of a network on the relations between a pair of its members can be appreciated by considering what keeps two people together. Scholars have observed that relationship stability can be attributed to the positive forces of *attraction* and to disengagement *barriers* (Johnson, 1973; Kelley, 1983; Levinger, 1976; Ryder, Kafka, & Olson, 1971). Attraction in a relationship is a function of the rewards and costs derived therefrom. Barriers include those social, economic, and moral considerations that impede an individual from leaving the relationship. Thus, two friends or lovers may remain together because they *want to* (i.e., are attracted to each other) or because they *have to* (i.e., are prevented from ending the relationship by extra-dyadic constraints).

Social networks have been assumed to affect both attraction and barrier forces in many ways. One might be attracted to a friend or lover, for instance, because the partner knows many people with whom one desires friendship. Likewise, becoming attracted to the members of the partner's network can escalate both romantic relationships and friendships (Eggert & Parks, 1986; Parks, Stan, & Eggert, 1983). In addition, involvement with a lover or friend's network implies communication with its members, which may reduce uncertainty about the partner (Parks & Adelman, 1983; Parks et al., 1983). Conversely, attraction to the partner might be diminished if interacting with his or her network is unrewarding. Networks can also act as barriers to disengagement. For example, two people

121

may remain friends or lovers even when attraction is low out of concern for how family and friends would react to disengagement.

Although attraction factors have been given more attention by researchers than barriers, evidence is mounting to support the importance of barriers in explaining relationship stability. Lund (1985) demonstrated that the barriers of commitment and past investments were more important than the attraction forces of love and rewards in predicting the continuity of dating relationships. A study of social networks in the Canadian city of East York revealed that 21% of East Yorkers' network ties were with people to whom they were not attracted, but with whom interaction was reinforced by other network ties (Wellman, Carrington, & Hall, 1988). McCarthy (1986) found that friendships within established social groups may be sustained more by the structure of those groups than by attraction at the dyadic level. Of course, changes in dyadic relations can also affect networks. For example, lovers tend to break away from some network members as their romantic bond strengthens (Johnson & Leslie, 1982; Milardo, Johnson, & Huston, 1983; Surra, 1985).

This study was conducted to address several gaps in our understanding of how an individual's network of friends constrains his or her dealings with another person in the network who has said or done something to cause conflict. Despite frequent calls by relationship scholars for such research, surprisingly little empirical work has been completed. Thus, the study reported here tests for the first time notions advanced by such noted scholars as Duck (1982), La Gaipa (1981), and Ridley and Avery (1979). Several of their speculations have been accepted as "taken-for-granted" truths by others, even in the absence of research support. Friendships were studied because most work on the influences of dyads and networks has focused on heterosexual romantic relationships. Findings from these studies may not apply to friendships, which do not typically involve assumptions of exclusivity or public rituals of commitment. The influences of friendship networks were studied with regard to *conflict* on the assumption that a network is most likely to exert influence when the relationships that compose it are undergoing change that might threaten stability (Salzinger, 1982).

HYPOTHESES

The hypotheses that are developed in the discussions that follow relate to four sets of issues. For clarity, the symbol P denotes the person reporting on the conflict (for instance, a subject in the study described later), whereas O represents the other person whose actions or words caused P to become dissatisfied in some way. The concerns addressed in this chapter can be summarized as follows: (a) When P becomes dissatisfied with friend O, how are P's responses to that dissatisfaction shaped by the degree to which O is a part of P's friendship network? (b) How does O's integration into P's network influence the extent to which P and O talk to devise ways to present their difficulties to the network? (c) Will the tendency of the members of P's network to intervene in the conflict between P and O be affected by the extent to which O is also a part of the network? and (d) Does the degree to which O is integrated into P's network influence P's desire to seek information about the network's feelings concerning the conflict and to take these feelings into account when deciding how to respond to the situation? Each of these concerns are discussed in turn.

Network Integration and Responses to Dissatisfaction

There is considerable evidence that the development of a social relationship leads to a combination of two individuals' personal networks. The construction of a joint network is a consequence of involvement with the partner's associates. Two literatures document intimates' tendencies to merge their separate networks: research on *network overlap* in romantic relationships and investigations of *transitivity* in group structure.

Marriage and family researchers have shown interest in the question of how two people attempt to bring their respective networks together as they move toward marriage. Milardo (1983) has argued that overlap helps couples to cultivate a shared view of themselves and their relationship and a common orientation toward their social environment. He was able to link changes in premarital couples' joint networks to relationship development and dissolution over a 3-month period (Milardo, 1982). Banks, Altendorf, Greene, and Cody (1987) found that *perceptions* of network overlap were positively related to intimacy, partner desirability, and dyadic adjustment in a sample of individuals who had recently broken off a romantic relationship. They also found that overlap leads to friendly, tentative strategies of disengagement. Perhaps one is forced to be nice in matters of disengagement to ensure that mutual friends are not lost after the romantic bond has been broken.

Transitivity research suggests that when one forms a close relationship with another person, there will be strong pressures to develop ties with the new intimate's friends. If A likes B, B likes C, and A comes to like C the relationship is *transitive*; an *intransitive* relationship is one in which the AB and BC ties are strong, but A does not care for C. The research on transitivity differs from network overlap research in a very important way. Investigations of transitivity typically assess the structure of relationships in a larger social group (e.g., a fraternity) and then compare the distribution of triad types against theoretical distributions based on random networks. Marriage and family researchers, on the other hand, investigate changes in the compositions of two people's networks during courtship.

There is now considerable documentation of the proclivity of people to form transitive relationships (Davis, 1970, 1979; Davis & Leinhardt, 1971; Hallinan, 1972, 1982). When intransitivity does occur, it tends to be associated with weaker ties (Hallinan & Felmlee, 1975). Although intransitivity is found far below chance levels in sentiment relations, it is not rare. Parks and Riveland (1987) found that 82% of high school and college students surveyed were involved in at least one triad in which they disliked the friend of a friend. Although the literature is replete with discussions of the causes of transitivity, there have been few studies of the relative merits of the various theoretical accounts. The most commonly advanced rationale for transitivity is derived from Heider's (1958) balance theory (Cartwright & Harary, 1956; see also Anderson, 1979). Imbalance (i.e., intransitivity) is assumed to cause psychological tension that motivates parties to restore transitivity.

Our own work has been greatly informed by the thinking of Feld (1981), who explained transitivity in sociological terms. His focus theory, which is compatible with balance theory, suggests that patterns of relations often stem from the focused organization of social interactions. A focus is "any social, psychological, or physical entity around which joint activities of individuals are organized" (Feld, 1981, p. 1025), such as a place of employment, a club, or a social establishment. Johnson (1982) referred to these foci as "lines of action" that structure network members' interactions. Positive sentiment is assumed to arise from "shared relations to foci [that] bring people together in a mutually rewarding situation which encourages the development of positive sentiments" (Feld, 1981, p. 1018). The theory implies that persons A and B may share a relationship with C because the three parties are connected by a shared focus. Thus, transitivity is considered a product of the number and form of foci that were responsible for the development of the relationships. Subsequent research suggests that the sharing of foci may account for both the formation of friendships and the tendency for intimates to be similar to one another (Feld, 1982, 1984).

One outcome of the preference for transitive relationships is increased *density*. The density of an individual's personal network is the percentage of potential ties in the network that actually exist. As a person's friends become friends themselves, the density of the network will increase. Salzinger's (1982) research has shown how density tends to beget density.

First, dense networks tend to limit the options of people; new friends tend to come from within the network, and access to "outsiders" may become limited. Second, a dense network reinforces the relationships composing it by promoting positive interactions and multiple friendship roles among its members that creates pressures to keep relationships intact.

The research just reviewed suggests that P's response to dissatisfaction with friend O is likely to be shaped by the extent to which O is integrated into P's network. We examined two forms of integration: *connectedness* and *shared foci/O-network*. *Connectedness* is the average strength of O's ties to the other people in P's network. At one extreme is the case of a fully connected friend who is very close to everyone in the network. At the other extreme is the friend who knows nobody in P's network. *Shared foci/O-network* refers to the number of activities and routines that the person causing dissatisfaction shares with the other members of P's network. In addition, we examined how the sharing of foci at the dyadic level—*shared foci/P-O*—constrains responses to conflict.

Several investigators assume that the integration of a person into one's network limits the options that one can take in response to dissatisfaction with that person. For instance, Salzinger (1982) speculated that the people in a tight-knit network will be pressured to continue their friendship for the sake of the network. In her longitudinal investigation of changes in students' friendship networks, Salzinger found that very few relationships in dense networks are terminated. Unfortunately, her data do not address the question of whether such pressures to preserve friendships are strong enough to influence antagonists' responses to conflicts, nor does this study shed light on the nature of such influences. Presumably, when friend O causes pain, P cannot terminate the bond without creating as many intransitive relationships as there are people to whom both P and O are close. According to La Gaipa (1982), the effect should be that the parties involved will prefer constructive responses to the situation that preserve the P–O relationship. With regard to the sharing of foci, a termination of the P–O relationship may be impossible unless P is willing to abandon those foci that have organized the relationship, thereby jeopardizing his or her ties to the other network members who also share those foci. On the other hand, if O shares very few foci with the members of P's network, then destructive responses to dissatisfaction become viable (Johnson, 1982). Finally, Duck (1982) noted that when one is conflicting with a person who is integrated into his or her network via close ties and shared foci, one may opt for a deescalated friendship characterized by reduced intimacy rather than for a complete severing of ties.

Up to this point, we have been referring to P's responses to his or her dissatisfaction with O without discussing these responses. Although

several disengagement researchers have reported typologies of such responses, we have based our work on the research of Rusbult and her
colleagues (Rusbult, 1980a, 1980b, 1983, 1987; Rusbult, Johnson, &
Morrow, 1986; Rusbult & Zembrodt, 1983; Rusbult, Zembrodt, & Gunn,
1982). These scholars classify responses to dissatisfaction into the categories exit, voice, loyalty, and neglect. *Exit* involves telling the partner that
the relationship is over, threatening to end the relationship, thinking
about terminating the bond, or drastically deescalating the relationship
through minimization of communication. *Voice* refers to responses in
which one expresses dissatisfaction to the partner with the intent of
improving the situation. The primary means of voice is problem-solving
discussions. *Loyalty* entails passively waiting for conditions to improve,
with the hope that the relationship's quality can be restored. For instance,
one might be silent about his or her dissatisfaction, avoid topics that are
likely to lead to conflict, or defend the partner from the criticisms of
others. *Neglect* is defined by actions that do not address the problems at
hand and allow the relationship to decay. Examples include not cooperat-
ing with the partner to resolve issues and criticizing the partner for things
unrelated to the problem. These four responses can be differentiated
along the dimensions *constructive–destructive* and *active–passive*. The first
discriminates voice and loyalty responses, which are intended to repair
the relationship, from exit and neglect responses, which threaten the
relationship. The active–passive dimension distinguishes exit and voice
from loyalty and neglect. Exit and voice are active; both entail taking
actions that directly impact on the problem causing dissatisfaction. Loyalty and neglect are considered passive because the actions that define
each do not directly pertain to the problem.

In this study, Rusbult's typology was used in lieu of other typologies
that can be found in the communication literature because it is parsimonious; has a theoretical basis in Investment Theory that has had considerable success in predicting people's responses to relationship difficulties;
is clearly communicative in nature; and recognizes that individuals can
take both constructive and destructive courses of action in response to
relationship problems, unlike other typologies that have incorporated
only termination responses to relational difficulties (e.g., Baxter, 1982;
Cody, 1982). Having described the constructive responses that we expect
to be associated with high connectedness and the sharing of many foci,
and the destructive responses predicted to accompany low connectedness
and few shared foci, our hypotheses can be stated formally:

H1:   Connectedness of *O* to *P*'s network will be positively related to
      the use by *P* of the constructive strategies of voice and loyalty in
      response to dissatisfaction with *O*.

H2: Connectedness of O to P's network will be negatively related to the use by P of the destructive strategies of exit and neglect in response to dissatisfaction with O.

H3: Those cases in which P and O do not sever their ties will be characterized by greater connectedness of O to P's network than will those cases in which the $P-O$ relationship is severed.

H4: The extent to which O shares foci with P's network will be positively related to the use by P of the constructive strategies of voice and loyalty in response to dissatisfaction with O.

H5: The extent to which O shares foci with P's network will be negatively related to the use by P of the destructive strategies of exit and neglect in response to dissatisfaction with O.

H6: Those cases in which P and O do not sever their ties will be characterized by a greater perception by P that O shares foci with the other members of P's network than will those cases in which the $P-O$ relationship is completely severed.

Collaboration

As two intimates seek a satisfactory solution to their troubles, they are often faced with the task of working out the social consequences of their problems (Duck, 1982; McCall, 1982). Given that it is often difficult to hide problems from mutual friends, two intimates may find it desirable to discuss ways in which their conflict will be presented to the network. The negative outcomes associated with relationship disengagement, together with friends' desires to minimize undesirable consequences of their problems for the network (La Gaipa, 1982), should lead to the construction of a positive account of the conflict that preserves both parties' integrity and promotes the well-being of the network. Furthermore, when one experiences dissatisfaction with a friend who also tends to be linked to one's other network members through friendship and common foci, it may be valuable to negotiate the manner in which future encounters are conducted. Pressures to provide a positive depiction of the conflict episode for the benefit of the network should be primarily determined by the extent to which the target person is a part of that network (Salzinger, 1982). After all, one's friends should be most concerned about the episode when they are close to both P and O and share foci with both individuals. Thus, it is expected that:

H7: Connectedness of O to P's network will be positively related to the extent to which P and O collaborate to present a positive view of the conflict and their relationship to others.

H8:   The extent to which O shares foci with P's network will be positively related to the extent to which P and O collaborate on how
to present the conflict and relationship to others.

Network Intervention

Duck (1982) observed that the dissolution of the relationship of two
members of a network is likely to be of great concern to the pair's mutual
friends and acquaintances. La Gaipa (1982) attributed this interest in the
private affairs of P and O to the fact that dyadic strife weakens the
structural integrity of the network. The effect, according to Duck (1984),
is that the network will favor *prevention* of dissolution. Salzinger (1982)
believed that this is especially likely to be the case in networks in which
most members are well-acquainted and share activities. Thus, when integration is high, the desire to minimize damage to the network may lead
its members to intervene as mediators to resolve the situation (La Gaipa,
1982). Furthermore, the network's ability to intervene is diminished
where only one party to the conflict is a participant in the friendship
network (Salzinger, 1982). The speculations of these scholars, when examined in the context of conflict between friends, lead to two hypotheses:

H9:   Connectedness of O to P's network will be positively related to
the proportion of friends in P's network who offer advice and
mediation assistance to P in an effort to resolve the source of
dissatisfaction in the $P-O$ relationship.

H10: The extent to which O shares foci with P's network will be positively related to the proportion of friends in P's network who
offer advice and mediation assistance to P in an effort to resolve
the source of dissatisfaction in the $P-O$ relationship.

Network Reaction, Information Seeking,
and Responses to Dissatisfaction

When a person forms a new relationship with another individual, friends
and family will often evaluate these people and the wisdom of pursuing
the relationship. Several investigations have sought to understand the
impact of network support and interference on a relationship's trajectory.
Most have focused on the responses of family and friends to a loved one's
courtship (e.g., Bates, 1942; Knox & Wilson, 1981; Sussman, 1953). By
and large, networks tend to be more supportive or neutral than negative
(Parks et al., 1983), with support being more forthcoming as courtship

advances (Ryder et al., 1971). Despite the suggestion that parental opposition might intensify a child's courtship—an outcome called the "Romeo and Juliet Effect" (Driscoll, Davis, & Lipetz, 1972)— most research indicates that courtship progress is associated with network support (e.g., Eggert & Parks, 1986; Lewis, 1973; Parks & Adelman, 1983; Parks et al., 1983), although direction of causality is open to debate (Leslie, Huston, & Johnson, 1986). Unfortunately, little is known about the importance of network support and opposition in the conduct of friendships. In the one study reported to date, Eggert and Parks (1986) found that expressed support from both the partner's network and one's own network was positively related to increases in similarity, commitment, intimacy, and interaction time in adolescents' friendships.

To summarize, there is evidence that people often seek out the opinions of their network when deciding whether to develop a relationship with a particular person. Duck (1982) believed that people may feel compelled to maintain a relationship with another person once that individual has become integrated into the network, even when they have come to question the relationship's viability. There is support for this conclusion with regard to romantic relationships, but its relevance to friendship is not yet known. If applicable, these studies suggest that when P becomes disenchanted with friend O, P may assess the reactions of other friends to a possible deescalation or termination of the $P–O$ relationship. The motivation to obtain such information should be a function of the extent to which O is a part of P's network and shares foci with the members of the network. The information received from the network about possible disengagement should be an important determinant of how an individual responds to dissatisfaction. Should one conclude that the network opposes disengagement, the use of constructive responses that seek to preserve the friendship should be expected. If one perceives little opposition from the network, then the use of destructive responses will be more likely. Thus,

H11: Connectedness of O to P's network will be positively related to the extent to which P makes an effort to assess the reactions of other network members to a possible redefinition of the $P–O$ friendship.

H12: The extent to which O shares foci with the other members of P's network will be positively related to the degree to which P makes an effort to assess the reactions of other network members to a possible redefinition of the $P–O$ friendship.

H13: P's perception of the strength of network opposition to disengagement with O will be positively related to the use by P of the constructive strategies of voice and loyalty in response to dissatisfaction with O.

H14: P's perception of the strength of network opposition to disengagement with O will be negatively related to the use by P of the destructive strategies of exit and neglect in response to dissatisfaction with O.

Implicit in Hypotheses 11 through 14 is the assumption that networks will show the most opposition to disengagement by P when O is connected to P's network and shares many foci with these people. Thus, we expect that

H15: P's perception of network opposition to disengagement from O will be positively related to the extent to which O is connected to P's network.

H16: P's perception of network opposition to disengagement from O will be positively related to the extent to which O shares foci with members of P's network.

METHOD

Subjects

Subjects were 161 female and 85 male college students recruited from the Department of Psychology subject pool at a public west coast university.

Procedures

Participants initially identified a friend who had said or done something during the preceding 5-week period that caused them to become dissatisfied with the friendship. Respondents then described the dissatisfying event and its effect on the relationship. Subsequently, each respondent provided a list of the 10 other friends to whom he or she felt closest. After describing their friendship networks subjects completed, in randomized order, the measures discussed here.

Measures

Connectedness. Connectedness was conceptualized as the extent to which person O, the individual whose words or actions caused the subject hurt, is integrated into P's friendship network. Each subject indicated how close O was to the other 10 friends he or she identified. The stipulation that 11 friends be listed, while arbitrary, is consistent with the research of Fischer (1982). In his survey of over 1,000 individuals, people reported an average of 11 friends. Using a modified form of Marsden and Campbell's (1984) procedure for measuring intensity of tie strength, each respondent indicated his or her perceptions of the closeness of all possible pairs of friends in the network on a 5-point scale:

1. strangers,
2. acquaintances,
3. casual friends,
4. good friends, or
5. best of friends.

From these ratings, a measure of connectedness was derived by *averaging P*'s perceptions of how close *O* was to *P*'s other friends. Connectedness scores thus had a theoretical range of 1.0, in the case where *O* was thought to be unacquainted with all of the subject's other friends, to 5.0, in the case where *O* was deemed to be best of friends with all of *P*'s other friends.

Shared Foci. To develop a procedure for assessing shared foci, it was first necessary to identify those factors that facilitate interaction between friends. A pilot study was carried out in which 327 students identified those foci that brought them together. In the study, 207 females and 120 males provided descriptions of 5,120 foci in the 1,592 friendships for which reports were made. A content analysis of these descriptions was carried out to develop a typology of shared foci. In the first step of typology development, a list of very specific categories was constructed using subjects' own words as labels when possible. The frequency with which each foci was reported was also noted. Second, the list was reduced further as more general categories emerged to account for similar types of foci. The following eight categories sufficiently represented the vast majority of the foci reported by our informants:

1. *shared athletic activities* (e.g., participation on the same sports team),
2. *courses* (e.g., enrollment in the same class),
3. *social establishments* (e.g., being "regulars" at the same tavern),
4. *living arrangements* (e.g., being roommates or living in the same dormitory),
5. *mutual friends,*

6. *religious organizations* (e.g., membership in the same church or temple),

7. *clubs/groups/associations* (e.g., belonging to the same political action group), and

8. *work* (e.g., coming into frequent contact with each other through work-related duties).

Respondents in the main study were given descriptions of each of the foci and were asked to check off any foci that *O* shared with them and with the other members of their network. From these reports, two variables were constructed. *Shared foci/P–O* was the number of foci that the respondent reported having in common with *O*. Values for this variable could range from 0 in the case where none of the foci were shared by *P* and *O*, to 8 in the case where all of the foci were deemed relevant in the *P–O* friendship. The second variable was the average number of foci that *O* shared with the other members of a respondent's network. This variable, which is referred to as *shared foci/O–network*, was computed by averaging the number of foci that *P* thought *O* shared with the other members of the subject's network. Thus, its potential range was also 0–8.

Responses to Dissatisfaction.   Exit, voice, loyalty, and neglect responses were assessed with four eight-item scales developed by Healey and Bell (chapter 2, this volume). Because the measures used by Rusbult and her colleagues were developed for romantic relationships, many of their items were not relevant to friendship. In contrast, Healey and Bell's scales were constructed specifically to assess responses to dissatisfaction in friendships and pretested in a sample of over 300 college students. The items composing each scale were selected from a larger pool of items based on the results of confirmatory factor analyses. They report *alpha* reliabilities of .85 for exit, .91 for voice, .84 for loyalty, and .78 for neglect. The exit scale includes items such as "I permanently cut off all contact with my friend"; the voice scale was composed of items like "We solved our problems by talking things over in a calm and polite manner"; the measure of loyalty consisted of items such as "I said nothing and waited for things to get better"; the neglect scale included such items as "I said and did things out of anger to make my friend feel bad." Responses were made on 7-point agree–disagree scales.

Collaboration.   The extent to which *P* and *O* worked together to construct ways to present their conflict and relationship to others in a positive way was assessed with an eight-item measure of collaboration reported by Healey and Bell (Chapter 2, this volume). This instrument includes four items that assess the extent to which P believes he or she and O collaborated to create an account for the conflict (e.g., "I talked with my friend about how we could explain our conflict to other friends"). The remaining four items assess the degree to which P collaborated with O to create rules for conducting their future interactions (e.g., "We made an agreement to be polite to each other so that others would not feel uncomfortable around us"). Healey and Bell expected these two sets of items to assess two independent modes of collaboration, but found via a confirmatory factor analysis that they best represent a single, more general measure of collaboration. As with the other measures, responses were made on 7-point agree–disagree scales.

Network Intervention. The tendency for subjects to turn to their network of friends for guidance in dealing with their problems with O was assessed by asking subjects to indicate who of the other 10 friends provided advice for dealing with the conflict. Each respondent also indicated which of these friends offered to mediate the problems he or she had with O. A subject's advice and mediation scores were the *proportion* of the other friends who gave advice or made offers to mediate the conflict.

Social Reaction Monitoring. This measure assessed subjects' *efforts* to gauge their friends' reactions to possible disengagement, *not* the content of these reactions. Subjects indicated from whom of the ten friends listed they had sought information about feelings concerning an alteration of the subject's friendship with O. This score was also represented as the *proportion* of friends for whom an attempt was made to assess reactions to disengagement.

Network Support–Opposition. This measure was designed to assess a subject's perceptions of friends' likely reactions to the disruption of his or her friendship with O. For each of the 10 friends, subjects rated on a 3-point scale their perceptions of the likely response of each friend at the time they were making decisions regarding the fate of their friendship. The scale was scored from 1 to 3 as follows: 1 = "would have supported an end to the friendship"; 2 = "would not have cared one way or the other if the relationship ended"; 3 = "would have been against an end to the friendship." The subject's perceptions of the 10 friends' expected reactions were averaged to construct a measure of network support and opposition.

Prior Attraction. Wheeless' (1978) 20-item Interpersonal Solidarity Scale was used to assess subjects' attraction to O prior to the conflict.

Subjects were instructed to respond to each item as they would have before their difficulties with O. Responses were made on 7-point agree–disagree scales. Wheeless reports an *alpha* reliability of .96 for the instrument.

Other Ratings.   In addition to the measures just described, each subject was also asked to make three other ratings and assessments. A rating of *conflict seriousness* was made on a 9-point semantic differential scale (1 = "not at all serious"; 9 = "very serious"). An assessment of the impact of the conflict on the friendship was made on a 5-point Likert scale; response categories ranged from: 1 = "I no longer talk to this person" to 5 = "we are actually closer than we were prior to the conflict." Because large values indicate a positive outcome, this variable is called *positive impact.* Finally, each respondent reported whether he or she *discussed* the conflict with any other friend.

RESULTS

Preliminary Analyses

Prior to undertaking tests of the specific hypotheses, several preliminary analyses were conducted. First, the exit, voice, loyalty, and neglect scales were subjected to a confirmatory factor analysis, using the LISREL-VI program (Jöreskog & Sorbom, 1984). The four-factor structure assumed to underly responses to the dissatisfaction questionnaire fit the data adequately [X^2 (458) = 1418.94, $p < .001$, x^2/df ratio = 3.09]; Wheaton, Muthen, Alwin, and Summers (1977) suggest that x^2/df ratio under 5.0 indicates a reasonably good overall fit. Second, reliabilities were computed to assess the internal consistencies of the scales used in the investigation. *Alpha* reliabilities were as follows: exit (.90), voice (.95), loyalty (.91), neglect (.84), collaboration (.93), and prior attraction (.93). Third, gender differences in the major variables of interest were examined (see Table 6.1). Females reported that a greater proportion of their network offered advice for dealing with the conflicts; they also rated their conflicts as more serious and as having a more negative impact on the relationship than did male respondents. Females were more likely to discuss their conflicts with other friends than were males; 75.2% of females, compared to 55.3% of males reported such discussions [$x^2(1) = 9.23$, $p < .003$]. Males reported that the person with whom they experienced conflict was better connected and shared more foci with their other friends. Males also perceived greater potential opposition to a weakening or severing

TABLE 6.1
Means and Standard Deviations of Measures

Measure	Females		Males		t (df)	p
	Mean	SD	Mean	SD		
Exit	17.89	10.26	16.67	9.19	0.92(243)	.36
Voice	29.25	13.33	30.92	12.02	−0.96(243)	.34
Loyalty	30.59	11.98	31.74	10.76	−0.74(244)	.46
Neglect	20.95	9.05	21.09	8.46	−0.12(244)	.90
Connectedness	2.40	0.69	2.59	0.78	−1.98(244)	.05
Shared foci/P-O	2.29	1.60	2.48	1.39	−0.93(244)	.36
Shared foci/O-network	1.24	.80	1.48	.94	−2.12(244)	.04
Collaboration	18.54	9.76	19.49	9.26	−0.74(244)	.46
Network advice	.27	.20	.19	.17	2.86(244)	.005
Network mediation	.07	.10	.05	.09	1.69(244)	.10
Assess network reaction	.16	.19	.12	.16	1.71(244)	.09
Network opposition	2.04	.57	2.19	.49	−2.07(244)	.04
Seriousness	5.53	2.26	4.69	2.20	2.80(244)	.006
Positive impact	3.15	.89	3.45	.79	−2.59(244)	.01
Prior attraction	100.19	19.84	99.86	19.66	0.50(244)	.62

of their bonds with the individual causing dissatisfaction. Correlations among measures are reported in Table 6.2.

Connectedness, Shared Foci, and Responses to Dissatisfaction

Connectedness. The first three hypotheses pertain to how *P*'s responses to dissatisfaction with *O* are constrained by the extent to which *O* is connected to *P*'s network by virtue of strong ties. Hypothesis 1, which predicted that connectedness would be positively related to *P*'s use of constructive strategies voice and loyalty in response to displeasure with *O*, received partial support. Voice and connectedness were modestly and positively correlated for both females ($r = .14$, $p < .04$) and males ($r = .21$, $p < .03$). However, connectedness was not associated with loyalty responses (females: $r = −.05$, $p < .29$; males: $r = −.03$, $p < .41$). The second hypothesis predicted that the connectedness of *O* to *P*'s network would be negatively related to *P*'s use of the destructive strategies of exit and neglect. Although there was a small, significant inverse relationship between connectedness and exit responses for the total sample ($r = −.12$, $p < .04$), the relationship was not significant when the data of females and males were analyzed separately (females: $r = −.12$, $p < .07$; males: $r = −.10$, $p < .18$). Connectedness was not significantly related to neglect responses (females: $r = .04$, $p < .32$; males: $r = .07$, $p < .28$). Overall, there is little evidence that connectedness is associated with people's use

TABLE 6.2
Correlations Among Measures (Decimal Points Have Been Deleted)

	1	2	3	4	5	6	7	8	9	10	11	12	13	14	15
1 Exit	—														
2 Voice	01	—													
3 Loyalty	−11	−46	—												
4 Neglect	58	−16	03	—											
5 Connectedness	−12	17	−03	00	—										
6 Shared foci/P-O	01	09	−01	07	17	—									
7 Shared foci/O-network	03	08	06	10	48	55	—								
8 Collaboration	32	42	−09	24	07	06	07	—							
9 Network advice	41	11	−09	33	12	13	21	19	—						
10 Network Mediation	28	13	−13	21	14	09	19	34	43	—					
11 Assess network reaction	38	13	−10	31	05	06	15	20	53	38	—				
12 Network opposition	−33	15	03	−22	24	06	11	−05	−20	−33	−12	—			
13 Seriousness	44	03	−02	25	−15	−05	−06	22	36	21	36	−24	—		
14 Positive impact	−56	19	03	−42	19	10	02	−07	−31	−15	−29	28	−37	—	
15 Prior attraction	−21	34	−09	−29	28	18	15	−05	−08	−09	−05	17	−03	36	—

Note: N = 246.
If $r > .11$, $p < .05$; if $r > .15$, $p < .01$; if $r > .19$, $p < .001$.

of destructive responses. However, there was a tendency for those who severed the relationship to do so when the person with whom they were experiencing dissatisfaction was less connected to the network. The 41 respondents who did not consider O to be a friend following the incident that led to dissatisfaction had a mean connectedness score of 2.28 (*SD* = 0.58), compared to a mean of 2.50 (*SD* = 0.73) for those 205 respondents whose friendships survived [$t(244) = -1.76$, $p < .05$]. Hypothesis 3 was thus supported.

Shared Foci. Hypothesis 4 predicted that the extent to which O shared foci with P's network would be positively related to the use by P of the constructive strategies of voice and loyalty in response to dissatisfaction with O. The hypothesis was not supported. Shared foci/O- network was not significantly associated with voice for females ($r = .08$, $p < .16$) or males ($r = .06$, $p < .29$); nor was shared foci/O-network related to loyalty for either gender (females: $r = .01$, $p < .46$; males: $r = .13$, $p < .12$). Hypothesis 5 predicted that O's sharing of foci with P's network would deter the use by P of the destructive strategies of exit and neglect. The hypothesis was supported for males; shared foci/O-network was significantly related to exit ($r = .18$, $p < .05$) and neglect ($r = .22$, $p < .03$). For females, this variable was not associated with exit ($r = -.04$, $p < .30$) or neglect ($r = .04$, $p < .33$). Hypothesis 6 predicted that those cases in which P and O do not sever their ties would be characterized by a greater perception by P that O shares foci with P's network than would those cases in which the $P–O$ friendship was ended. The results did not support this hypothesis [$t(244) = -0.73$, $p < .47$]. For those 41 respondents who no longer considered themselves friends with person O, the perceived mean number of shared foci with their network was 1.23 ($SD = 0.73$), whereas those 205 respondents whose relationships continued had a mean shared foci value of 1.34 ($SD = 0.88$).

Network Integration and the Coordination of Disengagement

Hypotheses 7 and 8 dealt with the influence of connectedness and shared foci/O-network on the tendency for two people in conflict to collaborate to devise ways to present the conflict and their friendship to others in a positive way. Hypothesis 7 predicted that connectedness would be positively related to the extent to which P and O engage in such collaborative efforts. The hypothesis received very modest support for males ($r = .18$, $p < .05$), but not for females ($r = .00$). Hypothesis 8 predicted that shared foci/O-network would be positively related to $P–O$ collaboration. No support was found for the hypothesis for females ($r = .02$, $p < .41$) or for males ($r = .13$, $p < .12$).

Network Intervention

Hypotheses 9 and 10 predicted that connectedness and shared foci would motivate network intervention in the $P–O$ conflict. Hypothesis 9 predicted that connectedness would be positively related to the proportion of friends in P's network who offered advice and mediation assistance to P in an effort to resolve the source of dissatisfaction in the $P–O$ relationship. The results provided weak support for the hypothesis. The correlation between connectedness and advice was significant for females ($r = .20$, $p < .01$), but not for males ($r = .04$, $p < .35$). The correlation between connectedness and mediation was a nonsignificant .10 ($p < .10$) for females and .25 ($p < .009$) for males. Thus, connectedness was associated with receiving advice for females and with receiving offers of mediation for males.

Hypothesis 10 predicted that the extent to which O shares foci with P's network would be positively related to the number of friends in P's network who offered advice and mediation assistance to P. The results provided support for the hypothesis. The correlation between shared foci/O-network and advice was .18 ($p < .01$) for females and .37 ($p < .001$) for males. The same pattern held for mediation (females $r = .20$, $p < .01$; males $r = .24$, $p < .05$).

Network Reaction, Network Opposition, and Responses to Dissatisfaction

Assessing Network Reactions. Hypotheses 11 and 12 predicted that P's efforts to assess network members' views of the situation would be influenced to a large extent by the degree to which O was integrated into P's network. Hypothesis 11 made the specific prediction of a positive relationship between connectedness and the degree to which P made an effort to assess the reactions of other network members to a possible redefinition of the $P–O$ friendship. The results did not support the hypothesis (females: $r = .10$, $p < .11$; males: $r = -.01$, $p < .46$). Hypothesis 12 predicted that the extent to which O shares foci with the other members of P's network would be positively related to the degree to which P made an effort to assess the reactions of other network members to a possible redefinition of the $P–O$ friendship. The results support the hypothesis for females ($r = .18$, $p < .01$) but not for males ($r = .13$, $p < .11$).

Network Opposition. Hypotheses 13 and 14 suggested that perceptions of the network's opinions about a possible disengagement is an important determinant of how an individual responds to dissatisfaction. Specifically, Hypothesis 13 predicted that P's perception of the strength of network opposition to disengagement with O would be positively related to the use by P of the constructive strategies of voice and loyalty in response to dissatisfaction with O. The results for the voice correlation supported the hypothesis for females ($r = .14$, $p < .04$), but not for males ($r = .14$, $p < .10$). The predicted relationship between network opposition and loyalty was not found (females: $r = .03$, $p < .35$; males: $r = .02$, $p < .41$). Hypothesis 14 predicted that P's perception of the strength of network opposition to disengagement with O would be negatively related to the use by P of the destructive strategies of exit and neglect in response to dissatisfaction with O. The data supported this prediction. Perceived network opposition was inversely related to exit for both females ($r = .37$, $p < .001$) and males ($r = -.20$, $p < .04$). Likewise, network opposition correlated significantly with neglect responses for both sexes (females: $r = -.19$, $p < .01$; males: $r = -.30$, $p < .01$).

Hypotheses 15 and 16 put to a test the assumption implicit in the preceding four hypotheses that networks show the most opposition to disengagement of P from O when O is part of the network. Hypothesis 15, which predicted that P's perception of network opposition to disengagement from O would be positively related to O's connectedness to P's network, was supported (females: $r = .19$, $p < .01$; males: $r = .31$, $p < .01$). Hypothesis 16 predicted that P's perception of opposition from the network to disengagement would be positively related to the extent to which O shares foci with the members of P's network. The results supported the prediction for females ($r = .14$, $p < .04$), but not for males ($r = .02$, $p < .44$).

Predictors of Exit, Voice, Loyalty, and Neglect

The failure of the connectedness and shared foci to constrain individuals' responses to dissatisfaction was disappointing and led us to wonder if the other characteristics of the conflict, the individual reporting on the conflict, or the network might be associated with any of the four responses. If connectedness and shared foci are not associated with exit, voice, loyalty, or neglect in any compelling way, what might predict reliance on these responses? What forces impact on a person's decision to use each of these modes of conflict resolution? These questions were addressed via stepwise regression analyses, in which the four responses were used as dependent variables in four separate analyses with the other variables in the study used as potential predictors.

As can be seen from Table 6.3, those situations in which exit responses tended to be used were ones in which the conflict was felt to be serious, where P–O collaboration occurred, where prior attraction to O was low, where network members felt compelled to offer advice, and where the network was not perceived as opposing disengagement. These five variables accounted for 43% of the variance in exit responses. Voice responses were predicted by a linear combination of P–O collaboration, high prior attraction, and perceived network opposition to disengagement. These three predictor variables together accounted for 31% of the variance in voice responses. The results for loyalty were disappointing. No variable could account for a significant portion of the variance in this response above and beyond that claimed by network mediation. Only 1% of the variance in loyalty was accounted for in the analysis. Finally, neglect tended to be used in response to dissatisfying events that were serious and involved an antagonist to whom respondents did not feel much attraction prior to the encounter. In addition, neglect responses were associated with obtaining advice from the network and with P–O collaboration. Approximately 26% of the variance in neglect responses could be accounted for by these four variables.

TABLE 6.3
Predictors of Exit, Voice, Loyalty, Neglect, and Collaboration

Dependent measure	Predictors	Adjusted R-square	F (df)	Beta
Exit	1 Seriousness	.33	121.98*** (1,244)	.428***
	2 Collaboration	.37	72.48*** (2,243)	.187***
	3 Prior attraction	.40	55.15*** (3,242)	−.151**
	4 Network advice	.42	44.57*** (4,241)	.145**
	5 Network opposition	.43	37.88*** (5,240)	−.134**
Voice	1 Collaboration	.17	50.50*** (1,244)	.438***
	2 Prior attraction	.30	53.39*** (2,243)	.348***
	3 Network opposition	.31	37.58*** (3,242)	.113*
Loyalty	1 Network mediation	.01	4.01* (1,244)	−.127*
Neglect	1 Seriousness	.15	44.16*** (1,244)	.280***
	2 Prior attraction	.22	35.49*** (2,243)	−.254***
	3 Network advice	.24	27.07*** (3,242)	.162**
	4 Collaboration	.26	22.17*** (4,241)	.137*
Collaboration	1 Voice	.17	50.50*** (1,244)	.413***
	2 Exit	.26	45.08*** (2,243)	.155*
	3 Network mediation	.30	36.66*** (3,242)	.203***
	4 Neglect	.32	29.91*** (4,241)	.175**

$*p < .05$; $**p < .01$; $***p < .001$.

Predictors of Collaboration

Given the failure of the two network integration variables to predict collaboration in any meaningful way, we examined via a stepwise multiple regression analysis other features of conflict situations that might be associated with P–O collaboration. Variables serving as potential predictors were the four responses to dissatisfaction, the network intervention variables, prior attraction, and the connectedness and shared foci measures. The results of the analysis are reported in Table 6.3. Four significant predictors emerged: exit, voice, neglect, and mediation from network members. Thus, P and O tended to work together in the construction of public accounts and rules for future interaction when they took action in response to the situation, as opposed to doing nothing (i.e., when they used exit, voice, and neglect responses in lieu of loyalty); and when the other members of their network showed enough concern about the conflict to offer mediation assistance. Approximately 32% of the variance of reports of P–O collaboration could be accounted for by these four predictors.

DISCUSSION

It has become common for scholars to observe that an understanding of disengagement necessitates research into network processes that contribute to relationship stability. The position typically advanced is that the dissolution of a relationship does not occur in a vacuum. Rather it is shaped by the other relationships in which it is embedded (Duck, 1982; Hinde, 1981; La Gaipa, 1981; Milardo, 1983, 1986, 1987). The results of this study, however, indicate that the impact of networks on decision-making processes during conflict may have been overstated, at least within the context of friendship. This section reflects on the results of this study, which suggest that network integration exerts little influence on how conflict at the dyadic level is resolved. Possible explanations for the findings that connectedness and sharing foci were not generally predictive of responses to dissatisfaction are considered.

Although partial support was found for the link of connectedness and shared foci to some responses to dissatisfaction, even the occasional statistically significant correlation was invariably weak. Several reasons for the failure of these two aspects of network integration to predict responses to dissatisfaction come to mind. First, it is possible that imbalance in peoples' ties to others does not cause sufficient levels of distress to motivate people to work toward balance. Recall that Parks and Riveland (1987) found that the majority of high school and college students surveyed were involved in at least one triad in which they disliked the friend of a friend. It may be that people can live with the imbalance that a decline in a relationship in the network may produce without much stress or consternation. As such, the extent to which one's friend is connected to the network or shares foci with the network may not be as potent a factor in one's approach to conflict resolution as has been assumed.

Second, the fact that connectedness and shared foci did not have strong associations with exit, voice, loyalty, and neglect suggests that when people make decisions about how to respond to dissatisfaction, they view the conflict as a dyadic issue rather than a network concern. Evidence for this proposition is especially strong for destructive responses. Dyadic and conflict variables proved in regression analyses to be more critical predictors of the exit and neglect responses than the network variables, which typically had smaller *beta* weights. The most significant predictor for exit responses was the seriousness of the conflict. Neglect responses were most strongly related to conflict seriousness and prior attraction. For voice, only one of the three significant predictors—network opposition—was a network variable; the other predictors were collaboration and prior attraction. Although the only significant predictor of loyalty responses was the network variable mediation, the correlation was very weak.

A third reason for the disappointing results for the integration–response hypotheses is that the people with whom respondents reported experiencing dissatisfaction were not usually integrated into subjects' networks to any great extent. The mean connectedness score of 2.45 reveals that O's typical involvement with P's other friends can be characterized as falling between "acquaintanceship" and "casual friendship." Likewise, the average number of foci that O shared with network members was less than 1.5. Future research should compare individuals' responses to the upsetting actions of well-integrated and poorly integrated members of their networks, while controlling for other variables that may co-vary with degree of integration.

Fourth, because relatively few conflicts were described that involved well-integrated friends, it is possible that network integration works not so much by shaping responses to a conflict, but by suppressing the conflict. For example, people may be more likely to adopt a "let it pass" rule when confronted with negative behaviors from an integrated individual than from a nonintegrated person. Or perhaps individuals may not allow a person who might be objectionable to other friends to become highly integrated into the network. Stated differently, network integration may influence the conflict process at an earlier stage than the one examined in this investigation. Finally, the possibility that connectedness and shared foci are important but were not operationalized well in this investigation is considered later.

Although this study suggests that the degree to which a person is integrated into one's network does not influence one's responses to dissatisfaction with that person very much, it would be a mistake to assume that the ways in which networks become involved are unrelated to these responses. First, there was a tendency for network members to offer advice and mediation services when subjects responded destructively. Second, perceptions of network opposition did seem to constrain subjects' use of destructive responses. In other words, for destructive responses it is not who O knows and what brings them together that matters. It is how those people are thought to value the $P-O$ tie that counts.

One of the entering assumptions of this investigation was that P and O work together to devise a public presentation of their conflict as a way of influencing network members' impressions of the situation. It was presumed that such efforts were intended to disguise the true nature of the conflict and minimize the network's concerns. We thus expected the network to be less inclined to offer advice or mediation for dealing with the situation when P and O had created accounts and rules for interacting with each other. Surprisingly, the $P-O$ collaboration was *positively* related to the degree to which P received advice and offers of mediation services. Collaboration was also related to the extent to which P attempted to assess other friends' reactions to the conflict. Thus, $P-O$ collaboration complements, rather than substitutes for, direct discussions with the network about the problem at hand. The motivation to talk with both the network and O about the conflict may be inspired by concerns that O might present a distorted version of the conflict to the network. As a consequence, P and O may be inclined to talk to the network as a way of monitoring the story that mutual friends hear about the conflict so that things can be set straight if necessary and the impact of damaging gossip can be mitigated.

The results of this study reveal strikingly few differences in the response tendencies of women and men. There were no differences between the sexes in the extent to which exit, voice, loyalty, or neglect responses were reported to have been used. The lack of differences evidenced in the study are especially noteworthy given that females reported more serious conflicts that had more damaging effects on their relationships. These results are at odds with previous investigations of responses to dissatisfaction, which have been carried out in dating relationships. Typically, the tendency in romantic attachments is for females to respond to dissatisfaction with voice and loyalty, whereas males tend to favor exit or neglect (Rusbult et al., 1982). One difference worth noting was that males reported conflicts with individuals who were more highly connected to their other friends and who shared more foci with those friends. This finding may reflect the tendency for males' friendships to be based on activities with groups, whereas females emphasize self-disclosure, personalism, and mutual support in friendship (e.g., Bell, 1981; Caldwell & Peplau, 1982). This finding is ironic given the fact that females were much more likely to discuss their conflicts with other friends. This may reflect the tendency for females to be more concerned with relationship discussions, presumably including discussions with the network (Davidson & Duberman, 1982).

The disappointing results for the variable connectedness raise concerns about the validity of the operationalization used in this investigation. Several findings suggest that the measure of connectedness used in this study is reasonable. First, and most basic, there was a moderate relationship between connectedness, assessed as the average strength of the tie of O to the other members of P's network, and the other measure of network integration used in this study—*shared foci/O-network*. Second, connectedness correlated with other variables in ways that should be expected. For instance, people who were connected to respondents' networks tended to be liked more by the respondents prior to the conflict. Likewise, respondents' reports of network opposition to a possible severing of the P–O bond were greatest when O had ties to those individuals.

Another question remains, however. Is the connectedness measure flawed by virtue of its reliance on P's *perceptions* of the strength of O's ties to other friends? The data collected here do not provide any basis for assessing the accuracy with which such reports are made. However, because respondents' decisions are presumably based on their *impressions* of the structure of their friendship networks and not on any objective reality, the use of perceptual data in deriving the measure of connectedness is reasonable. Nevertheless, the *actual* links among the members of an individual's network may exert influence on the course of a conflict even if that individual misunderstands the true nature of those ties. For example, in the case where the dissatisfying friend is perceived to be well-integrated into the network, but is actually not, the network would be unlikely to come forward with advice. The weak strength of the ties of O to the network precludes such interventions, and does so even when P overestimates these ties.

The two measures of shared foci developed for this study also appear to have been reasonable. The fact that connectedness (i.e., average tie strength of O to the network) correlated moderately with *shared foci/O-network* but very weakly with *shared foci/ P–O* provides evidence that these two variables are, in fact, assessing very different constructs. There is no reason to expect that just because P and O share many activities that bring them together that O must necessarily have strong ties with the network. However, O's sharing of foci with the network presumably strengthens the ties between O and the network on which the connectedness measure is derived. On the other hand, the very weak correlation between shared foci/ P–O and respondents' liking of O prior to the conflict is a source of concern. It may be that the sharing of foci with another individual and liking of that person is not as tightly coupled as has been assumed (Wellman et al., 1988).

Nevertheless, it is worth considering how the assessment of shared foci might be improved in future research. Several possibilities come to mind. First, the measurement scheme does not take into account the possibility that an individual may have multiple instantiations of interaction promoted by the same category of foci. Two people who share involvement in three different athletic organizations are treated equally with the measurement procedure used here as two people who share just one athletic activity. Second, no attempt was made to assess the importance to a relationship of a particular foci. Yet, it is self-evident that foci can differ considerably in their significance to be a dyad. Some foci, such as work, may create more *frequent* interaction than other foci, such as church membership, which may promote only weekly encounters. In addition, some foci may promote more *intense*, personal communication than others. Foci also differ in the *duration* of their existence. Some interaction facilitators, such as courses, operate for a short period of time; other foci, such as place of employment, may bring two people together in interaction for years. Beyond differences in the frequency and intensity of interactions promoted by foci, certain foci facilitate activities that are more *valued* than other foci. Joint participation in a valued foci may exert strong barriers to disengagement. Moreover, some foci are *intentional* interaction facilitators that are cultivated for the sole purpose of promoting interaction between two people, whereas others are incidental to the relationship. Finally, some foci such as work are not easily *substitutable*, whereas others can be replaced with relative ease (Johnson, 1982). The procedure used in this study treats as equivalent all foci despite these considerations. A better procedure for assessing shared foci may be to use respondents' own categories and have them estimate the interaction facilitating properties of each. It should be possible to weight a respondent's endorsement of a particular focus of interaction by considering its frequency, intensity, duration, value, intent, and substitutability.

Another limitation of the study is that the cross-sectional nature of the data collected here does not allow for precise descriptions of cause and effect. For example, the inverse relationship between exiting and receiving advice from the network can be explained in several ways. It may be that the network provides input *in response* to P's efforts to leave the friendship; that is, exiting may cause advice giving. Conversely, individuals who are contemplating the severing of a friendship tie may seek advice from other friends; that is, receiving advice from the network may precede and shape the use of exit responses. Future research should adopt longitudinal designs that follow the course of friends' conflicts from start to finish. It is only by assessing variables of interest at multiple points in time that the causal relationships among them can be sorted.

As with any study, the generalizability of results to other populations and contexts is an issue. First, several characteristics of the student sample may limit the applicability of the results to other populations. For instance, the level of investment in friendships at college may be affected by the view that such bonds are as transitory as the college experience itself. Conflict might consequently be conducted according to different rules and norms than would be found in a nonstudent population characterized by ties of longer duration. Adults may thus be more inclined than students to consider a friend's ties to other friends when deciding the course to be taken when that friend has caused hurt. Furthermore, the college environment offers plentiful alternative friendships for those who become dissatisfied with a friend. This being the case, the barriers against disengagement would be less constraining for students.

Many scholars have called for studies of the influence of networks on relationship development, maintenance, and deterioration. In this spirit, the present study has attempted to test empirically some commonly held assumptions about the dyad-network interface with regards to friends in conflict. Although some apparent influences were noted, the results taken as a whole indicate that friends resolve or fail to remedy their differences with limited input from other friends or consideration of their concerns. If networks constrain how friends deal with problems in their relationship, this study was unable to document such effects. As Wiseman (1986) observed, friendships are highly voluntary associations, and network integration does not appear to make friendly relations any less voluntary.

REFERENCES

Anderson, B. (1979). Cognitive balance theory and social network analysis: Remarks on some fundamental theoretical matters. In P. Holland & S. Leinhardt (Eds.), *Perspectives on social network research* (pp. 453–469). New York: Academic Press.

Banks, S. P., Altendorf, D. M., Greene, J. O., & Cody, M. J. (1987). An examination of relationship disengagement: Perceptions, breakup strategies and outcomes. *Western Journal of Speech Communication, 51,* 19–41.

Bates, A. (1942). Parental roles in courtship. *Social Forces, 20,* 483–486.

Baxter, L. (1982). Strategies for ending relationships: Two studies. *Western Journal of Speech Communication, 46,* 223–241.

Bell, R. (1981). Friendships of women and men. *Psychology of Women Quarterly, 5,* 402–417.

Bott, E. (1971). *Family and social network* (2nd ed.). New York: The Free Press.

Caldwell, M. A., & Peplau, L. A. (1982). Sex differences in same-sex friendship. *Sex Roles, 8,* 721–732.

Cartwright, D., & Harary, F. (1956). Structural balance: A generalization of Heider's theory. *Psychological Review, 63,* 277–293.

Cody, M. J. (1982). A typology of disengagement strategies and an examination of the role intimacy, reactions to inequity, and relational problems play in strategy selection. *Communication Monographs, 49,* 148–170.

Davidson, L. R., & Duberman, L. (1982). Friendship: Communication and interaction patterns in same-sex dyads. *Sex Roles, 8,* 809–822.

Davis, J. A. (1970). Clustering and hierarchy in interpersonal relations: Testing two graph theoretical models on 742 sociomatrices. *American Sociological Review, 35,* 843–852.

Davis, J. (1979). The Davis/Holland/Leinhardt studies: An overview. In P. W. Holland & S. Leinhardt (Eds.), *Perspectives on social network research* (pp. 51–62). New York: Academic Press.

Davis, J., & Leinhardt, S. (1971). The structure of positive interpersonal relations in small groups. In J. Berger (Ed.), *Sociological theories in progress* (Vol. 2, pp. 218–251). Boston: Houghton Mifflin.

Driscoll, R., Davis, K. E., & Lipetz, M. E. (1972). Parental interference and romantic love: The Romeo and Juliet effect. *Journal of Personality and Social Psychology, 24,* 1–10.

Duck, S. (1982). A topography of relationship disengagement and dissolution. In S. Duck (Ed.), *Personal relationships. Vol. 4: Dissolving personal relationships* (pp. 1–30). London: Academic Press.

Duck, S. (1984). A perspective on the repair of personal relationships: Repair of what, when? In S. Duck (Ed.), *Personal relationships. Vol. 5: Repairing personal relationships* (pp. 163–184). London: Academic Press.

Eggert, L. L., & Parks, M. R. (1986). Communication network involvement in adolescents' friendships and romantic relationships. In M. McLaughlin (Ed.), *Communication yearbook 10* (pp. 283–322). Newbury Park, CA: Sage.

Feld, S. L. (1981). The focused organization of social ties. *American Journal of Sociology, 86,* 1015–1035.

Feld, S. L. (1982). Social structural determinants of similarity among associates. *American Sociological Review, 47,* 797–801.

Feld, S. L. (1984). The structured use of personal associates. *Social Forces, 62,* 640–652.

Fischer, C. S. (1982). What do we mean by "friend"? An inductive study. *Social Network, 3,* 287–306.

Hallinan, M. (1972). Comment on Holland and Leinhardt. *American Journal of Sociology, 77,* 1201–1205.

Hallinan, M., & Felmlee, D. (1975). Analysis of intransitivity in sociometric data. *Sociometry, 38,* 195–212.

Hallinan, M. T. (1982). Cognitive balance and differential popularity in social networks. *Social Psychology Quarterly, 45,* 86–90.

Heider, F. (1958). *The psychology of interpersonal relations.* New York: Wiley.

Hinde, R. A. (1981). The bases of a science of interpersonal relationships. In S. Duck & R. Gilmour (Eds.), *Personal relationships. Vol. 1: Studying personal relationships* (pp. 1–22). London: Academic Press.

Johnson, M. P. (1973). Commitment: A conceptual structure and empirical application. *Sociological Quarterly, 14,* 395–406.

Johnson, M. P. (1982). Social and cognitive features of dissolving commitment to relationships. In S. W. Duck (Ed.), *Personal relationships. Vol. 4: Dissolving personal relationships* (pp. 51–73). London: Academic Press.

Johnson, M. P., & Leslie, L. (1982). Couple involvement and network structure: A test of the dyadic withdrawal hypothesis. *Social Psychology Quarterly, 45,* 34–43.

Jöreskog, K. G., & Sorbom, D. (1984). *LISREL VI: Analysis of linear structural relationships by the method of maximum likelihood.* Moorseville, IN: Scientific Software, Inc.

Kelley, H. H. (1983). Love and commitment. In H. H. Kelley, E. Berscheid, A. Christensen, J. H. Harvey, T. L. Huston, G. Levinger, E. McClintock, L. A. Peplau, & D. R. Peterson (Eds.), *Close relationships* (pp. 265–314). New York: Freeman.

Knox, D., & Wilson, K. (1981). Dating behaviors of university students. *Family Relations, 30,* 255–258.

La Gaipa, J. J. (1981). A systems approach to personal relationships. In S. Duck & R. Gilmour (Eds.), *Personal relationships. Vol. 1: Studying personal relationships* (pp. 67–89). London: Academic Press.

La Gaipa, J. J. (1982). Rules and rituals in disengagement from relationships. In S. Duck (Ed.), *Personal relationships. Vol. 4: Dissolving personal relationships* (pp. 189–210). London: Academic Press.

Leslie, L. A., Huston, T. L., & Johnson, M. P. (1986). Parental reactions to dating relationships: Do they make a difference? *Journal of Marriage and the Family, 48,* 57–66.

Levinger, G. (1976). A social psychological perspective on marital dissolution. *Journal of Social Issues, 32,* 21–47.

Lewis, R. A. (1973). Social reaction and the formation of dyads: An interactionist approach to mate selection. *Sociometry, 36,* 409–418.

Lund, M. (1985). The development of investment and commitment scales for predicting continuity of personal relationships. *Journal of Social and Personal Relationships, 2,* 3–23.

Marsden, P. V., & Campbell, K. E. (1984). Measuring tie strength. *Social Forces, 63,* 482–501.

McCall, G. (1982). Becoming unrelated: The management of bond dissolution. In S. Duck (Ed.), *Personal relationships. Vol. 4: Dissolving personal relationships* (pp. 211–231). London: Academic Press.

McCarthy, B. (1986). Dyads, cliques, and conspiracies: Friendship behaviors and perceptions within long-established social groups. In R. Gilmour & S. Duck (Eds.), *The emerging field of personal relationships* (pp. 77–89). Hillsdale, NJ: Lawrence Erlbaum Associates.

Milardo, R. M. (1982). Friendship networks in developing relationships: Converging and diverging social environments. *Social Psychology Quarterly, 45,* 162–172.

Milardo, R. M. (1983). Social networks and pair relationships: A review of substantive and measurement issues. *Sociology and Social Research, 68,* 1–18.

Milardo, R. M. (1986). Personal choice and social constraint in close relationships:

Applications of network analysis. In V. J. Derlega & B. A. Winstead (Eds.), *Friendship and social interaction* (pp. 147–165). New York: Springer-Verlag.

Milardo, R. M. (1987). Changes in social networks of women and men following divorce: A review. *Journal of Family Issues, 8*, 78–96.

Milardo, R. M., Johnson, M. P., & Huston, T. L. (1983). Developing close relationships: Changing patterns of interaction between pair members and social networks. *Journal of Personality and Social Psychology, 44*, 964–976.

Parks, M. R., & Adelman, M. B. (1983). Communication networks and the development of romantic relationships: An expansion of uncertainty reduction theory. *Human Communication Research, 10*, 55–79.

Parks, M. R., & Riveland, L. (1987, May). *On dealing with disliked friends of friends: A study of the occurrence and management of imbalanced relationships.* Paper presented at the annual meeting of the International Communication Association, Montreal, Canada.

Parks, M. R., Stan, C. M., & Eggert, L. L. (1983). Romantic involvement and social network involvement. *Social Psychology Quarterly, 46*, 116–131.

Ridley, C., & Avery, A. (1979). The influence of social networks on dyadic interaction. In R. L. Burgess & T. L. Huston (Eds.), *Social exchange and developing relationships* (pp. 223–246). New York: Academic Press.

Rusbult, C. E. (1980a). Commitment and satisfaction in romantic associations: A test of the investment model. *Journal of Experimental Social Psychology, 16*, 172–186.

Rusbult, C. E. (1980b). Satisfaction and commitment in friendships. *Representative Research in Social Psychology, 11*, 96–105.

Rusbult, C. E. (1983). A longitudinal test of the investment model: The development (and deterioration) of satisfaction and commitment in heterosexual involvements. *Journal of Personality and Social Psychology, 45*, 101–117.

Rusbult, C. E. (1987). Responses to dissatisfaction in close relationships: The exit-voice-loyalty-neglect model. In D. Perlman & S. Duck (Eds.), *Intimate relationships: Development, dynamics, and deterioration* (pp. 209–237). Newbury Park, CA: Sage.

Rusbult, C. E., Johnson, D. J., & Morrow, G. D. (1986). Predicting satisfaction and commitment in adult romantic involvements: An assessment of the generalizability of the investment model. *Social Psychology Quarterly, 49*, 81–89.

Rusbult, C. E., & Zembrodt, I. M. (1983). Responses to dissatisfaction in romantic involvements: A multidimensional scaling analysis. *Journal of Experimental Social Psychology, 19*, 274–293.

Rusbult, C. E., Zembrodt, I. M., & Gunn, L. K. (1982). Exit, voice, loyalty, and neglect: Responses to dissatisfaction in romantic involvements. *Journal of Personality and Social Psychology, 43*, 1230–1242.

Ryder, R. G., Kafka, J. S., & Olson, D. H. (1971). Separating and joining influences in courtship and early marriage. *American Journal of Orthopsychiatry, 41*, 450–464.

Salzinger, L. L. (1982). The ties that bind: The effects of clustering on dyadic relationships. *Social Networks, 4*, 117–145.

Surra, C. A. (1985). Courtship types: Variations in interdependence between partners and social networks. *Journal of Personality and Social Psychology, 49*, 357–375.

Sussman, M. (1953). Parental participation in mate selection and its effects upon family continuity. *Social Forces, 32,* 76–81.

Wellman, B., Carrington, P. J., & Hall, A. (1988). Networks as personal communities. In B. Wellman & S. D. Berkowitz (Eds.), *Social structures: A network approach* (pp. 130–184). Cambridge University Press.

Wheaton, B., Muthen, B., Alwin, D., & Summers G. (1977). *Sociological methodology 1977* (p. 84–136). San Francisco, CA: Jossey-Bass.

Wheeless, L. R. (1978). A follow-up study of the relationships among trust, disclosure, and interpersonal solidarity. *Human Communication Research, 4,* 143–157.

Wiseman, J. P. (1986). Friendship: Bonds and binds in a voluntary relationship. *Journal of Social and Personal Relationships, 3,* 191–211.

II

CONFLICT RESOLUTION: CONSTRUCTIVE CONFRONTATION BEHAVIOR, INTERVENTION STRATEGIES, AND TEACHING TECHNIQUES

7

Confrontation Behaviors, Perceived Understanding, and Relationship Growth

Dudley D. Cahn
State University of New York at New Paltz

Published in the scholarly journals of several academic disciplines, numerous research studies attempt to answer the question: How do intimate partners constructively resolve interpersonal conflict?

Partners typically deal with interpersonal conflict by planning and engaging in negative and destructive communication practices (Fitzpatrick & Winke, 1979; Rands, Levinger, & Mellinger, 1981; Ting-Toomey, 1983). Although intimates tend to resort to negative strategies and tactics for resolving interpersonal conflicts, there are significant benefits to taking more constructive approaches. Barry (1970) described functional conflict patterns as integrative in nature and beneficial for intimate relationships. First, functional conflict patterns are viewed more positively than are dysfunctional patterns. Cupach (1982) reported that they are viewed as more competent than avoidance tactics, which in turn are viewed as more competent than more destructive tactics.

Second, functional conflict resolution patterns may increase male–female intimacy. Verbal disagreements produce increased agreement and greater understanding of other's perspectives than does avoidance (Knudson, Sommers, & Golding, 1980). It is clear from the typology developed by Rands et al. (1981) that couples find the intimate–nonaggressive pattern most satisfying because it results in greater *intimacy* in which the spouses feel closer, understand each other better, have fun making up, and tend to compromise.

Third, over the long run, functional conflict patterns reduce stress because they do in fact frequently resolve problems. As Rusbult, Johnson, and Morrow (1986) made clear, giving voice to one's problems and passive loyalty are more constructive problem-solving behaviors and are

153

more powerfully predictive of couple nondistress than are destructive behaviors like exiting from the relationship or neglecting one's partner. As Menaghan (1982) has shown, negotiation efforts may not initially reduce feelings of distress, but they are associated with fewer problems later.

Because of the emotional nature of intimate relationships, it is important to resolve interpersonal conflicts in a way that preserves or promotes:

- love; intense, positive feelings
- commitment; expectations that the relationship will continue
- expressions of affection, esteem, and recognition
- caring, concern, interest, fascination with the partner; orientation toward the partner
- desire to help the partner in material, tangible ways
- mutual interests and activities; continuing to enjoy being together, doing things together
- trust and disclosure; continuing to take the partner into one's confidence

My purpose is to extend to the study of intimates in conflict research on interpersonal relationship development that lends insight into the process of constructive conflict resolution. Specifically, I intend to argue that perceived understanding underlies relationship growth, to describe an instrument for measuring perceived understanding, to identify verbal and nonverbal communication behaviors that are associated with perceived understanding, and to explain how the Perceived Understanding Instrument may be used to identify confrontation behaviors that contribute to relationship growth.

THE ROLE OF PERCEIVED UNDERSTANDING IN RELATIONSHIP DEVELOPMENT

Perceived understanding, or the feeling of being understood, refers to an individual's assessment of his or her success or failure when attempting to communicate. A communicator's perceived understanding is thought to function as an intervening variable between specific listener feedback, behavioral reactions, or response style and relationship change for better or for worse.

A number of studies found that perceived understanding correlated with other known relationship growth variables. Following 20 minutes of initial interaction between paired acquaintances, Cahn and Frey (1982) found that perceived understanding correlated moderately with social attraction ($r = .47$), low with the task-attraction factor (.34) on McCroskey and McCain's (1974) measure of interpersonal attraction, and moderately (.50) with Giffin's (1968) Trust Differential. Recently, 228 individuals in the Mid-Hudson Valley in Upstate New York were asked to assess their romantic partner (Cahn, 1990). Increases in perceived understanding correlated with increases in the social and task dimensions of McCroskey and McCain's (1974) Interpersonal Attraction measure ($r = .57$ and .38, respectively; both $p < .01$) and Larzelere and Huston's (1980) measure of dyadic trust ($r = .56$; $p < .01$). Although perceived understanding appeared to correlate with other known relationship growth variables, the question arises as to its relative importance.

A key proposition is that, as relationships mature, perceived understanding becomes most important relative to other variables (Cahn, 1987). Initially, perceived understanding accounted for only 1%–1.5% of the total variance in interaction prior to the formation of an interpersonal relationship (Cahn, 1983). Other variables played a more important role in the formation of an acquaintanceship than did perceived understanding. However, in a later study of the relationship that developed over 15 weeks between teachers and students (Cahn, 1984), perceived understanding accounted for 44% of the total variance and ranked highest compared to other variables. These studies taken together suggested that perceived understanding may grow in importance compared to other relevant variables as a relationship develops. To test this proposition, Cahn (1989) separated subjects who were casually dating from married and engaged subjects to investigate the effects of perceived understanding on ideal mateness compared to ratings of the partner's intelligence, sense of humor, trustworthiness, and three dimensions of interpersonal attraction—social attraction, physical attraction, and task attraction. Results showed that for the casual dating group ($n = 69$), a nonsignificant slight relationship ($r = .18$; $p > .05$) was obtained between perceived understanding and ideal mateness, whereas significant ($p < .05$) and higher Pearson correlations were noted between ideal mateness and task attraction (.30), trust (.29), and sense of humor (.24). Thus, for the casual dating group, perceived understanding was not as important in assessing ideal mateness as other characteristics. However, for the married/engaged group ($n = 86$), a significant moderate correlation ($r = .66$; $p < .01$) was found between perceived understanding and ideal mateness. This correlation was higher than those found for all the other variables.

How does one explain this change? Perhaps a sequential change occurs in the criteria used to evaluate different stages of relationship development, similar to filter theories of attraction (Kerckhoff & Davis, 1962;

Murstein, 1977). For example, Cushman and Cahn (1985) posited a three-stage developmental model. At the first stage, a set of causal and normative forces interact to determine one's field of available partners. At the second stage, normative rules delimit further one's field to a group of approachables. At the third stage, normative rules delimit one's field to one or more reciprocals and forms the basis for interpersonal interaction rules that govern and guide the process of relationship growth at this stage. Cushman and Cahn argued that at the third stage, communication rules come into play and define the nature of that stage of relationship development. Thus, when communication rules govern the relationship, perceived understanding becomes most important relative to other variables. Similarly, Hecht and Marston (1987) found that the related concept of communication satisfaction varied with conversation time. They reasoned that the criterion of satisfaction later in conversations is one of understanding based on "signs of understanding." Earlier in conversations, however, the criteria of satisfaction are dependent on more superficial concerns: information exchange, compliments, and dyadic adjustment.

One implication of this line of research is that individuals should make a special effort to pay more attention to perceived understanding earlier in a developing relationship because of its importance later. Thus, along with concerns for trust, interpersonal attraction, and other factors, intimate partners should also be concerned if there is a low level of perceived understanding in the relationship. This low level may result from failure to use particular communication behaviors to deal with conflicts in intimate relationships in a way that produces perceived understanding and promotes intimacy.

Canary and Spitzberg (1989) claimed that conflict is unrelated to affect during relational escalation, although it is negatively related to affect during relational dissolution. They cited research evidence by Braiker and Kelley (1979) and Lloyd and Cate (1985) that showed how *love* was unrelated to conflict during relationship growth. To assess love, both studies used 10 items that measured feelings of belonging, closeness, attachment, interdependence, and sexual intimacy. Perceived understanding, on the other hand, which consists of eight feelings of being understood and eight feelings of being misunderstood (discussed later in this chapter) was found to correlate with increases in trust, interpersonal attraction, and communication satisfaction as couples moved from acquaintanceship through courtship to marriage (Cahn, 1989, 1990). Like Canary and Spitzberg's concept of perceived conflict competence, perceived understanding is proposed as an intervening variable that mediates between particular communication behavior and relationship growth.

MEASURING PERCEIVED UNDERSTANDING

The Perceived Understanding Instrument was developed and tested for reliability and validity (Cahn & Shulman, 1984). First, 224 students enrolled in basic communication courses at three Midwestern state universities described in writing a situation where they tried to make themselves understood and felt in fact that they were being understood and described the feelings they experienced during and immediately after the interaction, and wrote the same for a situation in which they felt that they were being misunderstood. These open-ended responses were content analyzed resulting in the selection of 60 items.

Next, 182 students enrolled in basic speech classes at three Midwestern universities Q-sorted the 60 items by placing them in nine categories that were designed ahead of time to approximate a normal curve from "most like feeling understood" to "most like feeling misunderstood." The researchers were struck by the similarity across subjects who tended to sort the items in almost the same pattern that suggested that respondents shared a similar view of where items should be placed along the continuum. Analysis revealed that eight items loaded highest at each end of the continuum. The "most like feeling understood" items were: satisfied, relaxed, pleasant, good, accepted, comfortable, happy, and important. The items identified with "most like feeling misunderstood" were: annoyed, uncomfortable, insecure, sad, sense of failure, dissatisfied, incomplete, and uninterested. The many terms that clustered in the middle were eliminated from further analysis because they were considered the most ambiguous by the individual sorters. Third, an instrument was constructed with eight scales for the Perception of Being Understood (PBU) and eight scales for the Perception of Being Misunderstood (PBM). A series of studies was conducted to test the validity of the PBU scale and reliability of the instrument (Cahn & Shulman, 1984). A copy of a version of the instrument appears in Table 7.1. This version is designed to measure feeling understood following a specific interaction between partners or communicators. Because it is possible to feel both somewhat understood and misunderstood in a single encounter, a composite score (FUM) is calculated by subtracting PBM from PBU.

How does the measure compare with measures of relationship and communication satisfaction. The Perceived Understanding Instrument (FUM) correlated moderately with the Locke–Wallace (1959) Marital Adjustment Scale's first item that is used as a global measure of relationship/marital happiness ($r = .48$; $p < .01$, $n = 228$). Earlier studies found that the unitary item correlated very highly with the multiple-item measure (Spanier, 1976). The Marital Adjustment Scale has good discriminate validity in cross-sectional studies (Lock & Wallace, 1959). Although

TABLE 7.1
The Perceived Understanding Instrument

Directions: You have just finished talking with (or listening to) _____. The following terms refer to feeling that are relevant when people attempt to make themselves understood by others. Please indicate the extent to which each term describes how you felt when and immediately after trying to make yourself understood by the person specified above. As you fill in the answer sheet, respond to each term according to the following scale:

(1) Very Little
(2) Little
(3) Some
(4) Great
(5) Very Great

You felt:

_____ 1. Satisfied
_____ 2. Relaxed
_____ 3. Pleasant
_____ 4. Good
_____ 5. Accepted
_____ 6. Comfortable
_____ 7. Happy
_____ 8. Important

_____ 9. Annoyed
_____ 10. Uncomfortable
_____ 11. Dissatisfied
_____ 12. Insecure
_____ 13. Sad
_____ 14. A sense of failure
_____ 15. Incomplete
_____ 16. Uninterested

PBU is the sum of 1 through 8, whereas PBM is the sum of 9 through 16. FUM = PBU−PBM.

the correlation with perceived understanding was positive, the first item of the Lock–Wallace Scale clearly measures something different from the Perceived Understanding Instrument. The Locke–Wallace Scale asks respondents to consider *everything* when evaluating their relationship happiness, whereas the Perceived Understanding Instrument deals specifically with several feelings, and the instrument's instructions are more limited.

Cahn (1990) reported that the Perceived Understanding Instrument correlates highly ($r = .75$; $p < .001$, $n = 245$) with the summated scales of the Communication Satisfaction Instrument (Hecht, 1978). Hecht and Marston (1987) report an internal reliability check for the Communication Satisfaction Instrument (Cronbach a of .72 in their study). However, Hecht's instrument contains only one item that requests communicators to evaluate the extent to which the message receivers understand them, and it does not ask them to report as many of their feelings associated with being understood or misunderstood as does the Perceived Understanding Instrument. Although the Perceived Understanding Measure includes satisfaction, it also includes seven other feelings normally associated with feeling understood and eight typically experienced when feeling misunderstood. Thus, the Communication Satisfaction Instrument measures more than just perceived understanding (i.e., did X provide support for what he or she said), whereas the Perceived Understanding Instrument measures more than just satisfaction.

THE IDENTIFICATION OF RELATIONSHIP GROWTH-PROMOTING CONFRONTATION BEHAVIORS

Future research on perceived understanding may provide insight into constructive conflict resolution behaviors of intimate partners. In theory, perceived understanding results from the way intimate partners resolve their differences. The focus here is on the pattern of communication behavior for dealing with conflicts that may result in perceived understanding and subsequent interpersonal growth.

To create conflict situations for observation, each member of a pair or couple could fill out Strodtbeck's (1951) Revealed Differences Form or simply list topics of disagreement. The question is: What communication conflict patterns are candidates for producing perceived understanding in one's partner? At least three lines of empirical research suggest particular verbal and nonverbal communication behaviors that should produce perceived understanding.

Research on "Ideal Partners"

"Ideal partners" tend to engage in particular communication behaviors that probably result in greater perceived understanding. A great deal of research on communication conflict patterns separates "ideal" from problem couples. Ideal couples are classified as functioning at a high level because their scores on any one of several measures of relationship happiness, satisfaction, or adjustment show that they are happy, satisfied, adjusted, nondistressed, and stable. Although their approach is easily criticized, some researchers assume that couples not seeking counseling meet these same standards.

Birchler, Weiss, and Vincent (1975) observed that ideal or nondistressed couples engage in more positive and fewer negatives during casual conversation and problem solving than do distressed couples. As Gottman, Markman, and Notarius (1977) have reported, nondistressed couples are likely to begin with a validation sequence, to avoid negative exchanges, and to end the discussion with a contract sequence. Rands et al. (1981) described a nonintimate–aggressive pattern. Higher rates of problem-solving, verbal, and nonverbal positive and neutral behaviors occurred in nondistressed couples than in distressed couples (Margolin & Wampold, 1981). Unhappy couples were found to be more coercive and less cognitive in their conflict discussions (Billings, 1979). Studying satisfied and dissatisfied couples, Gottman (1979) observed that unhappy couples were more likely to engage in cross-complaining sequences and less likely to engage in validation sequences. Ting-Toomey (1983) found that high marital adjustment interaction is primarily characterized by significant sequential patterns of confirming, socioemotional description, and instrumental questioning strategies. As Rausch, Barry, Hertel, and Swain (1974) made clear, couples who engage in constructive confrontation often do so by keeping the boundaries of conflict within a specific issue. In summary, research on ideal or nondistressed couples reveals numerous communication behaviors that likely produce perceived understanding when intimates attempt to deal with their differences.

Research on the Orientation of the Partners

The expressed orientation of partners toward their relationship and one another may produce perceived understanding. According to Rausch et al. (1974), who wins and who loses a conflict should be far less important than the process of mutual growth and understanding. In a relationship that carries strong emotional investment and that is projected as continuing, the conflict encompasses more than specific disagreements or problems. It moves toward practical planning, followed by emotional reconciliation between the partners, then to reaffirmation and consolidation in discussion of other joint activities, and finally turns toward questions of future coping with other conflicts.

In addition to the relationship, the expressed orientation toward a partner may also serve as a source of perceived understanding. People often view human interaction with either their own or their partner's concerns in mind especially during an interpersonal conflict when they frequently assume that their partner's concerns are in some way incompatible with their own (Cushman & Cahn, 1985). When an intimate is oriented only toward the partner, he or she may express this attitude through accommodation behaviors and by sacrificing many or even all of his or her own personal and individual needs, interests, and goals for those of the partner (Fry, Firestone, & Williams, 1983). When intimates are oriented toward only themselves, they may express this attitude by preventing their partners from satisfying their own concerns (Cahn, 1987).

Because expressions of self-only concerns *or* partner-only concerns interfere with the discovery of joint, mutually acceptable resolutions of conflict, it is important to simultaneously express concerns for both one-self and for the partner (Cahn, 1987; Cushman & Cahn, 1985). Expressions of a we–us orientation take the form of compromise, mediation, conciliation, and implementation procedures for resolving differences (Hawes & Smith, 1973).

Although intimate partners may have only their own or the other's concerns at stake, they may also be trusting or suspicious of one another. The more trusting one is of others who deserve that trust, the more optimistic and hopeful one becomes, the deeper one's relationships are with others, and the more comfortable one feels around them. According to Rogers (1961), the expression of positive feelings toward others takes the following forms: trusting behaviors, openness or disclosure, genuine regard or respect of others, an expressed concern for another, and behaviors indicating acceptance of others as they are. Conversely, the less trusting one becomes, the more one tries to dominate another or to withdraw from the interaction; the less faith one has in oneself and in humanity, and the greater is one's isolation and loneliness. Expressions of trust help and those of suspicion hinder the discovery of mutually agreeable conflict solutions that enhance intimacy.

Research on an Interpersonal Confrontation Ritual

Intriguing and innovative work by Katriel and Philipsen (1981) serves as a basis for developing an interpersonal confrontation ritual that should produce perceived understanding. The ritual consists of four steps. First, one intimate partner initiates the ritual by announcing the existence of a problem that may be worked out in communication. At this stage, perceived misunderstanding or the lack of perceived understanding may have led to meta-analysis in which one thinks about or discusses with a partner the answers to such questions as "What happened? What went wrong? Where did I fail? What should I have done? What am I supposed to do now?"

Second, there is an acknowledgment step where the partner indicates a willingness to discuss this problem thereby acknowledging its legitimacy. Although acknowledgment might be associated with perceived under-standing, avoiding, and ignoring the problem would probably produce feelings of misunderstanding.

Third, there is a negotiation step where the problem is stated and ex-plored from several points of view. As the initiator of the ritual, an intimate would engage in self-disclosure with an attitude of acceptance to both feedback and suggestions for change, whereas the other would indicate cooperation by listening with nonjudgmental, noninquisitive empathy.

Finally, there is a reaffirmation step in which the uniqueness of each partner is affirmed and the solution is found to be consistent with some valued principle of the initiator's self- concept, thus mitigating any threat to the initiator's identity. The fact that conflict resolution is not always possible is seen as threatening to a relationship. Both persons must clarify for each other and examine together the discrepant positions, personal needs, and individual interpretations, but they must reaffirm their intimate relationship to lessen the interpersonal threat posed by the differences.

Talking about problems, the relationship itself, and its interaction patterns appears to have a positive effect on couples' feelings (Acitelli, 1988). In addition, Knudson et al. (1980) found that open discussion by itself offered valuable outcomes such as increased agreement and increased understanding of the partner's perceptions. For partners who avoided issues and conflicts, there were negative outcomes such as decreased agreement and increased discrepancies between partners' perceptions. Because perceived understanding presumably depends in part on actual understanding, partners who engage issues and try to resolve them are expected to experience greater perceived understanding than those who avoid the issues.

CONCLUSION

Communication conflict behavior has traditionally been labeled as constructive or destructive. The position taken here is that the more constructive communication behaviors are candidates for producing perceived understanding that acts as an intervening variable between communication behaviors generally and relationship growth.

An instrument is described for measuring perceived understanding. The results of two studies offer modest support for the reliability and validity of both the perception of being understood (PBU) and the perception of being misunderstood (PBM) scales of the instrument. Research indicates that the instrument is useful for measuring the intensity of interpersonal relationships at different stages of development and for identifying communication behaviors that contribute to perceived understanding. With this measure and the identification of conflict resolution behaviors that may enhance perceived understanding, empirical researchers should be able to determine what confrontation behaviors promote relationship growth between intimates.

REFERENCES

Acitelli, L. K. (1988). When spouses talk to each other about their relationship. *Journal of Social and Personal Relationships, 5,* 185–199.

Barry, W. A. (1970). Marriage research and conflict: An integrative review. *Psychological Bulletin, 73,* 41–54.

Billings, A. (1979). Conflict resolution in distressed and nondistressed married couples. *Journal of Consulting and Clinical Psychology, 47,* 368–376.

Birchler, G. R., Weiss, R. L., & Vincent, J. P. (1975). Multimethod analysis of social reinforcement exchange between maritally distressed and nondistressed spouse and stranger dyads. *Journal of Personality and Social Psychology, 31,* 349–360.

Braiker, H. B., & Kelley, H. H. (1979). Conflict in the development of close relationships. In R. Burgess & T. Huston (Eds.), *Social exchange in developing relationships* (pp. 135–168). New York: Academic Press.

Cahn, D. (1983). Relative importance of perceived understanding in initial interaction and development of interpersonal relationships. *Psychological Reports, 53,* 923–9.

Cahn, D. (1984). Teacher-student relationships: Perceived understanding. *Communication Research Reports, 1,* 65–7.

Cahn, D. (1987). *Letting go: A practical theory of relationship disengagement and reengagement.* Albany, NY: SUNY Press.

Cahn, D. (1989). Relative importance of perceived understanding in developing male-female mate relationships, *Psychological Reports, 64,* 1339–1342.

Cahn, D. (1990). Perceived understanding and interpersonal relationships, *Journal of Social and Personal Relationships, 7,* 231–244.

Cahn, D. & Frey, L. (1982, November). *Interpersonal attraction and trust: The effects of feeling understood/misunderstood on impression formation processes.* Paper presented at the Annual Meeting of the Speech Communication Association.

Cahn, D., & Shulman, G. (1984). The perceived understanding instrument, *Communication Research Reports, 1,* 122–4.

Canary, D. J., & Spitzberg, B. H. (1989). A model of the perceived competence of conflict strategies. *Human Communication Research, 15,* 630–649.

Cupach, W. R. (1982, May). *Communication satisfaction and interpersonal solidarity as outcomes of conflict message strategy use.* Paper presented at the International Communication Association conference, Boston, MA.

Cushman, D., & Cahn, D. (1985). *Communication in interpersonal relationships.* Albany, NY: SUNY Press.

Fitzpatrick, M. A., & Winke, J. (1979). You always hurt the one you love: Strategies and tactics in interpersonal conflict. *Communication Quarterly, 27,* 3–11.

Fry, W. R., Firestone, I. J., & Williams, D. L. (1983). Negotiation process and outcome of stranger dyads and dating couples: Do lovers lose? *Basic and Applied Social Psychology, 4,* 1–16.

Giffin, K. (1968). Interpersonal trust in small-group communication. *Quarterly Journal of Speech, 53,* 224–34.

Gottman, J. M. (1979). *Marital Interaction: Experimental investigations.* New York: Academic Press.

Gottman, J. M., Markman, H., & Notarius, C. (1977). The topography of marital conflict: A sequential analysis of verbal and nonverbal behavior. *Journal of Marriage and the Family, 39,* 461–477.

Hawes, L. C., & Smith, D. H. (1973). A critique of assumptions underlying the study of communication in conflict. *Quarterly Journal of Speech, 62,* 423–435.

Hecht, M. L. (1978). The conceptualization and measurement of interpersonal communication satisfaction. *Human Communication Research, 4,* 253–264.

Hecht, M. L., & Marston, P. J. (1987). Communication satisfaction and the temporal development of conversations, *Communication Research Reports, 4,* 60–65.

Katriel, T., & Philipsen, G. (1981). "What we need is communication": "Communication" as a cultural category in some American speech. *Communication Monographs, 48,* 301–317.

Kerckhoff, A. C., & Davis, K. E. (1962). Value consensus and need complementarity in mate selection. *American Sociological Review, 27,* 295–303.

Knudson, R., Sommers, A., & Golding, S. (1980). Interpersonal perception in mode of resolution in marital conflict. *Journal of Personality and Social Psychology, 38,* 751–763.

Larzelere, R., & Huston, T. (1980). The dyadic trust scale: Toward understanding interpersonal trust in close relationships. *Journal of Marriage and the Family, 42,* 595–604.

Lloyd, S. A., & Cate, R. M. (1984). The developmental course of conflict in dissolution of premarital relationships. *Journal of Social and Personal Relationships, 2,* 179–194.

Locke, H., & Wallace, K. (1959). Short marital adjustment and prediction tests: Their reliability and validity. *Marriage and Family Living, 21,* 251–255.

Margolin, G., & Wampold, B. (1981). Sequential analysis of conflict and accord in distressed and nondistressed marital patterns. *Journal of Consulting and Clinical Psychology, 49,* 554–567.

McCroskey, J., & McCain, T. (1974). The measurement of interpersonal attraction. *Speech Monographs, 41,* 261–6.

Menaghan, E. (1982). Measuring coping effectiveness: A panel analysis of marital problems and coping efforts. *Journal of Health and Social Behavior, 23,* 220–234.

Murstein, B. I. (1977). The stimulus-value-role (SVR) Theory of dyadic relationships. In S. Duck (Ed.) *Theory and practice in interpersonal attraction* (pp. 105–127). New York: Academic Press.

Rands, M., Levinger, G., & Mellinger, G. D. (1981). Patterns of conflict resolution and marital satisfaction. *Journal of Family Issues, 2,* 297–321.

Rausch, H., Barry, W., Hertel, R., & Swain, M. (1974). *Communication, conflict and marriage.* San Francisco, CA: Jossey-Bass.

Rogers, C. (1961). *On becoming a person.* Boston: Houghton Mifflin.

Rusbult, C. E., Johnson, D. J., & Morrow, G. D. (1986). Impact of couple patterns of problem solving on distress and nondistress in dating relationships. *Journal of Personality and Social Psychology, 50,* 744–753.

Spanier, G. B. (1976). Measuring dyadic adjustment: New scales for assessing the quality of marriage and similar dyads. *Journal of Marriage and the Family, 38,* 15–28.

Strodtbeck, F. L. (1951). Husband-wife interactions over revealed differences. *American Sociological Review, 17,* 468–473.

Ting-Toomey, S. (1983). An analysis of verbal communication patterns in high and low marital adjustment groups. *Human Communication Research, 9,* 306–319.

8

The Psychological Reality of Marital Conflict

Nancy A. Burrell
University of Wisconsin–Milwaukee
Mary Anne Fitzpatrick
University of Wisconsin–Madison

opening quote?

Marital relationships are created, maintained, and changed through the communication that occurs between husbands and wives. It is through communication that married partners not only create a relational identity but also construct a shared reality (Berger & Kellner, 1964). The construction of a *shared reality*, broadly defined as a couple's sense of past, present, and a future, arises out of the mundane, daily conversations that couples have with one another about what people are like, what values are important, how specific goals (career/relational) are attained, what is just and unjust, and so forth. Thus, marital partners reshape their individual psychological realities into a conjoint marital reality. This is not to say that the construction of a joint marital reality precludes the couple experiencing interpersonal conflict. Rather, the act of defining a marriage specifies the nature, direction, intensity, and eventual outcomes of marital conflict. The widely diverse and frequent interactions of spouses provides an unlimited arena for conflict. A fact of marital life, conflict is frequently used to index the level of relational commitment or lack thereof.

The study of marital relationships from a theoretical position that argues for the construction of a conjoint marital reality through talk necessitates understanding how spouses comprehend marital messages. On purely logical grounds, it is obvious that the assignment of meaning to the communication behavior of one's spouse emerges from what one knows about marriage, and how such knowledge changes in response to events. Such organized bodies of knowledge become especially important in understanding the causes, directions, and outcomes of marital conflict.

The premise of this chapter is that a theoretical understanding of the causes of marital conflict is necessary before practitioners can develop programs to help couples manage conflict. We offer one such theoretical model by arguing that an extensive, empirically based marital typology created by Fitzpatrick and her colleagues represents various organized knowledge structures, or schemata, about the nature of marriage. These schemata affect marital conflict in two interrelated ways. First, the violation of a schematic principle by a married partner leads to physiological arousal and the display of negative affect. Conflict cycles begin in this manner. Second, schemata direct the attention, memory, and inference processes concerning marital messages. Hence these schemata affect the ongoing negotiation of disagreements and difficulties in marriage.

In this chapter, we discuss Fitzpatrick's typology of married couples, argue that the typology is psychologically real, and demonstrate how the typology when conceptualized as marital schemata accounts for marital conflict. Using this perspective, we suggest methods by which practitioners can help distressed couples to renegotiate their shared realities.

A TYPOLOGY OF MARRIAGE

According to Olson (1981), marital and family typologies constitute a major breakthrough for therapists/counselors based on the advantages (conceptually and methodologically) of integrating clinical practice, research, and theory. Olson argued that by focusing on couples and families defined along multidimensional criteria rather than on one or two variables, researchers identify more meaningful and stable relationships between variables. These results can be more easily translated into clinical interventions. Despite the utility of a marital or family typology, many of these typologies are not as helpful because they tend to be intuitively rather than empirically derived (Fitzpatrick, 1984). A decade of research by Fitzpatrick (1976, 1977, 1981, 1983, 1984, 1988) has established empirically a typology for characterizing married couples. (For a comprehensive discussion of the typology's development and validation see Fitzpatrick, 1988, *Between Husbands & Wives*.) Briefly, the procedures followed by Fitzpatrick in the typology's development were: (a) identifying significant conceptual areas in marital and family life, (b) developing measures that delineated dimensions of marital life, and (c) comparing spouses' relational definitions to determine couple types.

The Relational Dimension Instrument (RDI) identified three dimensions of married life: ideology (e.g., relational beliefs, values, and standards), interdependence (e.g., degree of connectedness), and conflict (e.g., behaviors of avoidance engagement). By comparing spouses' responses to the RDI, couple types were characterized as traditional, independent, separate, or mixed. If both spouses agree independently on their relational definition, they are categorized as pure types (i.e., traditional, independent, or separate), whereas husbands and wives who diverge in their perspectives of marriage are classified as mixed couple types.

Traditional couples hold conventional ideological values about relationships (e.g., wives change their last names, infidelity is unacceptable), demonstrate interdependence (e.g., share time, space, companionship), and describe their communication as nonassertive but engage in rather than avoid marital conflicts. By contrast, independents espouse nonconventional values about relational and family life (e.g., relationships should not constrain individual freedom), exhibit a high degree of sharing and companionship that qualitatively differs from traditional couples in that independents maintain separate physical space (e.g., bathrooms, offices), do not keep regular time schedules, yet tend to engage in rather than avoid conflict. Finally, couples who define themselves as separates are conventional on marital and family issues yet at the same time uphold the value of individual freedom over relational maintenance, have significantly less companionship and sharing (e.g., maintain psychological distance, reflect autonomy in use of space), and describe their communication as persuasive and assertive, but avoid open marital conflict.

Mixed couple types include spouses who define marital life differently according to ideology, interdependence, and communication. Approximately 40% of couples surveyed fall into one of the mixed types and no one mixed type predominates numerically (Fitzpatrick, 1988).

The delineation of a typology of marriage through the use of a carefully constructed and thoroughly tested self-report device that questions spouses about important dimensions of relationships would scarcely be worthy of notice without the variety of methods that have been employed to explore its ramifications. Specifically, direct observations have been made of conflict, control, and disclosure processes within marriages of the various couple types. Expectations about marriage reflected in the typology can help to describe the communication behaviors of the traditional, independent, separate, and mixed couple types during conflict. The following representation of the various couple types emerges from the research on conflict interactions.

Traditionals tend to avoid conflict more than they realize but, in general, are cooperative and conciliatory. For these couples, conflicts are somewhat easier to resolve because traditionals tend to argue about content rather than relational issues. Traditionals value parenting, spending time with each other in close proximity, and place marriage (duality) over independence. Of particular note is that although the husband in this marriage is very sex-typed in his interpersonal behaviors, this husband is able to self-disclose to his wife.

Independents are constantly renegotiating relational roles and each spouse resents a partner's attempt to avoid conflict by withdrawing. Independents value their careers, co-workers, and/or friends outside the relationship, and need their own personal space. These couples can disclose both positive and negative feelings to their spouses. The downside for independents is that because of their high expressivity, they experience serious conflicts with each other.

Separates touch base with partners regularly, but maintain both psychological and spatial distance. Most separates seek emotional support/ reinforcement outside the relationship. Overall, separates experience little direct conflict in their marriage for two reasons. First, because separate couples agree with one another on a number of basic family issues, they have less potential for disagreements. Second, separates appear unable to coordinate their interaction effectively to engage in a direct open discussion of disagreements. A separate spouse may display outright hostility but quickly retreat if a partner disagrees. In other words, separates rarely discuss conflict and withdraw immediately when spouses introduce stressful topics.

The conflict patterns of mixed couple types depend on the specific combination of relational definitions under scrutiny. For example, separate/traditionals rarely argue but when they do argue, the burden of initiating a discussion of difficult issues falls to the wife. In the traditional/ independent pairing, the wife is more likely to engage in conflict, whereas the traditional husband is more likely to be conciliatory and prone to compromise.

Individuals and subsequently couples have been categorized as one of several marital types. The categorization of a couple has predicted a variety of communication behaviors during both casual and conflict interactions. Regardless of the strong empirical support for the communication pattern differences of couple types during conflict, the typology remains an elaborate descriptive enterprise. Such descriptive formulations need to be replaced by theoretical formulations (Fitzpatrick, 1987a). In the next section, we frame the typology as marital schemata. This theoretical move allows us to make predictions about message processing, the effect of marital messages on memory, and how meaning is assigned.

TYPES AS SCHEMATA

Individuals have expectations about marital partners and the external world of marriage. For example, traditional couples anticipate that partners will spend time and expend psychological energy so that their marriage will work. By contrast, independents encourage one another to take risks, to develop networks outside the relationship, however, partners expect a higher quality of time spent together. Separates anticipate spending time with one another, yet cultivate psychological and/or emotional support outside their marriage. In a recent series of investigations, we explored the degree to which the categorization of couples into various marital types was psychologically real.

Psychological reality was demonstrated by examining the degree to which couples used significantly different codes in communicating with one another. These varying codes reflect different underlying views of the relationships between the speakers. Using the dialogues of 29 couples waiting for an experiment to begin, the data revealed that three relational definitions (traditional, independent, separate) were discriminated through linguistic indicators (Fitzpatrick, 1987a), representing significantly different codes. Specifically, separates used a pragmatic code (less complexity, more implicit meaning), and independents used a more elaborate code (less meaning is assumed, more self-references, greater verb and adverbial complexity). By contrast, traditionals who relied on a pragmatic code also used a high proportion of couple references (we, us) and significantly fewer personal pronouns than the other couples.

A second example of psychological reality was demonstrated by examining the degree to which members of the culture discriminated among the various types of couples and linked these discriminations to particular patterns of communication. Giles and Fitzpatrick (1984) reported that individuals have stable views of marital relationships that correspond to the typology. Also, individuals specified distinctly different types of messages exchanged between the various couple types. For example, respondents saw couples described as high on interdependency and conventional ideology as likely to be conciliatory and cooperative during conflicts.

Finally, psychological reality was demonstrated when married couples evaluated information outside the marriage according to their definitions of marriage. The television viewing of couple types affected both the amount and the kind of marital communication (Fallis, Fitzpatrick, & Friestad, 1984). Individuals' marital definitions operated to evaluate the relevance and then the consistency of television portrayals of male and female relationships.

The demonstrations that the typology represents psychologically real marital descriptions both to outsiders and to married people themselves suggests that the marital types may represent marital schemata (see also, Fitzpatrick, 1987b, 1988). That is, the typology may be summarizing important dimensions on which couples, and people in general, process and store information about marriage. The implications of considering couple types as schemata are particularly striking in the study of marital conflict. In the next section, we consider couple types as schemata and show how the dimensions that underlie the marital types (schemata) predict marital conflict patterns.

MARITAL SCHEMATA AND MARITAL CONFLICT

Whereas all relationships experience some degree of conflict, the mere presence of marital conflict, however, is not an unconditional sign of relational dysfunction. As Fitzpatrick (1988) has shown, many couples (e.g., up to one third of large research samples) not only agree to disagree, but actually look to their conflict as an important indication that their individual identities have not been subsumed in the relationship. The difference between the conflict-tolerant independent couples and the more conflict–avoidant traditional couples for whom conflict is problematic is one of meaning. Independent couples have established a shared understanding that within their relationship conflict equals success, or at a minimum, conflict is orthogonal to love and relational satisfaction.

Each of the three marital definitions (i.e., traditional, independent, and separate) defines a different schema of marriage. The RDI does not isolate all the important dimensions but it can uncover individuals who share the same schema of marriage. But how do these schemata differentially affect marital conflict?

The answer to this question requires us to decompose the attributes that make up the types. Subsumed within the typology are the three attributes along which each type is defined: degree of interdependency, ideology, and conflict tolerance. Whereas particular scores on each of these attributes combine to define one of the basic marital definitions, each attribute relates to a schematic interpretation of marital communication in different ways. *Interdependency* is a measure of how connected spouses are to one another in the organization of their daily lives. This attribute affects a schematic interpretation of marital conflict by predicting which couples are likely to experience a greater frequency and intensity of conflict. Both *ideology* and *conflict tolerance* affect a schematic interpretation of conflict because they are attributes spouses use to judge the relevance and consistency of various marital messages.

In the next section, we demonstrate how the three major attributes/ dimensions affect marital conflict. Interdependency affects the frequency, intensity, and emotional tone of marital conflicts; ideology affects the interpretation of messages as power, affection, or inclusion issues; and conflict tolerance affects the ongoing negotiation of conflict issues.

Interdependency and Arousal

Conflict is defined as the perception of incompatible goals and/or interference in attaining one's goals (Folger & Poole, 1984). Research suggests that the interruption of complex goal sequences causes emotional arousal. The amount of interruption guides the intensity and direction of one's affective reaction. Two people in a long-term intimate relationship are more likely to be interdependent and have a greater chance of interrupting each other's plans and violating each other's expectations. The interdependence established by couples directly affects the experience of emotion in close relationships. A necessary condition for the experience of emotion is the presence of physiological arousal (Berscheid, 1983, 1987). Physiological arousal occurs when an individual is interrupted in the completion of an organized behavioral sequence. After the interruption occurs and alternate routes to complete the sequence are blocked, emotion is experienced. The valence (positivity or negativity) of the experienced emotion depends on the context in which the interruption occurs. Positive affect results if the interruption: (a) is seen as benign or controllable, (b) leads to the accomplishment of a goal sooner than expected, or (c) removes something previously disruptive. Because interruptions are usually uncontrollable, it seems that the majority of "interrupts" lead to negative affect.

The concept of interdependence is central to understanding what the individual may or may not experience as an "interrupt." Individuals also have intrachain sequences or ongoing goal-directed activities that need to be completed once they have begun. Between spouses, there are sequences of events in a partner's intrachain sequence that are causally connected to one or more events in the other spouse's intrachain sequence. That is, couples develop a series of meshed interchain sequences that necessitate including the spouse as a partner to attain certain goals. The meshed sequences that require a spouse for completion may also be called *interchain* sequences (e.g., love making, marital conversations). Interchain causal connections are viewed as necessary, but not sufficient, conditions for emotion to occur because autonomic arousal occurs when an interchain connection is interrupted by lack of cooperation by the partner.

The more highly interdependent the couple, the greater the number of meshed intrachain (interchain) sequences. Thus, traditional husbands and wives simultaneously engage in highly organized intrachain sequences and the events in each person's chain facilitate the performance of the other's sequence. Because of meshing, traditionals perform numerous event sequences that are interconnected and highly organized often without the slightest interruptive hitch. Connections between traditionals are symmetrical in that each partner facilitates the completion of the organized behavioral sequences for the other partner. The connections between these couple types are also facilitative. Because of their meshed and mutually facilitative intrachain sequences, traditionals are significantly less likely than the other couple types to experience conflict in their marital relationships.

By contrast, separates have a marriage in which there are very few meshed intrachain sequences. This means that for separates few if any causal connections exist between the intrachain sequences simultaneously enacted by partners in this marriage. Separates display emotional withdrawal from one another during discussions of problems. Even when one spouse displays anger, the separate partner retreats from the discussion.

Independents represent couples with a number of nonmeshed sequences. The causal connections between the intrachain sequences interfere with the enactment of behavioral sequences for either spouse. Independents experience a greater range and intensity of arousal and are likely to be frustrated and angry by a partner's interference in achieving a specific goal. Each spouse openly expresses anger to each other.

The emotional state of each participant in the pure couple types (e.g., traditional/traditional) is symmetrical, in that the facilitation or interference in the completion of behavioral sequences is balanced equally between husbands and wives. Marital partners have the same level of interdependence in the marriage and, hence, are more similar in the emotional experiences that the marriage generates. Mixed couple types (e.g., traditional/independent) demonstrate that asymmetries do exist. In the separate/traditional relationship, for example, the traditional wife facilitates the completion of a number of intrachain sequences for her husband, although he does not facilitate the completion of numerous intrachains sequences for her.

Recently, a number of longitudinal studies concerning marital conflict suggest that marital conflict exerts s sleeper effect on marital satisfaction. The ability to negotiate with a spouse is, at times, not related to concurrent marital satisfaction but this ability can predict marital satisfaction years later (Kelly, Huston, & Cate, 1985; Markman, 1979, 1981, 1987). Results indicate that although a greater number of anger exchanges between spouses was correlated with less concurrent marital satisfaction, these anger exchanges predicted greater marital satisfaction 5 years later (Gottman & Krokoff, 1986). Overall, less satisfaction occurred for couples who had initially demonstrated defensiveness, stubbornness, or husband withdrawal.

Displays of anger between spouses present fewer problems for the long-term future than are displays of emotional withdrawal. Anger exchanges may be beneficial in the long run because they can facilitate the resolution of a conflict, whereas once a spouse has emotional withdrawal from the discussion of problematic issues, the resolution of difficulties between spouses is unlikely. The attribute of interdependency in the marital schemata predicts which couples are more likely to experience those differing emotional responses during marital conflict.

To summarize, goal blockage leads to arousal and the expression of either anger or emotional withdrawal. Schemata predict that independents are more likely to experience goal blockage, and therefore more likely to display anger in conflicts with their spouses. Because of their very different levels of interdependency, traditionals and separates are less likely to experience goal blockage and arousal, traditionals because they are so well meshed and separates because they are not well meshed and hence are emotionally withdrawn. In general, the expression of anger during conflicts appears to have a different functional relationship to marital satisfaction than does the exhibition of emotional withdrawal.

Ideology and Issue Definition

Relational disputes can take many forms. Between spouses, anything can become grist for the conflict mill. In other words, couples can be fighting about a particular content issue or they may "really" be fighting about a relational issue. In general, relational issues are one of three major types: distribution of privileges or power issues, affection or love issues, and inclusion or commitment issues.

The dimension of ideology defines the relevancy or irrelevancy of specific relational issues for a given interactant. For example, power issues may be particularly salient for a given spouse in that he or she tends to perceive a variety of messages as referencing a power dimension (on this dimension one may be dominant, submissive, or equal). For those issues that are relevant to a given spouse, a subsequent evaluation is made of the consistency or inconsistency of a given message with the marital schemata.

Power is the relational issue for independents. Independents are more likely to see ambiguous messages as relevant to a power dimension and to evaluate the degree to which the message is consistent with their egalitarian concepts. Affection and its expression is the relational issue for traditionals. Traditionals are sensitive to the degree of love and affection in their relationship and see a variety of verbal and nonverbal behaviors along an affection dimension. Separates respond to discussions in terms of their relevancy to an involvement or commitment dimension. Included in this dimension would be boundary issues.

Individuals with one of the three basic marital schemata tend to evaluate communication from a spouse according to its relevancy to one of these basic schemata. Traditionals, for example, would not respond to orders as a power move on the part of a spouse but would tend to interpret such messages in reference to affection. Indeed, for traditionals, giving orders may be a sign of affection between spouses and thus would be perceived as "relevant" to their schema yet very consistent with the underlying ideology of the marital type.

The evaluation of messages along these different continua is instructive in understanding conflict in mixed marriages or those where spouses have significantly different marital schemata. Following is a conversation between an independent/traditional couple type.

Bob: What kind of salad dressing should I make?

Joanne: Vinagrette, what else?

Bob: What do you mean, "what else"?

Joanne: Well, I always make vinagrette, but if you want make something else.

Bob: Does that mean, you don't like it when I make other dressings?

Joanne: No, I like it. Go ahead. Make something else.

Bob: Not if you want vinagrette.

Joanne: I don't. Make a yogurt dressing.

(Bob makes a yogurt dressing, tastes it, and makes a face.)

Joanne: Isn't it good?

Bob: I don't know how to make a yogurt dressing.

Joanne: Well, if you don't like it, throw it out.

Bob: Never mind.

Joanne: What never mind? It's just a little yogurt.

Bob: You're making a big deal about nothing.

Joanne: You are!

How could this couple have ended up having a fight about salad dressing? (In this marriage, Bob does all the cooking.) The spouses evaluated ambiguous messages along the continuum of relevance in their own marital schemata. Bob is an independent and so he interprets Joanne's first statement along a power continuum and sees her as being inconsistent with his view of the egalitarian nature of the marriage. In fact, he reads her first statement as demanding and bossy. Joanne, however, thought she was being affectionate as she intended her remark to suggest that Bob could decide. Her "what else" comment was meant to imply that she wasn't too imaginative when it came to salad dressing and she always made vinagrette. Bob interprets her next comment as another order to make a yogurt dressing. On the other hand, Joanne was simply showing interest and by saying "yogurt dressing," she meant make something else.

Throughout this admittedly trivial interaction, the independent spouse, Bob, saw his wife as becoming increasingly more demanding, whereas the traditional wife, Joanne, perceived her husband as becoming more hypersensitive and tempermental. Joanne viewed her communication as playful, affectionate, and agreeable. To summarize, those who share a marital schemata may disagree on the degree of consistency of a given message with their view of marriage but are at least responding along the same continuum. By contrast, couples with varying schemata perceive messages as relevant to a different underlying dimension.

Conflict Tolerance and Interaction Trajectory

Conflict is an inevitable part of marital interaction. With increased intimacy comes greater potential for anger and more vulnerability to hurt. Couples in the various types, however, have different views of the efficacy of engaging in open conflict and discussion of negative feelings with a spouse.

The dimension of conflict tolerance provides potential behavioral routines for spouses (Folger & Poole, 1984). In other words, schemata give partners an indication about how to proceed in the conflict episode and a "guesstimate" for predicting a conflict's resolution or stalemate. Traditionals have developed interaction scripts during conflict that follow an engagement, negotiation, and termination trajectory. These individuals engage in conflict only over serious issues, which we have defined previously as violations of affection issues, and can go immediately to problem-solving and information exchange interactions. Independents quarreling over the distribution of power often follow an engagement, escalation, reconciliation, negotiation, and termination trajectory. Conflicts are longer, more intense, and more likely to evoke unusual expressions of affection and renewed commitment to the relationship. Finally, separates who perceive issues in terms of involvement and want to keep the level of conflict minimal find goal interruptions either trivial or insoluble and perceive a high risk in conflict engagement. Thus, these individuals utilize a greater range of conflict avoidance behaviors than do others.

It may be that in a constructive/functional relationship, partners' marital schemas are more complete/detailed or that spouses have a variety of subroutines to use. For example, because independents are high on expressivity, they may have an extensive repertoire of subroutines to choose from in their marital schemata. Problematic for independents is the fact that escalation subroutines can become extremely intense and make movement to a conciliation phase difficult. The difficulty for traditionals is that they define issues as unimportant and hence avoid conflict about those issues. It becomes easy for traditional couples to deny difficulties by categorizing them as "unimportant." Because separates actively avoid conflict, perhaps their marital schemas are void of subroutines for constructive marital conflict or those subroutines may be sketchy and incomplete for relational partners.

Spouses may not be using the same knowledge structures (schema) to generate inferences about their conflict. As Kellermann and Lim (1989) suggested, a number of different schemas can be applied to a message (e.g., conflict episode) to help in the inference process. For example, Ted and Sally are fighting over Ted's transfer and subsequent relocation of the family. As partners process this conflict episode, they could be using a marital schema, a career schema, a person schema, and so forth. The point is that the activated schema will affect the judgments that individuals make. It may be that Sally's marital schema has been activated and she feels that Ted is placing career advancement ahead of their marriage. By contrast, Ted's person schema (about Sally) has been triggered and Ted interprets Sally's persuasive attempt to not leave the community as an irrational, unfounded fear. In this case, messages have cued varying schema to direct the inferential process and marital partners may be generating meanings that may or may not be intended by each other (Kellermann & Lim, 1989). As illustrated earlier, couples often have different marital schemata.

In this section, we have seen that marital schemata have direct and far reaching effects on the initiation, issue definition, and negotiation process used by couples during marital conflict. In the next section, we discuss several pragmatic implications of schema theory on marital interaction. Specifically, we consider what the practitioner can do to help resolve serious marital conflicts.

PRAGMATIC IMPLICATIONS OF MARITAL SCHEMA THEORY

Couples in clinical settings are trapped in dysfunctional conflict episodes and have sought professional help to change these relational trajectories. There are a number of reasons for seeking help and, to complicate the task of the practitioner even more, individual husbands and wives may have different treatment goals. For example, one spouse may want to end the marriage and the other to preserve it or both may seek the help of a mediator to resolve a child custody dispute. Regardless of the issue under discussion, however, using the schema theory of marital interaction implies that a practitioner should adopt a cognitive paradigm for helping couples deal with conflict. The goal of the interventionist is to change the psychological reality of the participants. In other words, the practitioner needs to help the client redefine various stimuli. Work needs to be focused on how evaluations are made of incoming communication between spouses in the hope of eventually changing behaviors.

A context for redefining the psychological reality of a marital relationship is with a marriage counselor/therapist. In this setting the goal of the interventionist is to change unrealistic attributions/expectations to realistic ones when partners admit to dysfunctional behavioral routines/cycles. Both Ellis (1962, 1984) and Beck (1967, 1976) theorized that extreme emotional and behavioral reactions are triggered and maintained by unrealistic cognitions. These irrational cognitions stem from illogical, imprecise, and/or rigid processing of information. Hence, the goal of therapy is the need to challenge and ultimately change unrealistic cognitions replacing them with more rational/realistic ones (Forsterling, 1985). Homework is assigned to clients in order to gather data to test their dysfunctional thinking. A large portion of cognitive therapy is spent on logically analyzing marital partners' conclusions drawn from their interactions/observations of one another. The therapist assumes quite an active role, questioning and challenging the irrational beliefs that lead to destructive emotions and conflict episodes. In short, cognitive therapists assume that not stimuli but cognitive processing, evaluation, and organization largely (but not exclusively) determine emotional and behavioral reactions of marital partners. Therefore, cognitive approaches to therapy assume that dysfunctional behavioral and emotional reactions can be modified by changing intervening cognitions (Forsterling, 1986).

Three specific tacks can be taken based on marital schema theory. First, the practitioner needs to consider helping spouses to understand anger or emotional withdrawal. Because anger or emotional withdrawal during marital conflict emerges from the degree of interdependency in a relationship, it is difficult to imagine how a practitioner could change the underlying organizational bases and goal interruptions that occur between couples in a few sessions. Research in the context of divorce mediation suggests some possibilities. In child custody/visitation disputes, mediators structure the interaction between distressed couples to interrupt the destructive communicative exchanges. Jones (1987) examined the nonverbal vocal affect in 36 divorce mediations. Results of a lag-sequential analysis indicate that when a mediator uses neutral nonverbal affect, disputants are not significantly affected. However, when a mediator uses negative nonverbal affect, disputants reciprocate with negative nonverbal affect. Jones concluded that a mediator's behaviors act as emotional cues. Disputants anticipate that the mediator will remain calm. When these expectations are violated (e.g., the mediator responds with anger or intensity), the disputants respond with the same negative affect (e.g., act similarly). The same patterns of reciprocity occurred in disputant–disputant communicative exchanges.

Clear implications for practitioners' (e.g., mediators, counselors, therapists) intervention strategies can be deduced from Jones' findings. First, professionals should practice restraint in terms of vocal affect/intensity to reduce nonverbal tension between distressed couples. Second, clinicians should promote positive nonverbal affect between spouses to engender more of the same behavior. Third, practitioners should monitor the level of vocal affect (positive, negative, and neutral) as the session progresses. Professionals can gauge the emotional intensity of couples to frame appropriately timed interventions (Jones, 1987). Finally, the practitioner needs to help spouses to define ambiguous messages from one another along similar relevancy and consistency dimensions.

As we have seen, individuals with different marital schemata define issues in their conflict along different relevancy continua (i.e., power, affection, inclusion). Research in the context of divorce mediation sheds light on what the practitioner can do to help couples in reference to the "hidden issues" of their conflicts. Divorce mediation sessions were content analyzed for the types of issues that disputing couples forwarded (Donohue, Lyles, & Rogan, 1989). Couples that reached agreement addressed factual/interest issues, whereas deadlocked couples focused on value/emotional issues. Donohue and his associates reported that mediators in the agreement condition focused twice as much on interests as on facts, with minimal discussion of values or relational issues. By contrast, in the nonagreement condition the mediator split evenly between fact and interest interventions, with little time focused on values or relational issues. Deadlocked couples often used factual disputes to disguise relational disputes.

Frequently marital conflict is triggered by how something is said rather than what was said. According to Brown (1986) nonverbal channels are: (a) constantly monitored as they seem to communicate primarily affective information, (b) reflective of personal relationships, and (c) an index of attitudes toward others. Practitioners need to help spouses deal with the inherent ambiguity of nonverbal messages. The same nonverbal cues can easily be interpreted as power, affiliation, or inclusion depending on the context, the relationship between the communicators, the presence (absence) of other cues, the timing, and so forth (Patterson, 1985). In addition, one's marital schemata predisposes a spouse to interpret the mate's messages along a given continuum.

Marital counselors/therapists need to focus distressed couples on their nonverbal communication because the research indicates that distressed and nondistressed couples are best discriminated by their use of nonverbal rather than verbal channels (Gottman, 1979). Further, discrepant messages occur more frequently in the communication of the unhappily married. Negative communication of unhappy couples is more intense (i.e., negative on more channels) than those of happy couples (Noller, 1984). And, as we have seen the particular negative interpretations depend on whether the individual possesses a traditional, independent, or separate schemata of marriage.

What distressed couples frequently need is a reorientation and/or renegotiation of such relational parameters as control, trust, and intimacy (Donohue, Allen, & Burrell, 1985, 1988). Practitioners work with distressed couples by structuring therapy or mediation sessions. For example, divorce mediators establish ground rules for the conduct of the session to prevent spouses fighting for control (Burrell, Donohue, & Allen, 1988). As couples begin to resolve their conflict, trust increases based on the fact that partners are bargaining in good faith. Finally, mediators help redefine husband and wife roles. Conflict within a marriage can be explored as consisting of two features: the content of substantive issues of disagreement (Hocker & Wilmot, 1985) and the process by which the disagreements are enacted (Sillars, 1986).

Furthermore, the practitioner needs to help spouses develop more detailed and functional conflict interaction subroutines, especially negotiation skills. Noller (1984) pointed out that distressed couples are unskilled negotiators and problem solvers because their marital communication usually breaks down long before they reach the negotiation stage. Essentially, distressed couples become involved in cycles of negativity described earlier (Jones, 1987; Noller, 1982, 1984). The practitioner working from a cognitive paradigm sets up situations in which the participants themselves can achieve some positive result (no matter how small) through their own interaction. When participants begin to attribute their successful negotiation of an issue to their own actions, this success feeds back to other conversations. In this way, the practitioner may subtly begin to change, for example, the separate's fear of open conflict and sense that issues are not resolvable.

Skilled negotiators not only have a repertoire of conflict styles but are familiar with a variety of methods to resolve conflict. Many distressed couples tend to use only one style, and then find conflicts insoluable when their style is inappropriate (Noller, 1984). Another approach, then, in improving couples' negotiating skills involves learning different styles of conflict resolution (Epstein & Williams, 1981; Jacobson, 1981; Mace & Mace, 1974). The marital counselor/therapist can function as a teacher who instructs couples about the skills of negotiating and/or how to fight fairly (Bach & Wyden, 1969; Dayringer, 1976). Some interesting links can be made from the bargaining and negotiation research. Scholars have suggested that negotiation becomes a learning process for participants (Cross, 1977, Pruitt, 1981). Negotiators learn what tactics work best for them, which moves should be considered carefully, and how to interpret the opposition's maneuvering. Similarly, marital partners recognize their strengths when arguing, which tactics have failed, what issues are worth fighting over, and, in general, how to read their spouse. Negotiators develop expectations about the conflict, especially about their roles as the bargaining session unfolds (Burrell, 1987; Pruitt, 1981; Rubin & Brown, 1975). Marital partners also have expectations about married life and their roles in that partnership. Skilled negotiators are skilled interpreters of the communication process (Donohue, 1981). By contrast, partners who are poor communicators have problems in negotiation and decision making.

Based on marital schema theory, we have suggested a few techniques that practitioners can utilize to help couples resolve their difficulties. Armed with an assessment of the marital schemata of his or her clients, a practitioner can better design an intervention program to help couples.

CONCLUSION

Marital schemata help to specify the nature and organization of information relevant/irrelevant to partners and the marriage. Not just isolated cognitive structures, these schemata guide the interpretation of marital communications. In this chapter, we have argued that marital schemata can predict the onset, duration, intensity and relational issues in a marital conflict as well as the prototypical conflict interaction trajectory.

Therapists, marital counselors, and divorce mediators teach their clients about constructive and destructive communication. Various methods for resolving conflicts are explored. Behavioral routines are practiced to help partners learn to relate better. Without a sense of the marital schemata held by the participants, however, the type of help that we offer couples exists in a vacuum. Dealing with couples who suffer from emotional withdrawal and a sense that conflict is futile is a significantly different proposition than dealing with couples who are enraged with one another. Similarly, the interpretations that couples place on messages must be paramount in our design and in the implementation of programs to improve marital communication.

REFERENCES

Bach, G. R., & Wyden, P. (1969). Marital fighting: A guide to love. In B. N. Ard & C. Ard (Eds.), *Handbook of marriage counseling* (pp. 313–321). Palo Alto, CA: Science and Behavior Books.

Beck, A. T. (1967). *Depression: clinical, experimental, and theoretical aspects.* New York: Harper & Row.

Beck, A. T. (1967). *Cognitive therapy and the emotional disorders.* New York: International Universities Press.

Berger, P., & Kellner, H. (1964). Marriage and the construction of reality. *Diogenes, 46,* 1–24.

Berscheid, E. (1983). Emotion in close relationships. In H. Kelley, E. Berscheid, A. Christensen, J. J. Harvey, T. L. Huston, G. Levinger, E. McClintock, L. A. Peplau, & D. R. Peterson (Eds.), *Close relationships* (pp. 110–168). New York: Freeman.

Berscheid, E. (1987). Emotion and interpersonal communication. In M. E. Roloff & G. R. Miller (Eds.), *Interpersonal processes: New directions in communication research* (pp. 77–88). Newbury Park, CA: Sage.

Burrell, N. (1987). *Testing a model of mediation: The impace of disputants' expectations.* Unpublished doctoral dissertation, Michigan State University, East Lansing, MI.

Burrell, N., Donohue, W. A., & Allen, M. (1988). Gender-based perceptual biases in mediation. *Communication Research, 15,* 447–469.

Brown, R. (1986). *Social psychology: The second edition.* New York: Guilford.

Cross, J. G. (1977). Negotiation as a learning process. *Journal of Conflict Resolution, 21,* 581–606.

Dayringer, R. (1976). Fight fair for change: A therapeutic use of aggressiveness in couple counseling. *Journal of Marriage and Family Counseling, 2,* 115–30.

Donohue, W. A. (1981). Analyzing negotiation tactics: Development of a negotiation interact system. *Human Communication Research, 7,* 273–287.

Donohue, W. A., Allen, M., & Burrell, N. (1985). Communication Strategies in mediation. *Mediation Quarterly, 10,* 75–89.

Donohue, W. A., Allen, M., & Burrell, N. (1988). Mediator communicative competence. *Communication Mongraphs, 55,* 104–119.

Donohue, W. A., Lyles, J., & Rogan R. (1989). Issue development in divorce mediation. *Mediation Quarterly, 24,* 19–28.

Ellis, A. (1962). *Reason and emotion in psychotherapy.* Secaucus, NJ: Citadel Press.

Ellis, A. (1984). The essence of RET–1984. *Journal of Rational-Emotive Therapy, 2,* 19–25.

Epstein, N., & Williams, A. M. (1981). Behavioral approaches to the treatment of marital discord. In G. P. Scholevar (Ed.), *The handbook of marriage and marital therapy* (pp. 219–286). New York: Spectrum

Fallis, S. I., Fitzpatrick, M. A., & Friestad, M. (1984). *Nonverbal anxiety indicators in marital interaction research.* Unpublished manuscript, Center for Communication Research, University of Wisconsin–Madison, Madison, WI.

Fitzpatrick, M. A. (1976). *A typological examination of communication in enduring relationships.* Unpublished doctoral dissertation, Temple University, Philadelphia, PA.

Fitzpatrick, M. A. (1977). A typological approach to communication in relationships. In B. Rubin (Ed.), *Communication yearbook 1* (pp. 263–275). Rutgers: Transaction.

Fitzpatrick, M. A. (1981). A typological approach to enduring relationships: Children as audience to the parental relationships. *Journal of Comparative Family Studies, 12,* 81–94.

Fitzpatrick, M. A. (1983). Predicting couples' communication from couples' self reports. In R. N. Bostrom & B. H. Westley (Eds.), *Communication yearbook 7* (pp. 49–82). Beverly Hills, CA: Sage.

Fitzpatrick, M. A. (1984). A typological approach in marital interaction: Recent theory and research. In L. Berkowitz (Ed.), *Advances in experimental social psychology* (Vol. 18, pp. 1–47). Orlando, FL: Academic Press.

Fitzpatrick, M. A. (1987a, May). *The effect of marital schemata on marital communication.* Paper presented at International Communication Association, Montreal, Canada.

Fitzpatrick, M. A. (1987b). Marital interaction. In C. R. Berger & S. Chaffee (Eds.), *Handbook of communication science* (pp. 564–618). Beverly Hills, CA: Sage.

Fitzpatrick, M. A. (1988). *Between husbands & wives: Communication in marriage.* Beverly Hills, CA: Sage.

Folger, J. P., & Poole, M. S. (1984). *Working through conflict.* Glenview, IL: Scott Foresman.

Forsterling, F. (1985). Attributional retraining: A review. *Pscyhological Bulletin, 98,* 495–512.

Forsterling, F. (1986). Attributional conceptions in clinical psychology. *American Psychologist, 41,* 275–85.

Giles, H., & Fitzpatrick, M. A. (1984). Personal, group and couple identities: Towards a relational context for the study of language attitudes and linguistic forms. In D. Schiffrin (Ed.), *Meaning, form and use in context: Linguistic applications* (pp. 253–277). Washington, DC: Georgetown University Press.

Gottman, J. M. (1979). *Marital interaction: Experimental investigations.* New York: Academic Press.

Gottman, J. M., & Krokoff, R. (1986). *Marital interaction: A longitudinal view.* Unpublished manuscript University of Washington, Seattle, WA.

Hocker, J. L., & Wilmot, W. W. (1985). *Interpersonal conflict* (2nd ed.). Dubuque, IA: Wm. C. Brown.

Jacobson, N. S. (1981). Behavioral marital therapy. In A. S. Gurman & D. P. Kniskern (Eds.), *Handbook of family therapy* (pp. 556–591). New York: Brunner/Mazel.

Jones, T. S. (1987, June). *Nonverbal vocal affect in divorce mediation: An examination of differences in use and sequential structuring in successful and unsuccessful sessions.* Paper presented at the International Conference at the Conflict Management Group, Fairfax, VA.

Kellermann, K., & Lim, T. S. (1989). The role of knowledge structures in message processing. In J. J. Bradac (Ed.), *Message effects in communication science: Contemporary approaches* (pp. 1–53). Newbury Park, CA: Sage.

Kelly, K., Huston, T. L., & Cate, R. M. (1985). Premarital relationship correlates of the erosion of satisfaction in marriage. *Journal of Social and Personal Relationships, 2,* 167–178.

Mace, D., & Mace, V. (1974). *We can have better marriages if we really want want.* London: Oliphants.

Markman, H. J. (1979). Application of a behavioral model of marriage in predicting relationship satisfaction. *Journal of Consulting and Clinical Psychology, 547,* 743–749.

Markman, H. J. (1981). Prediction of marital distress. *Journal of Consulting and Clinical Psychology, 49,* 760–762.

Markman, H. J. (1987). Prediction and prevention of marital distress. In K. Hahlweg & M. V. Goldstein (Eds.) *Understanding major mental disorder: A contribution of family interaction research* (pp. 253–284). New York: Family Process Press.

Noller, P. (1982). Channel consistency and inconsistency in the communications of married couples. *Journal of Personality and Social Psychology, 43,* 732–741.

Noller, P. (1984). *Nonverbal communication and marital interaction.* New York: Pergamon.

Olson, D. H. (1981). Family typologies: Bridging family research and family therapy. In E. E. Filsinger & R. A. Lewis (Eds.), *Assessing marriage: New behavioral approaches* (pp. 74–89). Beverly Hills, CA: Sage.

Patterson, M. (1985). The evolution of a functional model of nonverbal exchange. In R. Street & J. N. Cappella (Eds.), *Sequence and pattern in communicative behavior* (pp. 190–205). London: Edward Arnold.

Pruitt, D. G. (1981). *Negotiation behavior.* New York: Academic Press.

Rubin, J. A., & Brown, B. R. (1975). *The social psychology of bargaining and negotiation.* New York: Academic Press.

Sillars, A. L. (1986). Interpersonal perception in relationships. In W. J. Ickes (Ed.), *Compatible and incompatible relationships* (pp. 277–305). New York: Springer-Verlag.

The Interplay of Cognition and Excitation in Aggravated Conflict Among Intimates

Dolf Zillmann
University of Alabama

AGGRAVATED CONFLICT

Recent sociological research has successfully penetrated the shroud of secrecy that, in the past, has conceded much violent action in the American family and in similar cohabitation arrangements. The revelations defined a domain of social problems of enormous gravity. Violent action among siblings (e.g., Gelles, 1979; Pagelow, 1984; Patterson, 1984), by parents or caretakers against children (e.g., Finkelhor, 1986; Gelles, 1974; Gil, 1973; Pagelow, 1984) and adolescents (e.g., Libbey & Bybee, 1979; Pagelow, 1984), among husband and wife or other sexual intimates living together (e.g., Dobash & Dobash, 1978, 1979; Lincoln & Straus, 1985; Shupe, Stacey, & Hazlewood, 1987; Straus, Gelles, & Steinmetz, 1980), and against aging and elderly cohabitants (e.g., Berg & Johnson, 1979; Goldsmith & Goldsmith, 1975) proved to be more frequent than had been thought. Violence among sexually intimate cohabitants, especially violent action by men against women in these relationships, proved to be particularly frequent and devestating in its consequences (e.g., Chapman & Gates, 1978; Dobash & Dobash, 1978, 1979; Dutton, 1987; Gelles, 1979; Pagelow, 1984).

Violence among intimates takes many forms. It invariably entails verbal abuse (e.g., Shupe et al., 1987). From such abuse it escalates to grabbing, shaking, shoving, slapping, punching, kicking, clawing, scratching, biting, choking, and strangling. Objects are thrown about with destructive intentions, and they are used as weapons to inflict injury

187

more effectively (e.g., Sedlak, 1988; Shupe et al., 1987). Violent men tend to make threats to their victim's life. They are known to batter pregnant companions, often causing miscarriages (e.g., Gelles, 1979; Shupe et al., 1987). Violent men also tend to become sexually abusive of female intimate partners, forcing on them sexual actions to which they object or that they deem repugnant (e.g., Faulk, 1977; Finkelhor & Yllo, 1985; Gelles, 1979; Russell, 1982). Violent assaults among sexual intimates occasionally result in death. Such killing is characteristically exceedingly brutal and gruesome (e.g., Wolfgang, 1958; Zillmann, 1979).

Dobash and Dobash (1978) provided a classification of victimization in the family context that indicates the relative magnitude of various forms of violence among intimates. According to their scheme, wife assault takes up three quarters of all domestic violence. The prevalence of child assault is about 11%. Parent assault is surprisingly high with 7%. Sibling assault amounts to about 5%. Husband assault occurs least frequently with only about 1%.

For the prime category, wife battering, it has been estimated that such violence occurs in 50%–60% of all couples (Straus, 1978). About half of these cases are believed to entail unidirectional violence, almost all of which victimizing women. In the other half of cases, both men and women are believed to be actively engaged in the violent action (Straus et al., 1980). Mostly on the basis of this information, Pagelow (1984) estimated that there are about 12 million mutually abusive husbands and wives in the United States. Also, Walker's (1978, 1979) contention that about half of all adult women who live with male sexual intimates are at least once beaten by them has been used to project that more than 20 million women are victims of some degree of abuse (Pagelow, 1984).

Estimates of women who are trapped in relationships where they are repeatedly victimized by their male companions are somewhat more conservative. Pagelow (1984) believes that 25% of all women cohabiting with male partners are battered with some regularity. Russell (1982) believes this ratio to be 21%. Considering only violent actions that meet the legal definition of assault, the percentage is about 11 (Straus et al., 1980). For about half these women, violence of more severe consequence proves to be a yearly occurrence or is even more frequent (Schulman, 1979). Habitual assault of women by their cohabiting male sexual intimates is thus placed at about 5% (Dutton, 1987).

All these estimates are based on imperfect samples. Many abused persons, possibly the most severely abused ones, are unwilling to reveal their plight to interviewers. It has been assumed (e.g., Gelles & Straus, 1985), therefore, that most estimates understate the amount of violence that is actually perpetrated among intimates. However, the enormity of the problem is apparent even when only the most conservative estimates are accepted.

Numerous investigators consider stress from sources external to a relationship, mostly from occupational conditions, implicated in the perpetration of much of the violence (e.g., Elmer, 1979; Farrington, 1980; Gelles & Straus, 1979). Alcohol intoxication is similarly considered a major contributing factor (e.g., Bowker, 1983; Pagelow, 1984; Shupe et al., 1987). Finally, the so-called home of orientation, with regard to tolerance and practice of violence, is thought to contribute greatly to the formation of violent dispositions (e.g., Gelles & Straus, 1985; Pagelow, 1985; Shupe et al., 1987).

Oddly, in considering the circumstances that lead to impulsive violence among intimates it is generally recognized that violence is not a reaction to immediate, life-threatening conditions. It is, instead, a reaction to continuing and escalating annoying stimulation that characteristically starts with seemingly trivial disagreements. In delineating prototypical violent action among intimates, Shupe et al. (1987) stated that: "arguments and conflicts usually are nonsubstantive (that is, over minor issues or over implied or unspoken issues). The arguments escalate in rapid fashion to physical violence" (p. 42). Gelles (1974) similarly suggested that, as a rule, the immediate circumstances do not warrant violent action, and that such action is better "explained as arising out of the buildup of stress and frustration" (p. 74).

The common elements in characterizations of this kind are these:

1. In many instances, acute conflict among intimates grows from insignificant disagreements.

2. Persistence in such disagreements escalates to intense feelings of annoyance and anger that eventually foster emotional outbursts and violent action.

3. Because the violent action cannot be deemed commensurate with any apparent provocation by the victim, "external" factors are considered to mediate the violence.

The general reference to stress and frustration (as the critical external factors) does not provide an adequate or acceptable explanation of the escalation process, however. The evidence concerning the effects of frustrating experiences on aggression is quite negative (Bandura, 1973; Quanty, 1976; Zillmann, 1979). In particular, the building up of frustration is popular belief rather than established fact. Stress is more likely a contributor to aggression. However, if the stress concept is not operationalized in measurable terms, it is bound to become the same patently postmortem explanation as frustration: As there are not too many who can claim to be stress and frustration free, any violent action could be justified (and, in retrospect, "explained") as the result of these omnipresent forces.

There is a great need, then, to complement the existing descriptive accounts of family violence with specific and validated explanations of the critical processes involved. The escalation of the experience of annoyance, because it so frequently creates the propensity for destructive violent action, may be considered the crucial process that is to be understood. I consequently focus theory and research on this process. At first, the escalation of annoyance and anger is investigated in physiological terms. The cognitive implications of the physiological changes that characterize the escalation process are explored thereafter. The interdependence of physiological and cognitive responding is analyzed in impulsive violent actions. The development of a propensity for violent behavior is examined in this context. Finally, strategies to minimize the occurrence of violent outbursts among intimates are considered.

ANGER ESCALATION

With few exceptions, violence among intimates is an emotional affair. Disagreements, in which the parties in conflict perceive themselves to be treated unfairly, unjustly, dishonestly, demeaningly, rudely, or brutally, produce feelings of acute anger toward companions. These feelings of anger are accompanied by significant elevations of the level of sympathetic excitation in the autonomic nervous system, and these excitatory changes are known to facilitate aggressive inclinations and actions (Zillmann, 1979, 1988).

In general terms, it is the recognition of endangerment that gives rise to aggressive dispositions and behaviors that are associated with increased sympathetic activity. Confronted with social or environmental conditions that threaten welfare and well-being, individuals respond in a fight-or-flight manner (Cannon, 1929). They act on these conditions, either by attacking them in hopes of defusing the threats they pose, or by escaping from them in hopes of eluding these threats. Whatever the option taken, individuals seem set to resolve emergencies of the specified kind through vigorous action. This partiality for action is the result of accelerated anabolic processes that generate the energy for a burst of vigorous action. The cited increase in sympathetic activity is a salient aspect of this behavior energization.

There can be little doubt that the tendency to respond with vigorous action to endangerment has served us well in our ancient past. However, the social conditions of contemporary society have severely compromised the adaptive utility of the fight-or-flight reaction. In fact, former utility has turned to present-day futility. Responding "emotionally" to threats to self-esteem, social status, social power, or economic standing not only tends to lack adaptive value, but can be counterproductive and maladaptive. Responding in this fashion to intimates who threaten fair and equitable arrangements is likely to be particularly maladaptive. An obvious reason for this is that social intimacy removes, for all practical purposes, the flight option from the fight-or-flight paradigm. Intimates usually cannot resolve conflict by escaping the social arrangements in which they live. Flight is a one-time, final solution only. It tends to terminate membership in the social aggregate in which conflict is to be resolved. Most intimates are thus left with the fight end of the paradigm, along with the archaic agonistic response tendency to take vigorous action against parties who threaten their self-interest. The choice becomes one between fighting and not fighting—the latter in the sense of abandoning an assertive course of action, of yielding, and of acquiescing to the attainment of valued conditions and commodities by others. Apparently, a great many emotionally aroused individuals have great difficulty mastering such submission to the selfish interest of others.

In the analysis of the bodily conditions that favor conflict resolution by vigorous action it is useful to distinguish between excitation mediated by the adrenomedullary system and excitation mediated by the adrenocortical system (Leshner, 1978). Activity in the adrenomedullary system, through the release of catecholamines and their fast but short-lived hyperglycemic effect, provides energy for essentially one behavioral engagement. The energization is said to be *phasic* or *episodic*. It is energy for one course of vigorous action, such as in fight, flight, coition, or other emotional experiences and behaviors (Zillmann, 1986). Activity in the adrenocortical system, mainly through the release of glucocorticoids and their hyperglycemic effect, also generates energy, but does so for extended periods of time. This energization is said to be *tonic*. Such tonic energization is part of the coping response to social and environmental stressors.

As one would expect, in the production of their sympathomimetic effect the two systems operate in an integrated fashion. Heightened activity in the adrenocortical system usually defines the undercurrent for acute emotions. It places the organism in a state of increased action readiness. It creates, essentially, superior conditions for aggressive responsiveness, and it does so tonically—that is, for extended periods of time. Emotional reactions build on this foundation. Phasic excitation from heightened activity in the adrenomedullary system combines with tonic excitation, and this combination creates emotional reactions of potentially great intensity.

It is important to recognize that the correspondence between the duration of tonic or phasic excitation, on the one hand, and the time course of the stimulation that induces the excitatory reactions under consideration, on the other, is far from perfect. This imperfection is mainly the result of the humoral nature of the mediating agents (Zillmann, 1983).

Stressful stimulation fosters heightened adrenocortical activity only after a considerable latency period. More importantly, the activity may persist for hours and days after the termination of the stressful stimulation. Individuals suffering from stress that is induced outside the intimate social sphere thus do bring home conditions conducive to the escalation of emotional experiences and behaviors.

Analogously, emotion-inducing stimulation fosters heightened activity in the adrenomedullary system only after some latency. The latency is a matter of seconds, however, and has little, if any, practical significance. The period of time by which the excitatory reaction outlasts the emotional stimulation is again more important. The time beyond the cessation of emotional stimulation is a matter of minutes. These minutes may seem unimportant, but turn out to be crucial in the escalation of anger.

Escalating conflict can be conceptualized as a sequence of provocations, each triggering an excitatory reaction that materializes quickly and that dissipates slowly. As a second sympathetic reaction occurs before the first has dissipated, the second reaction combines with the tail end of the first. As a third reaction occurs before the second and first reactions have dissipated, this third reaction combines with the tail ends of both earlier reactions. In general, the excitatory reaction to a provocation late in the escalation process rides the tails of all earlier reactions. (See Zillmann, 1983, 1984, for a more complete exposition of this paradigm of excitation transfer.) The combination of residual sympathetic excitation with the excitation in response to a particular provocation produces emotional experiences and behaviors that are incommensurate with the provocation. Sympathetic excitation is at "artificially" high levels, producing overly intense feelings and reactions.

The intensification of anger and aggressive behavior by residual sympathetic excitation from reactions unrelated to the instigation of aggression has been demonstrated in numerous experiments (Zillmann, 1979, 1984). Suffice it here to indicate the nature of these demonstrations.

Aggressively instigated men were, for instance, subjected to strenuous physical exercise or not and then, while excitation from exercise was still in evidence, provided with an opportunity to retaliate. Retaliatory aggression was found to be greatly enhanced by residual arousal unrelated to provocation (Zillmann, Johnson, & Day, 1974; Zillmann, Katcher, & Milavsky, 1972). In similar research, provoked men and women were exposed to differently arousing, pleasant or unpleasant films and then given a chance to retaliate. The intensity of retaliatory aggression was consistently found to be proportional with the magnitude of residual excitation from ulterior sources (e.g., Bryant & Zillmann, 1977; Cantor, Zillmann, & Einsiedel, 1978; Ramirez, Bryant, & Zillmann, 1982; Zillmann, 1971; Zillmann, Hoyt, & Day, 1974).

APPRAISALS

The primary function of cognition is to guide behavior. The immediate objective of such guidance is the avoidance of harm and the minimization of aversion. The maximization of gratification is, of course, a further objective.

Awake and alert individuals continually monitor their environment for conditions posing threats and for opportunities to gain gratification. Based on their experience with pertinent circumstances, they recognize prevailing action contingencies and *anticipate* aversion or gratification as the result of particular contemplated courses of action as well as of contemplated inaction. Table 9.1 summarizes anticipations that influence and control aggressive actions.

Under ordinary circumstances, the anticipation of the consequences of one's contemplated aggressive action fosters the inhibition of the action. Probable social reproach, for example, might be expected to result

TABLE 9.1
Anticipations in the Cognitive Guidance of Aggressive Behavior

Appraisal of Circumstances	*Appraisal of Consequences*
Contingencies of reward and punishment	Anticipation of gratification or aversion
Coercive contingencies	Anticipation of success[a] or failure[b]
Stable abilities and inabilities of self	Anticipation of success or failure
Transitory abilities and inabilities of self	Anticipation of success or failure
Opposing situational forces	Anticipation of cost[c]
Punitive and retaliatory potentialities of others	Anticipation of cost
Contingencies of social approval and reproach	Anticipation of gratification or aversion

[a] Success ultimately translates into attainment of gratification or removal of aversion.
[b] Failure ultimately translates into removal of gratification or attainment of aversion.
[c] Cost ultimately translates into aversion.
(Adapted from Zillmann, 1979. Reprinted with permission.)

in intensely noxious experiences and be deemed unacceptable. Such reproach, then, might be considered more noxious than inaction or the consequences of other nonaggressive reactions. Or the attack on someone might be feared to prompt retaliatory action likely to inflict even more severe suffering. On the other hand, knowledge of superior strength and fighting skill, together with the belief that the victim is unlikely to resist or retaliate, would be most conducive to uncurtailed violent action.

It is important to recognize that appraisals and repeated reappraisals of the circumstances in which individuals find themselves modify excitatory activity. Threats and dangers produce excitedness. So do anticipations of threats and dangers. The excitedness, in this case, is part of a preparatory emotional reaction that is to facilitate vigorous coping reactions once their need materializes. However, as the conditions change and the threats and dangers are reappraised and deemed less severe or inconsequential, excitatory activity serves no cause and promptly dissipates. In accordance with theory and research evidence (Zillmann, 1979) it may be expected that this dissipation lowers the propensity for destructive behavior. But it may also be expected that information that prevents individuals from appraising threats and dangers as deliberate acts against them personally will forestall the strong preparatory excitatory reactions that personal attacks would necessitate. Noxious treatments that catch individuals by surprise, and for which they have not prepared coping reactions, are known to produce particularly intense excitatory and emotional reactions (Leventhal, 1974). However, noxious treatments that can be anticipated, and for which individuals are prepared or can prepare, especially when these treatments can not be attributed to deliberate malevolence of others, are unlikely to instigate intense emotions.

The indicated influence of cognition on excitatory activity, along with its effect on the experience of anger and hostile behavior, has been demonstrated in an investigation by Zillmann and Cantor (1976). Male subjects were severely provoked by a rude same-gender experimenter and later given an opportunity to harm him. In one condition, the subjects received no information about circumstances that could have made their tormentor's behavior appear less hostile or assaultive. His rudeness seemed deliberate, and the subjects had no alternative to appraising it as a personal attack. In the other condition, information of mitigating circumstances was provided. The rude experimenter was said to be under a lot of stress from his preliminary doctoral examination. In one of these conditions, the subjects received the mitigating information prior to being mistreated. In the other, they received it after the mistreatment.

In the case of prior communication about mitigating circumstances, any seemingly hostile action on the part of the experimenter was *preappraised*. His actions could be attributed to stress and frustration deriving from conditions unrelated to the subjects' behavior. His rudeness did not have to be construed as a personal attack, and subjects did not have to ready themselves for such an attack. Compared with the control condition in which mitigating information had not been communicated, subjects should appraise the situation as less threatening. As a result, their excitatory reactions should be subdued, their experience of annoyance should be less severe, and they should be less inclined to take strong retaliatory measures.

In the case of the later communication of the same mitigating information, the subjects had suffered the full impact of the experimenter's rudeness. Excitatory reactions were comparatively strong, and experiences of annoyance were intense. The reception of the mitigating information eventually fostered a *reappraisal* of the circumstances. This reappraisal should remove the personal, deliberate, and arbitrary component from the mistreatment. Once such recognition materializes, excitation, now expendable, should start to dissipate, and the experience of annoyance should diminish. However, related research (Bryant & Zillmann, 1979) has shown that intensely felt anger may instigate retaliatory intentions, and that these intentions may be executed "in cold blood" long after recovery from acute anger. Reappraisal is thus unlikely to curtail retaliatory action as effectively as preappraisal.

In the experiment, excitatory activity was monitored at critical times between provocation and retaliation. Sympathetic excitation was ascertained in peripheral manifestations (blood pressure, heart rate). The findings show that subjects who had prior knowledge of mitigating circumstances were relatively unperturbed by the mistreatment they received. Sympathetic excitation never reached high levels, and it dissipated to particularly low levels. In contrast, the mistreatment prompted extreme excitatory reactions in subjects without such prior knowledge. The communication of mitigating information after the mistreatment apparently fostered a reappraisal that initiated and accelerated excitatory recovery. Excitation quickly fell below levels in the control condition in which subjects had not received mitigating information. But the reappraisal clearly failed to lower excitedness to levels comparable with those in subjects who had prior knowledge of the mitigating circumstances.

The severity of retaliatory actions proved to be proportional to levels of sympathetic excitation at the time these actions were taken. Persons who received mitigating information prior to being mistreated showed considerable compassion for their tormentor. On the other hand, persons who had received this information after having suffered the full blow of this treatment were almost as punitive with their tormentor as those who never learned of mitigating circumstances.

The investigation clearly demonstrates the influence of appraisals on excitation, emotional experiences such as anger, and hostile, harmful behaviors. It also has important implications for communicative efforts at curtailing hostilities and preventing destructive reactions. Obviously, if punitive actions in response to noxious happenings are to be minimized and averted, information about mitigating circumstances that may exist must be presented, and it is imperative that communication of such information occurs prior to the onset of aversive stimulation.

COGNITIVE DEFICIT

It is recognized, apparently in all cultures on earth, that people occasionally perpetrate violence "in the heat of passion," and that they usually regret their actions as soon as the extreme excitatory activity that invariably accompanies these actions has subsided (Averill, 1982; Zillmann, 1979). Laws regulating violent, destructive behavior characteristically show leniency for persons who committed their transgressions in states of extreme excitedness. Compassion for those who maim and kill "in the heat of anger" can be so great that the temporary loss of cognitive control, manifest in what seems to be a total disregard for consequences other than the accomplishment of the intended destruction, is deemed a form of insanity. But regardless of the merits of such characterizations, it should be clear that in much conflict among intimates agonistic emotions do reach extreme excitatory intensity; and behavior-guiding cognitions, in line with the blind-passion truism, may be expected to suffer considerable impairment.

The physiological mechanics of the cognitive incapacitation associated with rage and violent action have been the subject of ample speculation. It has been suggested, for instance, that small amounts of the catecholamines that mediate sympathetic excitation in the peripheral structures, especially norepinephrine, cross the brain blood barrier and affect central processes (Rothballer, 1967) that favor immediate action against threats and dangers. However, the operation of specific processes of this kind has not been demonstrated as yet, and it would seem prudent to invoke, instead, well-established mechanisms that are capable of explaining the cognitive deficit that characterizes actions perpetrated under extreme excitatory conditions.

The inverted-U relationship between arousal and behavioral efficiency (e.g., Easterbrook, 1959; Freeman, 1940; Malmo, 1959) may be considered a model that has withstood the test of time. For extremely high levels of excitation it simply projects a cognitive preoccupation with the behavioral emergency at hand. This preoccupation comes at the expense of attention to nonimmediate, potentially secondary aspects of the emergency and its resolution. The "cognitive deficit" that accompanies extreme excitedness thus concerns the reception and processing of information that has no immediate utility for the fight-or-flight reaction. Applied to violent conflict, this means that many of the cognitions that mediate the inhibition of violent action are no longer executed, and that, consequently, rage and violence can find expression. Table 9.1 lists the critical cognitive processes, especially anticipations, that are likely to be impaired or become defunct. Anticipations, by definition, are projections of consequences of contemplated events and actions. They are complex cognitive operations and, as excitation escalates, likely to fail. And as anticipations of cost, failure, and aversion resulting from one's action become defunct, the basal, if not archaic, actions favored by high excitedness go unopposed and can be pursued.

Evidence for the indicated impairment of the cognitively mediated inhibition of aggressive behavior comes from an investigation by Zillmann, Bryant, Cantor, and Day (1975). In this investigation, male subjects were or were not strongly prearoused by invigorating strenuous physical exercise. The exercise consisted of riding a bicycle ergometer. Reactions to this task had shown it to be affectively neutral. Subjects neither particularly liked nor disliked the assignment, and none of them found it irritating, tiresome, or unreasonable. The subjects were then instigated to aggression by a male experimenter's abusive behavior and eventually provided with an opportunity to retaliate. Just prior to getting their opportunity to get even, a female confederate had occasion to enter the laboratory, calling the experimenter to the phone. He left with a snide remark, giving her a chance to comment on the fact that he was under a lot of stress from exams.

At moderate levels of excitation, such mitigating information should be received, processed, applied to the circumstances, and ultimately curtail hostile, retaliatory actions. This aggression- reducing effect of mitigating information has been observed in numerous studies (e.g., Burnstein & Worchel, 1962; Pastore, 1952; Rule, Dyck, & Nesdale, 1978; Zillmann & Cantor, 1976). At very high levels of excitation, however, the effect should not materialize because of cognitive incapacitation.

The findings were as expected. Mitigating information strongly reduced retaliatory hostility at moderate levels of excitation. This outcome corroborates the earlier findings. The novel finding concerns the behavior at high levels of excitation. At these levels, the provision of mitigating information proved to be without appreciable effect on hostile behavior.

Unanticipated data from this investigation suggest that mitigating information is similarly received but is processed differently at different levels of excitation. The prearoused subjects apparently comprehended the information, but rejected it vehemently. Upon the confederate's revelation of stress from exams, these prearoused subjects uttered assessments like "That's just too bad!". Other utterances expressed the same sentiment, but in so doing used the strongest vulgarities the English language has to offer. The expression of such vulgarities is, of course, a characteristic accompaniment of much impulsive agonistic behavior. Regardless of the intensity of the language used, however, the comments seem to suggest that acutely angry, extremely excited persons become unforgiving. Such persons are determined to fight back. They seem obsessed with the desire to reciprocate harm and "get even" with their tormentor, and they appear to become oblivious to consequences such as social condemnation of their actions and likely reprisals by their opponent. In this connection, it has been suggested that excessive excitedness may foster an illusion of power and invulnerability that inspires and facilitates aggressive action (Zillmann, 1979). Notwithstanding these proposals, the effects of extreme excitedness on particular cognitive processes have not been demonstrated and may prove elusive in future exploratory efforts. What has been demonstrated is that cognition that operates to curtail hostile behavior at moderate levels of sympathetic excitation fails to operate in this manner at extreme levels of excitation.

Cognition that serves to inhibit and curtail violent action is, of course, not only influenced by changes in sympathetic activity. The so-called "mind-altering" drugs have a direct impact on the proficiency of cognitive operations, especially on operations involved in monitoring events in the environment and in preparing rationally sound response strategies. In the explorations of violence among intimates, alcohol is the drug to be considered. Ethanol intoxication is a condition under which a large portion of violent, abusive behavior occurs (e.g., Kantor & Straus, 1987; Leonard, Bromet, Parkinson, Day, & Ryan, 1985; Pagelow, 1984).

Experimental research has shown with consistency that the provocation of alcohol-intoxicated persons leads to stronger aggressive reactions than does the same provocation of sober persons (Taylor & Leonard, 1983), presumably because of a relaxation of inhibitions resulting from the impaired anticipation of consequences. An investigation by Leonard (1989) suggests that intoxicated persons are particularly insensitive to cues that under normal circumstances convey the victim's unwillingness to continue fighting, and that aggravated conflict often continues and escalates because of this intoxication-generated insensitivity.

Related research (Zillmann & Bryant, 1989) indicates that alcohol intoxication facilitates aggression most when the provocation predates the intoxication. Male subjects were either aggressively instigated prior to ethanol ingestion or thereafter. With time between provocation and retaliation kept constant, they eventually, but always while intoxicated, were given an opportunity to aggress against their tormentor. Table 9.2

TABLE 9.2
Effects of Provocation Prior to Versus After Alcohol Intoxication
on Aggressive Behavior

Behavior Sequence	Provocation/Intoxication Treatment		
	Provocation No Intoxication	Provocation Intoxication	No provocation Intoxication
Prior provocation	45.3[b]	64.2[d]	34.3[a]
Later provocation	44.2[b]	53.3[c]	34.7[a]

Note: The scores represent the average accumulated intensity of a set of hostile responses. Means associated with different letter superscripts differ significantly at $p < 0.05$ by Neuman-Keuls' test.
(From Zillmann & Bryant, 1989.)

summarizes the findings. As can be seen, ethanol intoxication intensified aggressive reactions in both sequences: intoxication/provocation and provocation/intoxication. However, in the latter sequence, aggression proved to be facilitated to a markedly greater degree than in the former sequence.

These findings suggest that intoxication may impair the processing of provocations and personal attacks, or it may hamper the formation of retaliatory dispositions and strategies, or both—all in addition to clouding the anticipation of consequences of aggressive actions. Sober persons, in contrast, suffer the full blow of demeaning treatments and assaults, construct plans for retaliatory action, and commit themselves to them. Such persons, once disinhibited by intoxication, then execute their pre-intoxication plans. The sociological literature (e.g., Bard & Zacker, 1971; Bowker, 1983; Pagelow, 1984) is laden with examples of violence perpetrated under these circumstances. It has been argued, in this connection, that alcohol intoxication is used, often deliberately, as an excuse for violent action. Gelles (1974), for instance, suggested that, because drinking is a "socially approved excuse for violent behavior, . . . individuals who wish to carry out a violent act become intoxicated *in order to carry out the violent act*" (p. 117). The findings are certainly consistent with this possibility of intentionally shifting blame from self to liquor ("I didn't know what I was doing . . . I was drunk," Gelles, 1974, p. 117).

IMPULSIVE AGGRESSION

Theories of impulsive aggression (e.g., Averill, 1982; Berkowitz, 1974; Gelles, 1974; Zillmann, 1979, 1988) invariably focus on three factors: loss of cognitive control, high levels of arousal or excitation, and the seemingly unwarranted use of force in dealing with social conflict. A theory proposed by Zillmann (1979) posits specific interdependencies between these factors. Excessive sympathetic activity from the instigation of emotions is expected to foster an impairment of cognitive behavior guidance; and this impairment, in turn, is expected to foster a reliance on well-established behavior patterns or habits. Obviously, the cognitive incapacitation can be brought about by alternative means, such as ethanol intoxication, and eventuate a similar reliance on habits. Violent action depends, however, on a sufficient amount of sympathetic activity and coordination; it cannot be expected for intoxication to the point of physical incapacitation.

The important consideration is that, as conflict escalates and sympathetic activity reaches extreme levels, individuals become less proficient in devising coping responses whose conception requires complex cognitive operations. Much practiced and well-rehearsed reactions now offer themselves. They constitute a fallback or default system for failing cognitive guidance. The situation is comparable to panic in a schoolhouse fire. Students who practiced the fire drill are likely to find their way out, and students who did not are bound to pound locked doors.

For violence among intimates this means that hyperexcited persons, or excited persons whose cognitive capabilities are reduced by toxins, will resort to performing basic behaviors that have been reinforced in the past. Those who succeeded with aggression, who were able to resolve conflict to their advantage by brutalizing others, will be sure to take this course of action again. Others who failed with aggression—who, instead of being victorious, became victims of brutality—are likely to exhibit actions, or rather inactions, that are commonly subsumed under the heading of "learned helplessness" (Seligman, 1975). Although vastly different, both types of actions are impulsive in the sense that behavior is quasi-automatic and devoid of rationality. And once such impulsive, quasi-automatic behavior dominates social conflict, efforts at resolving the conflict through persuasion and bargaining are abandoned, the conflict becomes physical, and resolutions are pursued and possibly achieved by brute force.

CALLOUSNESS, HABITS, AND INTIMACY

If, at the level of impulsive behavior, well-formed habits play such a significant part, the question arises as to how coercive, violent habits evolve. How are they formed? How are they maintained?

Much emphasis has been placed on the development of callous, aggression-encouraging attitudes (e.g., Huesmann & Eron, 1986), especially on the development of such attitudes in young men who seek to dominate their gender counterparts (e.g., Mosher & Sirkin, 1984; Zillmann & Weaver, 1989). But the formation of aggressive dispositions and habits has also been explored in terms of winning and losing in conflicts arising among intimates. There can be no doubt that those for whom aggression works, mostly because of superior strength and agility, are more likely to become aggressors than are those for whom it fails (e.g., Olweus, 1984; Patterson, 1979, 1984), and that aggressive dispositions and habits, once they are formed, are highly stable and persistent (e.g., Olweus, 1984; Robins, 1978).

Ironically, the place of cohabitation, the home, turns out to be the main stage on which impulsive aggression is observed, tried, practiced, "perfected," and reinforced—in short, learned. The home is where frictions develop and heated conflict comes about with regularity. Preventive intervention from third parties is very much ruled out by societal precepts of privacy. These precepts also minimize the likelihood of social reproach and punitive action against persons who resort to violence. Aggressive action is thus protected, to a high degree, from outside influences.

It should not surprise that, under these conditions, the physically strong and agile are tempted to use their endowment to their advantage against the weak and meek, and that their temptation grows with repeated success in the use of force. The sociological notion that abuse gravitates to the *greatest power differential* (Finkelhor, 1986; Pagelow, 1984) applies in a truly physical sense: The physically strongest are most likely to victimize the physically weakest. Findings, such as decreasing child abuse with increasing victim age (Steinmetz, 1977) or more extensive wife battering by especially fit and well-trained military men than by their civilian counterparts (Shupe et al., 1987), would seem to support such a contention.

The power differential between children and adults is obvious enough. The fact that it also exists for gender constellations generally, and that it is part and parcel of much of the abusive violence that men perpetrate against women, is often overlooked, however.

Granted that numerous women are stronger and faster than numerous men, it is nonetheless true that, on average, men outrun, outjump, outlift, outpush, and outpunch women (McWhirter & McWhirter, 1977). Fighting skills favor the male skeletal-motor build. Added the culturally created and supported male eagerness to develop these skills, the result is that, on the whole, men are better hand-to-hand fighters than women. Nowhere is this more evident than in the bedroom, where sexual intimates quickly learn who has the power to do what to whom. Men are known to take advantage of their physical superiority and, if need be, push, shove, and beat their partners into compliance with their particular desires. The so-called "battering rapes" and "obsessive rapes" among cohabitants are cases in point (Finkelhor & Yllo, 1985). Because sexual activities are most private and most shielded against third-party witness or intervention, coercion by physical means enjoys the strongest protection in this context. Impulsive actions are further favored by high levels of sympathetic excitation that accompany sexual arousal (Zillmann, 1986). It is thus conceivable that the use of physical coercion starts in connection with sexual activities and then generalizes to all less protected domestic confrontations.

COMMUNICATION AND DISENGAGEMENT

What can be done to curtail impulsive violence among intimates? In particular, what can be done through communication?

The discussed research sensitizes us to critical events in the escalation of conflict and points to communicative intervention strategies.

First of all, the research indicates how the escalation of emotional arousal in conflict situations—the escalation that creates the propensity for impulsive violent action—can be averted or held to a minimum. Those who bring bad news, who have to disclose disturbing and upsetting happenings, must make every effort to convey existing mitigating circumstances at the earliest possible time. The communication of information that shows that annoying conditions were not deliberately created and/ or not intended to harm the victim specifically, should prove effective in preventing intense emotional reactions. Similarly, the communication of plans of action specifying how to cope with the aversive situation, and how to minimize its impact, should prove useful in holding excitatory activity to moderate levels.

Second, the research demonstrates the futility of arguing with persons exhibiting "cognitive deficit" because of extreme emotional arousal, intoxication, or a combination thereof. Aggravated conflict cannot be resolved by rational means—at least not by the parties in conflict. The violence-curtailing strategy that is called for is *cautious disengagement.* Confrontational strategies are known to create great difficulties (Wilson, 1982). If pursued into escalated conflict with potentially violent persons who show impaired cognition, such strategies virtually guarantee the eruption of violence.

Cautious disengagement does not mean passivity, however, especially not communicative passivity. Meeting arguments with silence usually conveys stubborn adherence to a particular stand and can infuriate annoyed persons. Difficult as it may be not to pursue one's vital interests, nor to insist on specific interpretations of circumstances and on one's rights, aggravated conflict is best resolved by signaling that one understands the other's agony, that one sees merit in the other's point of view, and that the other's goals are legitimate and actions toward it justified—all this to the extent possible (i.e., without becoming dishonest and deceptive).

Cautious disengagement means acquiescing, by communicative means but not by deeds, to unreasonable demands by an infuriated, potentially dangerous intimate opponent. It means yielding, but only temporarily. The strategy is based on the premise that equitable arrangements cannot be achieved during aggravated conflict, and that confrontational persistence poses danger. The foremost objective must be the defusion of that danger. Emotional outbursts have to be waited out. Excitation eventually must return to moderate levels, and the effect of toxins does wear off. Once conditions have normalized, negotiations towards resolving the unresolved conflict can and should resume—in fact, if equitable arrangements are to be achieved, they must resume.

Finally, it must be acknowledged that practicing cautious disengagement faces one major obstacle: Persons pursuing this strategy may find themselves quickly engulfed in a conflict, become excessively aroused, and then suffer a loss of cognitive control in their own behavior. Abandonment of the disengagement strategy is the likely result of this loss of guidance.

Such a development is best prevented by preparedness for aggravated conflict (Leventhal, 1974). Comprehension of the futility of solving anything by arguing with exceedingly excited or intoxicated persons should produce a firm determination not to insist on one's perceptions and judgments—especially not on one's rights. Creating similar dispositions in our cohabitants through educational efforts at times of dispassion and repose should also prove useful.

However, the most effective way of preventing violent eruptions is indicated by the principle of *passive inhibition* (Scott, 1958; Zillmann, 1988). It simply suggests not to form aggressive habits by not performing aggressive acts. If aggressive acts are not performed, they obviously cannot be reinforced or otherwise strengthened. And if aggressive habits are not formed, such habits cannot break through in the heat of passion. In other words, if habits of violent action have not been established, they cannot constitute a fallback system for failing cognition in aggravated conflict among intimates.

The recommendation to resist all temptations to use physical force in the pursuit of selfish interests, so that this use will not become automatic in times of crises, is primarily directed, of course, at those strong enough to succeed in imposing their will on others. The literature on abusive behavior leaves no doubt about the fact that many in this category never attempted to curtail their power or failed miserably when trying. The focus on such failure, on the ubiquity of battering, creates the impression that the violent abuse of the weak by the strong in intimate relationships is inevitable—or the rule, at least. Such impression is unwarranted, however (Dutton, 1987). The large majority of people—men, women, parents, and caretakers alike—who could exploit the physical power differential to their advantage, do *not* erupt into violent action when affronted by difficulties, provocations, mistreatments, and injustices. The majority manages to cope with trying circumstances without resorting to violence. Hopefully, this majority will grow as people learn to read correctly the cues that signal "cognitive deficit" in others involved in aggravated conflict, as they strengthen their determination not to argue with persons showing such deficit and to appease them instead, and perhaps most importantly, as they conscientiously practice the passive inhibition of aggressive acts of any kind in all situations of conflict.

REFERENCES

Averill, J. R. (1982). *Anger and aggression: An essay on emotion.* New York: Springer-Verlag.

Bandura, A. (1973). *Aggression: A social learning analysis.* Englewood Cliffs, NJ: Prentice-Hall.

Bard, M., & Zacker, J. (1971). Assaultiveness and alcohol use in family disputes: Police perceptions. *Criminology, 12*(3), 281–292.

Berg, W. E., & Johnson, R. (1979). Assessing the impact of victimization: Acquisition of the victim role among elderly and female victims. In W. H. Parsonage (Ed.), *Perspectives on victimology* (pp. 58–71). Beverly Hills, CA: Sage.

Berkowitz, L. (1974). Some determinants of impulsive aggression: Role of mediated associations with reinforcement for aggression. *Psychological Review, 81,* 165–176.

Bowker, L. H. (1983). *Beating wife-beating.* Lexington, MA: Lexington Books.

Bryant, J., & Zillmann, D. (1977). The mediating effect of the intervention potential of communication on displaced aggressiveness and retaliatory behavior. In B. D. Ruben (Ed.), *Communication Yearbook, 1* (pp. 291–306). New Brunswick, NJ: ICA-Transaction Press.

Bryant, J., & Zillmann, D. (1979). Effect of intensification of annoyance through unrelated residual excitation on substantially delayed hostile behavior. *Journal of Experimental Social Psychology, 15,* 470–480.

Burnstein, E., & Worchel, P. (1962). Arbitrariness of frustration and its consequences for aggression in a social situation. *Journal of Personality, 30,* 528–540.

Cannon, W. B. (1929). *Bodily changes in pain, hunger, fear and rage: An account of researches into the function of emotional excitement* (2nd ed.). New York: Appleton-Century-Crofts.

Cantor, J. R., Zillmann, D., & Einsiedel, E. F. (1978). Female responses to provocation after exposure to aggressive and erotic films. *Communication Research, 5*, 395–411.

Chapman, J. R., & Gates, M. (1978). *The victimization of women.* Beverly Hills, CA: Sage.

Dobash, R. E., & Dobash, R. P. (1978). Wives: The "appropriate" victims of marital violence. *Victimology, 2*(3/4), 426–442.

Dobash, R. E., & Dobash, R. P. (1979). *Violence against wives: A case against patriarchy.* New York: The Free Press.

Dutton, D. G. (1987). Wife assault: Social psychological contributions to criminal justice policy. In S. Oskamp (Ed.), *Applied Social Psychology Annual. 7: Family processes and problems: Social psychological aspects* (pp. 238–261). Newbury Park, CA: Sage.

Easterbrook, J. A. (1959). The effect of emotion on cue utilization and the organization of behavior. *Psychological Review, 66*, 183–201.

Elmer, E. (1979). Child abuse and family stress. *Journal of Social Issues, 35*(2), 60–71.

Farrington, K. M. (1980). Stress and family violence. In M. A. Straus & G. T. Hotaling (Eds.), *The social causes of husband-wife violence* (pp. 94–114). Minneapolis: University of Minnesota Press.

Faulk, M. (1977). Sexual factors in marital violence. *Medical Aspects of Human Sexuality, 11*, 30–38.

Finkelhor, D. (1986). *A sourcebook on child sexual abuse.* Beverly Hills, CA: Sage.

Finkelhor, D., & Yllo, K. (1985). Rape in marriage: A sociological view. In A. J. Lincoln & M. A. Straus (Eds.), *Crime and the family* (pp. 121–133). Springfield, IL: Charles C. Thomas.

Freeman, G. L. (1940). The relationship between performance level and bodily activity level. *Journal of Experimental Psychology, 26*, 602–608.

Gelles, R. J. (1974). *The violent home.* Beverly Hills, CA: Sage.

Gelles, R. J. (1979). *Family violence.* Beverly Hills, CA: Sage.

Gelles, R. J., & Straus, M. A. (1979). Violence in the American family. *Journal of Social Issues, 35*(2), 15–39.

Gelles, R. J., & Straus, M. A. (1985). Violence in the American family. In A. J. Lincoln & M. A. Straus (Eds.), *Crime and the family* (pp. 88–110). Springfield, IL: Charles C. Thomas.

Gil, D. G. (1973). *Violence against children: Physical child abuse in the United States.* Cambridge: Harvard University Press.

Goldsmith, J., & Goldsmith, S. S. (Eds.). (1975). *Crime and the elderly.* Lexington, MA: D. C. Heath.

Huesmann, L. R., & Eron, L. D. (Eds.). (1986). *Television and the aggressive child: A cross-national comparison.* Hillsdale, NJ: Lawrence Erlbaum Associates.

Kantor, G. K., & Straus, M. A. (1987). The "drunken bum" theory of wife beating. *Social Problems, 34*, 213–230.

Leonard, K. E. (1989). The impact of explicit aggressive and implicit nonaggressive cues on aggression in intoxicated and sober males. *Personality and Social Psychology Bulletin, 15*, 390–400.

Leonard, K. E., Bromet, E. J., Parkinson, D. K., Day, N. L., & Ryan, C. M. (1985). Patterns of alcohol use and physically aggressive behavior. *Journal of Studies on Alcohol, 46*, 279–282.

Leshner, A. I. (1978). *An introduction to behavioral endocrinology.* New York: Oxford University Press.

Leventhal, H. (1974). Emotions: A basic problem for social psychology. In C. Nemeth (Ed.), *Social psychology: Classic and contemporary integrations* (pp. 1–51). Chicago: Rand McNally.

Libbey, P., & Bybee, R. (1979). The physical abuse of adolescents. *Journal of Social Issues, 35*(2), 101–126.

Lincoln, A. J., & Straus, M. A. (1985). *Crime and the family.* Springfield, IL: Charles C. Thomas.

Malmo, R. B. (1959). Activation: A neuropsychological dimension. *Psychological Review, 66,* 367–386.

McWhirter, N., & McWhirter, R. (1977). *Guinness sports record book, 1977–78.* New York: Sterling.

Mosher, D. L., & Sirkin, M. (1984). Measuring a macho personality constellation. *Journal of Research in Personality, 18,* 150–163.

Olweus, D. (1984). Development of stable aggressive reaction patterns in males. In R. J. Blanchard & D. C. Blanchard (Eds.), *Advances in the study of aggression* (Vol. 1, pp. 103–137). Orlando, FL: Academic Press.

Pagelow, M. D. (1984). *Family violence.* New York: Praeger.

Pastore, N. (1952). The role of arbitrariness in the frustration- aggression hypothesis. *Journal of Abnormal and Social Psychology, 47,* 728–731.

Patterson, G. R. (1979). A performance theory for coercive family interaction. In R. B. Cairns (Ed.), *The analysis of social interactions: Methods, issues, and illustrations* (pp. 119–162). Hillsdale, NJ: Lawrence Erlbaum Associates.

Patterson, G. R. (1984). Siblings: Fellow travelers in coercive family processes. In R. J. Blanchard & D. C. Blanchard (Eds.), *Advances in the study of aggression* (Vol. 1, pp. 173–215). Orlando, FL: Academic Press.

Quanty, M. B. (1976). Aggression catharsis: Experimental investigations and implications. In R. G. Geen & E. C. O'Neal (Eds.), *Perspectives on aggression* (pp. 99–132). New York: Academic Press.

Ramirez, J., Bryant, J., & Zillmann, D. (1982). Effects of erotica on retaliatory behavior as a function of level of prior provocation. *Journal of Personality and Social Psychology, 43,* 971–978.

Robins, L. N. (1978). Sturdy childhood predictors of adult anti-social behavior: Replications from longitudinal studies. *Psychological Medicine, 8,* 611–622.

Rothballer, A. B. (1967). Aggression, defense and neurohumors. In C. D. Clemente & D. B. Lindsley (Eds.), *Aggression and defense: Neural mechanisms and social patterns: Vol. 5. Brain function* (pp. 135–170). Berkeley: University of California Press.

Rule, B. G., Dyck, R., & Nesdale, A. R. (1978). Arbitrariness of frustration: Inhibition or instigation effects on aggression. *European Journal of Social Psychology, 8,* 237–244.

Russell, D. E. H. (1982). *Rape in marriage.* New York: Macmillan.

Schulman, M. (1979). *A survey of spousal violence against women in Kentucky.* Washington, DC: U. S. Department of Justice, Law Enforcement Assistance Administration.

Scott, J. P. (1958). *Aggression.* Chicago: University of Chicago Press.

Sedlak, A. J. (1988). The effects of personal experiences with couple violence on calling it "battering" and allocating blame. In G. T. Hotaling, D. Finkelhor, J. T. Kirkpatrick, & M. A. Straus (Eds.), *Coping with family violence* (pp. 31– 59). Newbury Park, CA: Sage.

Seligman, M. E. P. (1975). *Helplessness: On depression, development, and death.* San Francisco, CA: Freeman.

Shupe, A., Stacey, W. A., & Hazlewood, L. R. (1987). *Violent men, violent couples.* Lexington, MA: Lexington Books.

Steinmetz, S. (1977). *The cycle of violence: Assertive, aggressive, and abusive family interaction.* New York: Praeger.

Straus, M. A. (1978). Wife beating: How common and why? *Victimology, 23*(4), 443–458.

Straus, M. A., Gelles, R. J., & Steinmetz, S. K. (1980). *Behind closed doors: Violence in the American family.* Garden City, NY: Anchor.

Taylor, S. P., & Leonard, K. E. (1983). Alcohol and human physical aggression. In R. G. Geen & E. I. Donnerstein (Eds.), *Aggression: Theoretical and empirical reviews. Vol. 2. Issues in research* (pp. 77–101). New York: Academic Press.

Walker, L. E. (1978). Battered women and learned helplessness. *Victimology, 23*(4), 525–534.

Walker, L. E. (1979). *The battered woman.* New York: Harper Colophon.

Wilson, G. D. (1982). Feminism and marital dissatisfaction. *Individual Differences, 3,* 345–347.

Wolfgang, M. E. (1958). *Patterns in criminal homicide.* Philadelphia, PA: University of Pennsylvania.

Zillmann, D. (1971). Excitation transfer in communication-mediated aggressive behavior. *Journal of Experimental Social Psychology, 7,* 419–434.

Zillmann, D. (1979). *Hostility and aggression.* Hillsdale, NJ: Lawrence Erlbaum Associates.

Zillmann, D. (1983). Transfer of excitation in emotional behavior. In J. T. Cacioppo & R. E. Petty (Eds.), *Social psychophysiology: A sourcebook* (pp. 215–240). New York: Guilford.

Zillmann, D. (1984). *Connections between sex and aggression.* Hillsdale, NJ: Lawrence Erlbaum Associates.

Zillmann, D. (1986). Coition as emotion. In D. Byrne & K. Kelley (Eds.), *Alternative approaches to the study of sexual behavior* (pp. 173–199). Hillsdale, NJ: Lawrence Erlbaum Associates.

Zillmann, D. (1988). Cognition-excitation interdependencies in aggressive behavior. *Aggressive Behavior, 14,* 51–64.

Zillmann, D., Bryant, J., Cantor, J. R., & Day, K. D. (1975). Irrelevance of mitigating circumstances in retaliatory behavior at high levels of excitation. *Journal of Research in Personality, 9,* 282–293.

Zillmann, D., & Bryant, J. (1989). *Effects of ethanol intoxication before versus after provocation on aggressive behavior.* Unpublished manuscript, University of Alabama, Tuscaloosa, AL.

Zillmann, D., & Cantor, J. R. (1976). Effect of timing of information about mitigating circumstances on emotional responses to provocation and retaliatory behavior. *Journal of Experimental Social Psychology, 12,* 38–55.

Zillmann, D., Hoyt, J. L., & Day, K. D. (1974). Strength and duration of the effect of aggressive, violent, and erotic communications on subsequent aggressive behavior. *Communication Research, 1,* 286–306.

Zillmann, D., Johnson, R. C., & Day, K. D. (1974). Attribution of apparent arousal and proficiency of recovery from sympathetic activation affecting excitation transfer to aggressive behavior. *Journal of Experimental Social Psychology, 10*, 503–515.

Zillmann, D., Katcher, A. H., & Milavsky, B. (1972). Excitation transfer from physical exercise to subsequent aggressive behavior. *Journal of Experimental Social Psychology, 8*, 247–259.

Zillmann, D., & Weaver, J. B. (1989). Pornography and men's sexual callousness toward women. In D. Zillmann & J. Bryant (Eds.), *Pornography: Research advances and policy considerations* (pp. 95–125). Hillsdale, NJ: Lawrence Erlbaum Associates.

Cultural Diversity in Intimate Intercultural Relationships

Gary Fontaine
University of Hawaii

In making a recent major theoretical contribution to the understanding of communication in interpersonal relationships, Cushman and Cahn (1985) argued that "the contemporary problem of communication is how to ensure cooperation among people who are diverse in perspectives and interdependent in regard to the resolution of mutual problems" (p. 11). There may be few persons that better typify this challenge than those involved in intimate intercultural relationships such as intercultural marriages. They commonly represent extremes of diversity and, as with any marriage, are continuingly engaged in attempts to resolve a broad range of mutual problems over an extended time period. Similarly, Fontaine and Dorch (1980) argued that a

> primary reason for focusing on *close* intercultural relationships is that for such relationships to remain stable over time, the partners must have developed workable strategies for dealing with diversity and/or be receiving benefits that offset the greater costs. Identification of these strategies and benefits should have fruitful implications for improving the quality of other diverse, less intimate but important intercultural encounters. (p. 230)

There has been a recent increase in research on intercultural couples—particularly marriages—paralleling their increased frequency. Unfortunately, however, few studies have contributed significantly to our understanding of the role communication plays in bridging the gap created by differing cultures. Thus, intercultural research has yet to realize the potential just discussed.

Many of the studies in the area (particularly the early ones) focused on the frequency, demographics, motives, and relative stability of intercultural marriage (e.g., Carter & Glick, 1976; Glick, 1972; Lampe, 1982; Nitta, 1988). For instance, although "intercultural" marriage is increasing in the mainland United States, it represents just over 1% of all U.S. marriages. In Hawaii, however, it is remaining stable at 35% to 40% of all marriages. Interpretation and comparability of these rates is problematic because operational definitions of *intercultural* vary greatly: Studies focus variously on *interracial, interethnic, inter country of origin, international, interreligious,* and so forth.

Some research has attempted to identify the types of problems intercultural couples face (e.g., Graham, Moeai, & Shizuru, 1985) and, in some cases, the special benefits they provide (e.g., Brislin, 1983; Fontaine, 1986; Fontaine & Dorch, 1980; Rivers & Fontaine, 1979). The two most comprehensive review works on the subject do a bit of each (Stuart & Abt, 1973; Tseng, McDermott, & Maretzki, 1977). They do deal somewhat with strategies for handling diversity, but largely with anecdotal methods and little theoretical umbrella that would allow us to generalize. Two studies that do focus on such strategies are by Hunt and Coller (1957) on Filipino wives of U.S. servicemen and a more recent one by Kim (1977) with Asian wives of U.S. servicemen.

Even those studies that have dealt with strategies have again used the different operational definitions of intercultural mentioned previously that—without any theoretical tie among them—make comparison of findings difficult. Thus, studies have generally used fairly obvious demographic indicants of culture rather than attempted to determine if the participants in the relationships did, in fact, differ in their perceptions of the world, their relationship, and the tasks in it.

In contrast to the studies just mentioned, this chapter describes strategies for dealing with diversity in intercultural intimate relationships, presents a theoretically derived optimal strategy for doing so, and examines empirical evidence for that strategy. It then describes the key communication-related skills necessary for participants in intimate intercultural relationships to use the strategy effectively. Finally, implications for the role of counseling in facilitating the development of these skills is discussed. The overall objective is to suggest a theoretical framework that can usefully structure future research on intercultural couples. Thus, the chapter is directed to teachers and students who are interested in better understanding strategies for handling diversity effectively and to helpers and counselors who are looking for theoretically derived methods for best assisting couples in dealing with the cultural diversity in their relationships.

STRATEGIES FOR DEALING WITH CULTURAL DIVERSITY

Recently Fontaine (1989) presented several commonly described strategies for dealing with cultural diversity in a broad range of tasks in a variety of relationships. Some of the theoretical issues dealt with were relevant primarily to those engaged in relatively short-term interactions such as those encountered on an international assignment in business or diplomacy or delivering a service to a culturally different client domestically. These are contexts in which the *tasks* to be completed are generally more central than whatever *relationship* must be established to complete them. Many of the issues, however, have an equal relevance to effectiveness in intimate intercultural relationships in which the relationship may be more important than any specific tasks within it. The purpose here is to highlight some of these latter issues.

The intercultural literature describes the following general strategies for dealing with cultural diversity: We sometimes deal with it by attempting to complete tasks "our way" (the same way we always do in our home culture) because we do not recognize cultural differences or we feel that "our way" is best; we sometimes attempt to do it "their way" (i.e., "when in Rome do as the Romans"); or we sometimes try to "compromise" (do some of it "our way" and some "their way"). I suggest, however, that these commonly described strategies are rarely the ones used by those consistently effective interculturally. This is so primarily because each requires at least some participants to become skilled fairly quickly in another culture's ways of completing tasks. But it has taken natives a lifetime to learn to do it "their way:" Outsiders are not going to learn to do such tasks very well in a 1-day orientation or a 1-week training program. So, in such cases, "their way," "our way," and "compromise" (requiring each to learn at least some of the other's way) could not be the basis of consistent effectiveness interculturally (Fontaine, 1989).

Further, in intercultural relationships one does not interact with a nation, race, ethnicity, or culture on any *macro*level. One does so with specific people on the specific tasks required by the relationship (be it business, diplomacy, or a marriage). Thus, the wisdom of relying on generalized descriptions of how people do things at the macroculture level is questionable. Again, there must be other strategies on which effective relationships are based. I suggest that dealing with diversity consistently effectively requires developing intercultural *microcultures* (IMCs) within which participants from different cultures can negotiate, make decisions, advise, manage, supervise, teach, train, resolve conflicts, or communicate *between* cultures (Fontaine, 1989).

IMCs are shared ways of completing tasks based on the *ecologies* of those tasks that must be completed in a relationship. The ecology consists of the social, biological, and physical environment in which the tasks are completed. Task participants must arrive at a way to do the task that is not necessarily the way either of them would normally do it within their own culture, but in a way that is adequately tuned to the task ecology they face—one important characteristic of which in intercultural relationships is that they commonly differ in expections about how to do such tasks. Although on individual occasions "our way," "their way," or some "compromise" might work (i.e., be a useful IMC), we must remember that it works because of its appropriateness to the ecology on that occasion—not because it is *the way* to do it effectively generally.

In addition to being more effective because it is tuned to the task ecology, an IMC strategy tends to deflate the conflict and resentment often produced by alternative strategies. With these latter strategies, the way of doing things is based on who has the most power. Whether a participant is successful in imposing "our way" or is forced to accept "their way," the power conflict usually results in a residue of resentment that affects subsequent interactions. With an IMC strategy participants can see that the criterion for selecting a way to do things is the *appropriateness to the task* ecology rather than the power of the participants.

STRATEGIES IN INTIMATE INTERCULTURAL RELATIONSHIPS

In intimate intercultural relationships diversity is typically encountered in values, the meaning of "marriage," stereotypes and prejudices, food and drink, sex, male–female relationships, time, place of residence, politics, friends, neighbors and the community, finances, in-laws, religion, childrearing, language, dealing with stress, language/communication, illness, marital goals and objectives, decision making, conflict resolution, and so forth (see also Markoff, 1977; Romano, 1988). There is evidence that intimate intercultural relationships approach such diversity with the same range of strategies as previously identified. For instance, Tseng (1977) described "one-way adjustment" and Romano (1988) described "obliteration" and "submission" in ways similar to "our way" and "their way" strategies. Both authors stressed that although these strategies are common they rarely work in the long run. Tseng described "alternative," "simultaneous," "mid-point," and "mixing" strategies as forms of "compromise." Romano used the latter term. Again, as Romano pointed out, although in principle this strategy might be good, in practice it does not work well because one gives up some of his or her important interests or principles to another making the dimension of power salient in the relationship.

Tseng described "creative adjustment" and Romano described "consensus" in a manner similar in some respects to building IMCs. In the former, participants "invent an entirely new way because old ones are incompatible or otherwise undesirable" and they need to be "open-minded enough to see that many other aways of living exist in the world, and [are] willing to try new things and to make necessary changes" (p. 102). In the latter:

> consensus is related to compromise in that it implies a give-and-take on the part of both partners; but it is different in that it is not a trade-off but an agreement, and no scores are kept. In a consensus model neither partner sacrifices things which are essential to his or her well-being—as often happens in other situations. (p. 124)

Thus, both Tseng and Romano described strategies that address issues related to the relationship ecology but neither explicitly identifies the role of the microculture–ecology link. There is evidence, however, that some couples do attempt to make just such a link. Hunt and Coller (1957) found "a decided tendency toward the development of a specialized type of culture which had significant variations from either the American or the Filipino pattern" (p. 229). This specialized culture addressed the particular ecology these couples faced.

The descriptions of Tseng and Romano and the findings of Hunt and Coller center more on the partners' agreeing on ways to deal with diversity across many tasks than on addressing each task individually as the IMC model suggests. This makes sense because the stability of a long-term relationship provides a relatively consistent ecology (the same partners, the same families, the same neighbors, the same community factors, the same cultural differences, etc.) over time and can thus allow more habitual ways of completing tasks to develop and be effective. In such cases, I call the strategy an intercultural *organizational* culture (or IOC) rather than *micro*culture. In this respect, the optimal strategy may be somewhat different from the IMC strategy described in Fontaine (1989) and applied to the relatively shorter term relationships in international assignments in business or diplomacy. An example of such a strategy is presented here.:

> In a 2-year-old marriage between an American husband and his Taiwanese wife, a problem developed in how each could effectively communicate displeasure with something the partner did. The husband would typically try to confront his wife verbally and directly (as is typical in the United States), leading her to either become violently defensive or withdraw completely from the discussion. She, on the other hand, would attempt to

indicate her displeasure by changes in mood and eye contact (typical of Chinese culture) that were either not noticed (or uninterpretable) by her husband. Thus, neither "his way" nor "her way" was working and they could not see any realistic way to "compromise."

Unfortunately, the couple was newly arrived in Hawaii and did not have access to relatives nor the time to develop close friends locally who could serve as third-party "intermediaries" in their conflicts—a strategy commonly used by intercultural couples. Out of apparent frustration, in this case, the wife began writing her complaints on little notes—always including reaffirmation of her love—and leaving them around the house for her husband to find. He then could appreciate her concerns and alter his behavior without a verbal confrontation. Similarly, he began leaving notes—often by writing on the bathroom mirror—and she began to better appreciate his perspective. They thus developed and used an IOC for resolving conflict that was tuned to the ecology of their particular relationship. It worked, but it was not the customary way for either Chinese or Americans to resolve problems. Further, it would be quite likely that as they got to know each other better, or as they made new friends, or as they had children that might intercept the the notes, or if they moved to another location, this IOC might become less ecologically appropriate. In such cases, perhaps the third-party intermediary might be more useful. Thus, relationship ecology can change over time.

In another sense, of course, intimate intercultural relationships are related to many aspects of international assignments. Many intercultural marriages involved international "assignments" in which one spouse or sometimes both are living outside their home country and everything said about long-term international assignments is relevant to them. These relationships are the focus of Romano (1988), and she identified several types of them:

Those in which partners meet in the country of one of the partners and remain there.

Those in which partners meet in the country of one of the partners, marry, and move to the country of the other.

Those in which partners meet and remain in or move to a country that is not home to either of them.

The first is typical of foreign students, the second of military personnel stationed overseas, and the third of those in business or diplomatic communities. The first and second generally provide strong social support for doing things "our way" or "their way." Romano noted that many couples feel that living in a third country is "the only (or ideal) way for intercultural marriages to succeed" (p. 53). This may be the setting most conducive to developing an IOC.

A SENSE OF PRESENCE

When completing tasks in relationships with others *in our own culture* we are often much less than 100% "present" psychologically. Our mind may be occupied by things that happened on the way to the task, previous tasks, the next one, characteristics of the people or facility unrelated to the task, a problem at home, how badly we need a vacation, and so forth. We are not "tuned-in" to the ecology of the immediate task. Because so many tasks are routine and predictable, we do not need to be. We can get by on being 25% "present"; each task can be successfully completed by applying rules that have become habitual.

But when dealing with those from *another culture* many tasks are not routine. At least one new and important characteristic of the task ecology is involved—the way *others* expect to do things. Because their expectations are often *unpredictable* beforehand we rarely have the opportunity for adequate preparation: We must be prepared to "do it on the spot." Because ecologies so often *change* even as we are "doing it," we need to monitor them continuously. Because there is always the danger— particularly at times of stress or frustration—of falling back on *habits* developed in the past and probably ineffective interculturally, we need to monitor our own behavior as well. To be interculturally effective, we need to be more involved, perhaps 100% *present*! I suggest, then, that a key skill interculturally is *a sense of presence*—an awareness of the necessary, possible, and desirable in each task (Fontaine, 1989).

Unlike *attention*, which involves a *narrow* focus on one or a few specific characteristics of the task ecology, a *sense of presence* involves a *broad* focus on all potentially relevant characteristics. For instance, in a multicultural classroom it is not adequate for the teacher to attend to one cue alone (e.g., student-to-teacher eye contact) to determine if students are interested in and understanding the material. The teacher may need to additionally monitor student-to-student eye contact, student-to-book eye contact, note taking, facial expressions, talking among students, general activity level, and so forth. They may all have implications for student attentiveness—and different implications for different cultures! The teacher in the intercultural classroom needs a sense of presence.

A sense of presence is in some ways related to *empathy*—the ability to "get into the other person's shoes" and see how the world looks and feels to another person (Brislin, 1983). However, although awareness of the perceptions and feelings of others is certainly part of a sense of presence, developing IMCs requires more: We may need to know more than just "our way" and "their way," because neither may work well with culturally different participants. We need to be aware of a broader range of ecological characteristics than cultural differences alone to select the best way to proceed (e.g., the role of family, friends, and other potential support groups, the organization for which we work, community expectations, financial resources, and so forth).

Fontaine and Dorch (1980) stressed that intercultural couples have a larger source of potential problems and more variable potential causes of those problems than intracultural couples. Thus, the former require more "presence" to identify problems and the likely causes of those problems. Most studies of causal attribution in intracultural relationships (e.g., Jones & Nisbett, 1971; Orvis, Kelley, & Butler, 1976) indicate a decided tendency to attribute problems to dispositional characteristics of the partner (e.g., "they are lazy," or "abusive," or "don't listen," or "don't like me," etc.). To the degree that intercultural partners do have heightened senses of presence, we would expect them to be more open, flexible, or variable in their attributions and consider the importance of ecological factors other than just dispositional personality characteristics of their partner (e.g., situational and cultural factors). As Brislin (1983) suggested:

> If people . . . engage in intimate contact, then they must engage in some thinking from the others' point of view. The people would inevitably learn about some of the less visible situational factors and would incorporate these into their explanations . . . and that people who have had intercultural friendships and romances will give more situational explanations of behavior. (p. 10)

The limited research on causal attribution in *inter*cultural relationships suggests that that may well be the case. Brislin (1981) found that in a variety of samples (from Hawaii, New Jersey, and Newfoundland) those who had experienced intercultural friendships or romances used more situational explanations. Situational factors were operationally defined as characteristics of the task, the actions of other people, and the physical setting.

Goldstein (1983) did not find more situational attributions for younger ($\bar{x} = 21$) university students having had *only* intercultural versus *only* intracultural romantic relationships. However, she did find that older students ($\bar{x} = 25$) reporting a history of *both* intra- and intercultural relationships did indicate more situational attributions over the status of their current relationship than younger students had. And most interestingly she found that, for the older students in an intercultural relationship, the longer the relationship the greater the percentage of situational attributions. Given that both intercultural and intracultural relationship subjects gave more dispositional than situational attributions (74% vs. 72% for younger students and 57% vs. 65% for the older students, respectively), this finding indicates that those older students in the (arguably) more successful longer term intercultural relationships had more balance between situational and dispositional attributions. Such, of course, would be predicted if presence were an important relationship skill that enabled them to develop IOCs in those task areas critical to relationship survival.

One of the problems of presence is the high energy required to maintain it. For short-term tasks, that probably is not a problem. But for long-term tasks or for many tasks continually encountered in an intimate relationship, it could be a major drain on the partners' energy. It could have, then, long-term destabilizing effect on the relationship. Thus, ironically, the use of one key intercultural skill—necessary in the short term—could be damaging in the long term. It may explain some of the "Romeo and Juliet effect" noted by Rubin (1973) and Fontaine and Dorch (1980) that, although shorter term intercultural couples reported more love and greater satisfaction with their relationship, longer term couples did not. Perhaps, in part, they just get worn down by the challenge of attempting to maintain high presence.

Thus implied, is the importance for those engaged in intimate intercultural relationships—and perhaps any long-term intercultural relationship—to move from the task to the organizational level of culture with respect to how they complete tasks in their relationship. As presented earlier, the relatively consistent ecology can allow for these more habitual ways of doing things to be effective.

COMMUNICATION SKILLS

Because intercultural couples are often more disparate in their perceptions associated with the relationship and because the development of effective IOCs are *mutual* partner responsibilities a particular emphasis is placed on the importance of communication. Yet, ironically, cultural differences in perceptions for how to communicate can make communication, itself, more difficult. Cultures prescribe what may be discussed and when. Many cultures do not expect affection to be verbalized and are suspicious when it is; others expect it to be verbalized and are mistrustful if it is not. Cultures differ in the concern for honesty versus harmony when communicating and the directness with which messages are worded. There is also a vast array of differences in meanings attached to verbal and nonverbal symbols, the relative reliance on these symbols, and the meaning of silence.

Romano (1988) stressed importance of communication skills in intercultural marriage and notes that most of the couples she interviewed:

> cited the ability to communicate as being one of the most essential ingredients of success in marriage, though admitting that it took a lot of work, patience and care. . . . Something few of them actually identified, but which was universally present in the better communicators, was clarity of thought: they themselves knew what they were trying to say and so were able to keep at it until they were sure that they had communicated the right message. Those who were less clear in their own minds (especially regarding what they expected from one another and what they wanted from the relationship) had a harder time communicating. (pp. 136–137)

This observation also interestingly indicates a possible relationship between communication skills and a sense of presence: Those more aware of the relationship ecology were better able to communicate with one another within the relationship.

Rohrlich (1988) reviewed the quite scanty literature on communication in intercultural marriages and noted several areas of research and types of methodologies. She stressed the necessity for evaluation and dyadic decision making as communication skills necessary to implement the adjustment styles mentioned by Tseng (1977) and others. She stressed the importance of "careful listening, unbiased questioning and tactful expressing" (p. 42) and noted that these are unlikely to have been skills taught in both or either of the partner's upbringing.

When communicating with others from our own culture we usually assume that the symbols used mean the same to them as they do to us and our attempts at both information exchange and social influence are based on this assumption. But because of our different experiences with symbols a given symbol will *never* mean exactly the same thing to anybody else! Nevertheless, we can often get away with the improper assumption that others understand precisely what we mean. Interculturally we rarely can! For those in intimate intercultural relationships, skills in information exchange and social influence must be supported by an array of other communication skills.

If the partners are from cultures with different languages often the first communication skill required is *matching language*. Whereas in some intercultural contexts such as business or diplomacy, participants have the option of retaining an interpreter, that is rather impractical and otherwise inappropriate for those in intimate relationships (although the field is full of anecdotes about the use of bilingual friends to translate love letters—and even marriage contracts—in budding relationships). One of the partners usually learns the language of the other. The major language matching concerns are then those associated with communicating when one partner is not using his or her *primary* language.

The person for whom the language is not primary must expend much more effort speaking and listening and as a consequence will tire and loose concentration more quickly, interpret meanings ideosyncratically, loose the train of reasoning, and so forth. Generally, a long relationship discussion or argument in our own language leaves us fatigued. We should be able to empathize with the frustration and fatigue experienced by marriage partners when the language is *not* their own and every phrase requires maximal concentration! These couples must speak slowly, have more breaks, and get more feedback from one another. They must learn to attribute many of their problems to these language difficulties (even if they *can* speak the same language) rather than the more common tendency to attribute them to their partner's lack of intelligence, education, manners, social skills, or some other inadequacy.

Another important communication skill, particularly in the early stages of relationship development, is *ritual matching*. A ritualistic message is designed to communicate that we know what is appropriate for a person like us to say to a person like them in a situation like this. We show we are *competent* in our culture. The meaning does not lie in the content of the message. Thus, when we say "good morning" to a colleague the comment should *not* be understood to mean that we think it is a good morning or even that we wish him or her to have a good morning. It means that we know that that is the appropriate message to convey to a colleague first thing in the morning in our culture.

In intercultural relationships the chief importance of matching ritual is as a *cultural test*: If partners speak the same language, are they from the same culture? If they exchange ritual smoothly—if one asks if the other would like a beer and receives a smooth reply ("Sure would!")—it indicates that they are at least at some level culturally similar. They could then proceed to share task information, cautiously confident that the words used would have similar meaning to both. If the exchange of ritual goes less smoothly—the partner replies "No, I'd rather have tea with clover honey"—they have a problem! The lack of ritual matching indicates that they may not be sufficiently similar culturally and the future sharing of information is unlikely to go smoothly: They must *first* share perspectives. *values*

Perspective sharing involves exchanging the perspective from which each partner is approaching a task and from which they are attributing meaning to events and symbols. It is particularly important when partners are coming from different cultures. Perspective sharing produces an *awareness* of the perspective of the other person. At a minimum, such an awareness is a necessary prerequisite to both exchanging information and persuasion. In an intercultural relationship without an understanding of the perspective from which the partner is giving and receiving information, that "information" is at best meaningless, at worst misleading.

An important aspect of perspective sharing involves what Hall (1981) referred to as low- and high-context communication. In *low-context* communication the burden of information exchange lies in the symbols themselves (the words) such that if anything very complex must be communicated it takes lots of words often arranged complexly. *High-context* communication on the other hand relies heavily on the context of the interaction (including the partners' shared experience and their relationship to one another) to convey information: The symbols only serve as "cues" to the salient aspects of the context. In high-context communication the meaning of the symbols cannot be fully understood without reference to that context. Cultures differ significantly in the extent to which they use generally high- versus low-context communication. In intercultural relationships, additional communication problems occur when one partner is from a culture with a high-context language and the other a low-context language. The former is overwhelmed with words while trying to ascertain what the words are cueing, making it seem that the partner is "all words and no substance." The latter is looking for words and gets far too few of them to make any sense of things, making the partner seem "inscrutable." In both cases, there is a need to match the level of context between partners.

Further, low-context cultures commonly place the burden of communicating a complaint on the person with the complaint. He or she is expected to make explicit what the problem is so the couple can discuss and do something about it. In high-context cultures, however, the burden is on the partner to discern from the relationship context the reason for an often very subtly expressed complaint. As a consequence, one partner is always frustrated by the other's refusal to "talk" and the other is overwhelmed with "talk" and the first's insensitivity. Neither feels "understood," an important ingredient in long-term, intimate relationships (Cahn, 1987).

A final skill supportive of information exchange and persuasion is *matching agendas*. That is, when the partners do talk, what do they talk about? In any discussion each partner has several agenda items he or she wishes to be dealt with. Those items are usually prioritized in some way. But the overlap of items and priorities is rarely perfect—or even good. What frequently happens is that one talks about his or her first agenda item while the other "fades out." When the first has finished the other talks and the first "fades out." Without matching agendas, discussions end with both partners happy because they both said what they wanted to say, but no information is *exchanged*. Nothing is being shared but *time*. Interculturally, because of likely differences in agenda items or at least their priorities, a much more prepared and explicit agenda may be required. Discussion of the agenda, itself, can be an important aspect of the dialogue.

As a final note on communication, although partners in intimate intercultural relationships may encounter more differences they may also be more prepared for them—thus engaging in more ritual, perspective, and agenda matching—than their intracultural counterparts. Consequently, they may be less ignorant of their differences than intracultural couples who all too frequently assume their partner looks at the world and their relationship as they do—only to be surprised and shocked when events prove otherwise.

STRESS MANAGEMENT SKILLS

All couples face stress: stress from sources outside and inside the relationship. Intercultural couples might be expected to suffer from more of both for reasons easily derived from the discussion thus far. Additionally, intercultural couples—at least initially in their relationship—are likely to experience the stress of "culture shock" (Furnham & Bochner, 1986) and, if one or both are living in a foreign country, "ecoshock" (Fontaine, 1989). Thus, as in so much of life, the success of these couples depends significantly on their skills to cope with stress.

There is no new or different type of stress management skill appropriate to intimate intercultural relationships. However, the partners must often have available a broader range of strategies to choose from than they might within their own culture. The reason is that the appropriateness of strategies differs markedly from culture to culture: drinking, praying, shopping, meditating, hiking, windsurfing, and suicide are not culturally universal in appropriateness. As Romano (1988) pointed out, different or conflicting styles for managing stress is a major problem for intercultural couples.

IMPLICATIONS FOR COUNSELING

In my previous work (e.g., Fontaine, 1989) I have noted that the skills described here cannot be just "screened for" or "trained for," but that effective international and intercultural interactions must be *managed* in terms of several or all of the programs through which assistance or intervention can be provided and with the objective of aiding in using an IMC strategy for handling diversity. These programs often include: screening and self-selection, orientation, training, organizational and social support, and arranging travel and accommodation (if required). Intimate intercultural relationships do not normally occur in a formal organizational setting in which these programs can be provided. There may still be some informal and personal screening (is this person good for me?), self-selection (can I do this?), orientation (what problems are we likely to encounter?). There is rarely any formal training for such relationships (although some may receive intercultural training for work-related purposes and that may help some—particularly if relocation to another country is involved). Kim (1977), for instance, recommended both orientation and language/culture training for Asian wives of U.S. servicemen. However, a key type of institutional intervention appropriate to the needs of many intercultural couples is counseling.

A great deal of recent progress has been made in defining the skills required for counselors to generally be more interculturally sensitive and specifying the types of training useful in providing those skills (Pedersen, 1981). Most focus in this work has emphasized skills for counselors to provide effective counseling to clients from a culture different from themselves (e.g., a Japanese-American social worker and a Vietnamese client). Little attention has focused, however, on the more complex context in which the clients themselves are from different cultures (as in an intercultural marriage) and at least one must be from a culture different from the counselor. There are some fairly explicit implications, however, from the issues addressed in this chapter for what counselors in this context could most effectively do to help those couples deal with the cultural diversity in their relationships.

To the degree that the use of IMCs or IOCs is the optimal strategy for consistent effectiveness in completing tasks in intimate intercultural relationships and thus presence, communication, and stress management skills are important, effective intervention by counselors should involve:

1. helping couples identify the range of tasks essential to maintaining a satisfactory relationship;
2. sensitizing them to the ecology of each of these tasks (including their parameters of acceptability and skill and their cultural differences in expectations for how to complete them);
3. helping them expand the range of alternative ways to complete each task beyond just their culturally based habits; and
4. helping them select an alternative that meets the ecological demands—that is tuned to the specific ecology within which tasks must be completed in their particular relationship.

There are a variety of ways this intervention could be provided ranging from an analytical "task-analysis" technique (Fontaine, 1989) to guided "experiential exercises" (e.g., Pedersen, 1981). The former involves the counselor helping participants develop lists for Steps 1 through 3 just mentioned and then for Step 4 select the alternative most supported by the ecology for each task. Once participants have completed the processes several times they report relative ease in bringing the technique back home and applying it as needed. A more experiential approach that shows promise is derived from Pedersen's triad model used frequently in training interculturally skilled counselors. Participants role play a task situation and the counselor interrupts as needed to identify behaviors that are inconsistent with the task ecology. The key, of course, is for the counselor to select from among the range of techniques, those most appropriate to the cultures, the relationships, and the individual characteristics of his or her particular clients.

REFERENCES

Brislin, R. W. (1983). The benefits of close intercultural relationships. In J. Berry and S. Irvine (Eds.), *Human assessment and cultural factors* (pp. 521–538). New York: Plenum.

Cahn, D. D. (1987). *Letting go: a practical theory of relationship disengagement and reengagement.* Albany, New York: State University of New York Press.

Carter, H., & Glick, P. C. (1976). *Marriage and divorce: A social and economic study.* Cambridge, MA: Harvard University Press.

Cushman, D. P., & Cahn, D. D. (1985). *Communication in interpersonal relationships.* Albany, NY: State University of New York Press.

Fontaine, G. (1986). The roles of social support systems in overseas relocation: Implications for intercultural training. *International Journal of Intercultural Relations, 10,* 361–378.

Fontaine, G. (1989). *Managing international assignments: The strategy for success.* Englewood Cliffs, NJ: Prentice-Hall.

Fontaine, G., & Dorch, E. (1980). Problems and benefits of close intercultural relationships. *International Journal of Intercultural Relations, 4,* 329–337.

Furnham, A., & Bochner, S. (1986). *Culture shock: Psychological reactions to unfamiliar environments.* New York: Methuen.

Glick, C. E. (1972). Interracial marriage and admixture in Hawaii. *Social Biology, 17,* 278–291.

Goldstein, S. B. (1983). *Attribution in intercultural relationships.* Unpublished Master's thesis, University of Hawaii, Honolulu, HI.

Graham, M. A., Moeai, J., & Shizuru, L. S. (1985). Intercultural marriages: an intrareligious perspective. *International Journal of Intercultural Relations, 9,* 427–434.

Hall, E. E. (1981). *Beyond culture.* Garden City, NY: Anchor.

Hunt, C. L., & Coller, R. W. (1957). Intermarriage and cultural change: a study of Philippine-American marriages. *Social Forces, 35,* 223–230.

Jones, E. E., & Nisbett, R. E. (1971). *The actor and the observer: Divergent perceptions of the causes of behavior.* Morristown, NJ: General Learning Press.

Kim, B. L. (1977). Asian wives of U.S. servicemen: Women in shadows. *Amerasia Journal, 4*(1), 91–115.

Lampe, P. E. (1982). Interethnic dating: reasons for and against. *International Journal of Intercultural Relations, 6,* 115–126.

Markoff, R. (1977). Intercultural marriage: Problem areas. In W. Tseng, J. F. McDermott, & T. W. Maretzki (Eds.), *Adjustment in intercultural marriage* (pp. 51–61). Honolulu, HI: University of Hawaii Press.

Nitta, F. (1988). *Kokusai kekkon*: Trends in intercultural Marriage in Japan. *International Journal of Intercultural Relations, 12,* 205–232.

Orvis, B. R., Kelley, H. H., & Butler, D. (1976). Attributional conflict in you couples. In J. H. Harvey, W. Ickes, & R. F. Kidd (Eds.), *New directions in attribution research* (Vol. 1, pp. 353–386). Hillside, NJ: Lawrence Erlbaum Associates.

Pedersen, P. (1981). The triad model: A cross-cultural coalition against the problem. In R. Corsini (Ed.), *Handbook of innovative psychotherapies* (pp. 840–854). New York: Wiley.

Rivers, N. M., & Fontaine, G. F. (1979). Friendships with Whites and status as predictors of Black students' satisfaction with an integrated university. *International Journal of Intercultural Relations, 3,* 227–231.

Rohrlich, B. F. (1988). Dual-culture marriage and communication. *International Journal of Intercultural Relations, 12,* 34–44.

Romano, D. (1988). *Intercultural marriage: Promises and pitfalls.* Yarmouth, MA: Intercultural Press.

Rubin, Z. (1973). *Liking and loving: An invitation to social psychology.* New York: Holt, Rinehard & Winston.

Stuart, I. R., & Abt, L. E. (1973). *Interracial marriage: Expectations and realities.* New York: Grossman.

Tseng, W. S. (1977). Adjustment in intercultural marriage. In W. Tseng, J. F. McDermott, & T. W. Maretzki (Eds.), *Adjustment in intercultural marriage,* (pp. 93–103). Honolulu, HI: University of Hawaii Press.

Tseng, W. S., McDermott, J. F., & Maretzki, T. W. (Eds.). (1977). *Adjustment in intercultural marriage.* Honolulu, HI: University of Hawaii Press.

Teaching and Learning the Skills of Interpersonal Confrontation

Rory Remer
Paul de Mesquita
University of Kentucky

The complexity of human interaction creates the inevitability of human conflict. How conflicts are recognized and resolved largely depends on a complex interpersonal communication process known as *confrontation.* Confrontation involves a process of face-to-face communication through which conflicts are uncovered and managed.

According to Egan (1986), confrontation is viewed as an interpersonal invitation to identify self-defeating and harmful defenses and to take advantage of opportunities to learn better ways of managing conflicts. Confrontation involves the skill of challenging an individual to identify ineffective defenses (interpersonal discrepancies, distortions, games, and smokescreens) and to achieve a sense of self-understanding resulting in a functional change in behavior.

In this chapter, confrontation is presented as a complex helping process of human interaction involving discrete skills that can be task analyzed for learning and training purposes. Although interpersonal conflict and confrontation skills have received considerable attention (e.g., Carkhuff, 1969; Coser, 1956; Deutsch, 1973; Egan, 1986; Filley, 1975; Putnam & Poole, 1987), specific instructional models for the teaching and learning of interpersonal confrontation skills are lacking. A six-stage confrontation process through which individuals learn to recognize ineffective interaction patterns, create opportunities for conflict resolution, and develop more adaptive interaction skills is presented. The model is derived from psychodramatic enactment theory (Hollander, 1968; Moreno, 1985) and delineates those essential skills related to successful conflict management.

There are a number of possible structures that could fit the process of interpersonal confrontation. The one employed here comes from the literature on psychodramatic theory—Hollander's (1968) Enactment Curve (see Fig. 11.1).

Briefly, psychodramatic theory characterizes life as a continuous series of enactments between and among people. Each enactment consists of a warm-up, the rise of the enactment proper to a catharsis of abreaction (the focusing/ releasing of energies toward a particular objective), the integration of those energies to a completion of the enactment (catharsis of integration), and a closure/withdrawal. If this process is not interrupted (i.e., continues through its completion with adequate time for all stages) the enactment will produce a spontaneous outcome (i.e., one that is creative, adequate, novel, within the parameters of the context in which it occurs and immediate, in the present). If the process is interrupted or inadequate in any of its phases it will result in "act hunger," a sense of incompletion. Our aim here is to help ensure that the uses of confrontation skills can be characterized as spontaneous acts, in the psychodramatic sense of the word (Moreno, 1985).

THE CONFRONTATION PROCESS AS A SPONTANEOUS ENACTMENT

As we conceive of confrontation, it is a process that begins far before the actual interaction, as used in the confrontation model outlined by Remer (1984) and Watson and Remer (1984). We outline the extended model

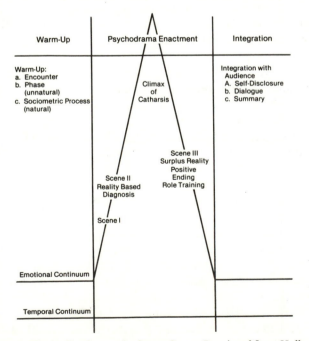

FIG. 11.1. The Hollander psychodrama Curve. Reprinted from Hollander (1968, p. 14) by permission of author.

briefly, as an introduction. At the same time we indicate how it parallels the Hollander (1968) Enactment Curve. Then we look at each stage of the confrontation process at greater length, giving an explanation/ rationale for its inclusion, indicating possible difficulties, and anticipating questions, as far as possible.

The confrontation process has six stages (see Fig 11.2). They are described on page 228.

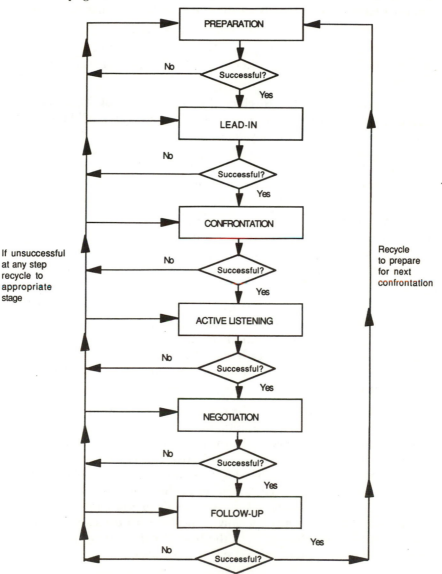

FIG. 11.2. Flow chart of confrontation process.

1. Preparation: includes: (a) judging whether the relationship is worth the investment of energy, (b) deciding the level or type of confrontation involved, (c) reviewing knowledge of self and the other(s) involved, (d) choosing the appropriate time, place and context, (e) planning the wording of the confrontation and lead-in, (f) readying oneself to switch mind sets from confronter to listener, and (g) pondering possible acceptable behavioral changes/contracts that might eventuate. This stage includes a large part, if not all, of the warm-up to the enactment.

2. Lead-in: primarily involves preparing those being confronted to engage in the confrontation stage. Although it is part of the enactment for the confronter, for the other(s) involved, it is their warm-up to the enactment phase.

3. Confrontation: the succinct, direct statement of the situation as perceived by the confronter. The form developed and validated by Remer (1984), with additional validation by Watson and Remer (1984), is employed to convey the specific source of concern (behavior of the confrontee) and the impact of that behavior on the confronter. This stage coincides with the culmination of the initial (rising) phase of the enactment to the catharsis of abreaction.

4. Active Listening: involves the switching of roles for the confronter to that of listener—understanding, clarifying, validating, and supporting the reactions of the confrontee. This stage corresponds to the initial decline of the enactment from the catharsis of abreaction toward integration.

5. Contract Negotiation: aims at finding an acceptable, mutually agreeable, mutually involving plan for the solution of the situation or a plan for its further exploration. The successful establishment of a contract can be considered the catharsis of integration (i.e. the focusing of energies toward a change in future enactments). It can also be the first step toward closure.

6. Follow-up: includes: (a) the restatement of the contract negotiated, (b) the verbal or written commitment of each person involved to the contract, (c) the expression of any reservations or questions, (d) the setting of a specific time to review and possibly to revise the contract, (e) the statement of the criteria by which the success or failure of the contract will be judged, (f) the actual execution of the evaluation, and (g) all the subsequent related actions taken as a result of the confrontation and evaluation. The follow-up not only coincides with the closure phase of the enactment, but also serves as the basis for the warm-up for further confrontation/enactment on this particular focus.

We would like to promise that the process is linear, but it need not be. There may need to be some degree of "looping back" should it become apparent that a particular stage has not been completed adequately enough to allow the subsequent stage (or stages) to be addressed and completed. More regarding this point is discussed as we address the individual stages in detail.

Preparation

Preparation is the most extensive and, in many ways, the most important stage of the confrontation process. It encompasses not only the readying for actual confrontation, but also the learning or reviewing of the mindset and behaviors that contribute to a spontaneous outcome. Thus, this stage addresses not only the specific confrontation, but the general attitude toward it as well. Preparation—literally and figuratively—is the foundation on which the confrontation process rests. Most of the time it is primarily a cognitive activity, including quite a bit of "self talk," planning, and cognitive rehearsal but can include other types of preparation, like behavioral rehearsal, too. For those just learning the process it also includes activities designed to overcome the innate reservations and misconceptions most people hold regarding the entire confrontation process. Accordingly, we discuss preparation in detail both generally and specifically.

General Aspects of Preparation

There are two general aspects to preparation. First is conceptualizing confrontation in a functional manner; second is learning to use that conception in a facile, acceptable way. Construing the confrontation process as assertive behavior affords both a compelling framework from which to operate and extensively researched methods for acquiring needed skills (Alberti & Emmons, 1974; Jakubowski, 1977a). Although a comprehensive discussion of assertiveness is not within the scope of this chapter, an overview—noting some of the most salient points—is in order.

Assertiveness. An assertive message is one that conveys a person's desires in a particular situation in a forthright way while respecting the rights and sensibilities of other people involved. This definition is easier to say than it is to implement, because the implementation is context specific.

Viewing a response relative to the ends of the assertive continuum allows a discrimination to be made more easily. On one hand there are passive responses that are certainly characterized by a type of respect for others, but which make one a doormat (e.g., "If you really wouldn't mind I'd like my lawnmower back some time in the next week or so. I really could use it"). On the other end are aggressive responses that are definitely non-doormat but show no regard for others (e.g., "Listen idiot, get me my bill now!"). Assertive responses lie somewhere in between. Just where must be judged in each instance by the respondent.

Using the idea of a confrontation as an assertive response somewhere along a continuum can help rid people of two popular misconceptions about confrontation. First it debunks the notion that confrontation must be an all or nothing proposition; second that it must be a "me first" or aggressive message. In addition, people can accept the strategy of starting toward the passive end of the continuum and then, if or when necessary, "upping the ante" (i.e., moving to increasingly more aggressive stances) as logical, functional, and safe.

Safety (not to be confused with the derogatory implication of "playing it safe" as passivity) is a point not often directly addressed in the assertiveness literature. Being assertive does *not* force a person to be reckless. Quite the contrary, having a working knowledge of assertive interventions means having the ability to choose when and where to use them. No one is suggesting that choosing not to confront an abusive drunk in a bar indicates any lack of assertiveness. What it indicates is a good knowledge of the limitations of the approach and a fair share of common sense.

Although recognition of the ability to choose when to act assertively and of the flexibility to accommodate to different situations are important in learning to be assertive, there is one final point to mention: Assertiveness implies action. To be assertive one must act assertively occasionally. To do otherwise is, at a minimum, allowing ones skills to wither for lack of practice; at a maximum it is deluding oneself that one has the capability to act assertively at all.

Self-Talk. Addressing the second general aspect of preparation, the use of the framework provided by assertiveness, is the concept of self-talk. Implicitly, and sometimes explicitly, it is a large component of assertiveness training approaches (Bass & Davis, 1988; Jakubowski, 1977b). Although being integral to assertiveness and, hence, to the confrontation process, self-talk is more extensive and more generally applicable in a variety of situations. The literature dealing with self-talk is both extensive and rich (e.g., Ellis, 1977; Mahoney, 1974; Meichenbaum, 1972a, 1972b, 1976, 1977). However, as in the case of assertiveness, only a brief commentary is within the present scope.

Self-talk, as might be inferred from the term itself, is verbalizing, either overtly or covertly, the inner messages we all send ourselves. It can consist of monologues, dialogues, or "group discussions." Where it differs from simple cognitions is in the consciousness of the process and in the control one exercises over it. Evidence suggests that it is an extremely effective and powerful tool (Meichenbaum, 1972b). It is an absolutely essential tool in confrontation for using the assertiveness framework to overcome the powerful, and usually hidden, messages learned and internalized early in life regarding confrontation.

Self-Talk: Fears and Misconceptions about Confrontation. Short of ignoring or denying frictions, if that is possible to do, they must be addressed. If not they will tend to build only to become worse and harder to face. Almost everyone recognizes this fact at some conscious level, yet few are willing to act. What stops them? Their self-talk, the messages they send themselves.

There are many reasons for not confronting, some legitimate, some only excuses. First, people do not know how. As is assumed about most communication, many people believe that being able to confront frictions should come naturally. They may convince themselves that their fear is because they are inept.

Second, they may be afraid, or at least highly anxious, about being inappropriate or being seen so. Particularly coming from a familial or cultural background where confronting problems directly was frowned on, they may have extremely strict internal injunctions against any form of directness and thus fear being ostracized.

They may tell themselves they will make a scene. Even if they believe they would be acting appropriately, they think others will be made uncomfortable by *their actions.* If that happens they fear they may be blamed for the situation.

Of course, everyone has seen an aggressive bully at some time. Who would want to be identified that way? So they may fear coming on too strong.

They may convince themselves that confronting will only make matters worse. In some situations, like those with drunks or abusers, they may be right and the self-talk is functional. Even in less drastic circumstances, however, they may fear that the others involved will not see their point of view or even disagree. They tell themselves that disagreement might threaten the relationship.

There are myriad other ideas, thoughts, conceptions, and beliefs that people have and tell themselves so they will not confront. Perhaps the most detrimental, however, is that they convince themselves that the problem will go away on its own. Although it might seem that way at times, the "problem" probably would not be a problem (i.e., someone be aware of it) if this strategy would work. The "ignore and hope-wish-pray" approach probably has already failed.

The main misconception about confrontation seems to be that it has to be all or nothing. This simply is not so. This should be obvious judging from the number of people who thought they had confronted only to have the other persons involved be completely unaware and unaffected by the "confrontation." Still people convince themselves they "must do it" or do nothing.

To allay some of this fear, and to lay the groundwork for correcting the misconceptions, myths, and faulty learning surrounding confrontation, it is helpful to have a framework from which to work, one that provides a convincing, logical, rationale for functional, accurate self-talk. The concept of assertiveness provides an excellent one.

How can these mental roadblocks to implementing the confrontation process be overcome? By using self-talk to assert the counter message that is logically supported by the assertiveness framework and by experience, observation, and safe experimentation. To counteract the messages mentioned here one might tell oneself:

"I am not inept. I can learn to be more assertive, like Lucy did."

"I am not inept. In fact, I can handle this situation much like I did the one last week with Ricky."

"I don't have to be like the rest of my family. I am a different person. I didn't like the way Fred handled that lawnmower problem. I'll find a better way."

"That's ok that I'm anxious. It will make me more sensitive to the people I'm confronting."

"My family won't stay mad at me forever. When they see my point and that my suggestion might make life easier, they'll come around."

"People may be a little uncomfortable. That's natural. But I don't cause their discomfort. As long as I handle this situation appropriately, they'll live and even be better for it."

"If Ethel thinks it's my fault, I can talk it out with her."

"Things won't change unless I do something. I'm already irritated. I think the situation is bad already. Bringing it out in the open will make it different, but certainly no worse than it will become if I let it go."

"It's ok if Rob disagrees with me. He's entitled to his opinion. We certainly can't work out a compromise unless he knows mine. Beside he might just see my side. Mary did and now we get along great."

"This doesn't look like a good time to confront Buddy. He really looks hassled. I'll tell him I'd like to talk to him later in his office when he's less pushed."

There are obviously many others, one to counter every unfounded rationalization for not confronting; and one to support every good reason.

Using the framework of assertiveness implemented through the use of self-talk we now address the specific aspects of the preparation stage of the confrontation process. In discussion we suggest, in part through giving examples, how these two general aspects of preparation might be employed.

Specific Aspects of Preparation

Whether to Confront. The decision whether to confront is not an easy one and should not be taken lightly. The impact of a confrontation on the relationship must be considered, because the relationship will change once the confrontation has occurred. There are two questions that must be answered affirmatively in order to proceed: "Is this relationship worth the time, effort and, perhaps, discomfort to me to carry this confrontation process through to completion?" and "Is this relationship strong enough to take a direct interaction?" Asking these questions may make the confrontation seem dire when it need not be. However, they must be asked because the result of well completed confrontation will be a strengthening of the relationship—a stronger, mutual commitment—while a confrontation with a negative outcome will probably result in distancing.

Taking Personal and Interpersonal Stock. Reviewing the personal resources and past history of both (or all) parties to be involved in the confrontation is essential to preparing adequately. Knowing one's own strengths and weaknesses, one's inclinations and present and future demands of one's life can go a long way toward deciding whether, when, and how to confront. Although the similar knowledge of the others concerned may not be quite as extensive or available, even recognizing this limitation is important in planning. Picking the best possible conditions—time, place, wording of the confrontation, and lead-in—and using self-talk to rehearse and motivate oneself will be grounded in this step.

Time, Place, and Context. All assertive confronters want to give themselves the best chance for a positive outcome. Thus, preparing includes consideration of such variables as time, place, and context. Confronting someone at a crowded restaurant who is rushing through lunch to get to a meeting is likely not to succeed. Alone, away from colleagues, when you have a half hour scheduled for talking things out has a much better probability of success.

Which brings up an important misconception, that confrontations must occur when the irritating situation takes place. Nothing could be further from the truth. It is important to be able to tell oneself to wait and plan well. However, it is also good to learn to schedule a confrontation for a specific time and place, and soon after the occurrence of the offending behavior, while the incident is still fresh (Napier, 1988).

Type of Confrontation. In dealing with the confrontation stage of the process proper we discuss the different types of levels of confrontation in more detail. Most legitimate confrontations are either interpretive or a combination of interpretive and observable (Remer, 1984; Watson & Remer, 1984). More important, however, is being able to distinguish between interpersonal confrontations and values conflicts. The former can be addressed using the skills we're discussing; the latter are out of the present realm.

Wording. This topic too is expanded later. However, the consideration of the phrasing of the confrontation, particularly the choice of the feeling description, the specification of the problem behavior, and the delineation of the personal consequences, is part of preparation. The wording is certainly influenced by taking stock. Using self-talk to rehearse, role-reverse with the confrontee (asking how I would react if someone confronted me this way), and generally examine the choices made helps hone confrontation.

Possible Changes/Acceptable Outcomes. The purpose of confronting is to ask for a change in a person's behavior. As we see when we talk about the contracts for change, it is best to remain flexible and open. The change should be important, not necessarily how the change is achieved. Still having in mind a goal and a way to suggest to achieve it is a necessary starting point. Inviting the confrontee to suggest a plan may also work and can certainly be a way to produce cooperation, but the confronter needs to be ready in case the confrontee is at a loss (after all, the confronter is prepared). Even if the confrontee has some ideas, having given this aspect some thought ahead of time will provide a basis for compromise until a mutually acceptable course of action is found.

Switching Modes. The most difficult aspect of the confrontation process for which to prepare is switching from the confronter stance to that of the listener/clarifier/supporter. Here both self-talk and practice are essential. Most of the preparation is geared toward helping a person become more self-oriented, toward building momentum. After delivering the confrontation a 180° change must occur, particularly if those being confronted do not have confrontation and listening skills themselves. The others involved have to be allowed to react and their reactions dealt with constructively. A good deal of prevention can be done through being proactive in the lead-in. This fact not withstanding, the confronter must be prepared to validate and cope with the confrontee's response, without backing off the confrontation. This end can best be achieved through using active-listening skills. To do so takes first telling oneself that the switch is necessary and then urging oneself to do it now! It also helps to remind oneself that the confrontation can either be repeated or elevated later, if need be.[1]

Lead-In

The lead-in stage, as the name suggests, consists of a statement made by the confronter to prepare the confrontee for the confrontation and, possibly, to agree on the structure of the interaction to follow. The lead-in message is important because it is related specifically to how the problem is perceived and consequently represented for problem solution (Witteman, 1988). To a large extent, a successful confrontation outcome depends on the initial interpersonal communication skills of the confronter used in overcoming the resistance of the confrontee (Parsons & Meyers, 1984). If done well, lead-in aids the confrontee's warm-up to create the best possible atmosphere for the confrontation, thus reducing resistance, increasing the spontaneity and the corresponding chances of a good outcome. Lead-in can help create a coordinational alignment that enhances communication accuracy that has been associated with greater overall satisfaction from the conflict (Papa & Pood, 1988).

What goes into the lead-in? According to Newell and Stutman's (1988) model of social confrontation, negotiating the expectations and rules of a relationship is a critical element and this element should be attended to during the lead-in. Therefore, this stage includes statements about the importance of the person(s) and the relationship(s) to the confronter; reinforcement of capabilities used in coping with previous difficult situations; acknowledgment of the discomfort atten-

---

[1]Exercises designed to facilitate the learning and practice of confrontation skills are available from the authors for each stage of the confrontation process.

dant in confrontations for both (all) those involved; and requests/ suggestions for how the confrontation interaction will be structured. A sample lead-in might be as follows:

> We've been friends for a few years now and have been through a few uncomfortable times in our relationship. I've always appreciated your honesty with me and I always want to be direct with you too. I have something to say that will probably be uncomfortable for both of us. Please hear me out and think about what I've said. Then I want to hear your reaction and see if we can work out some way to address my concern. All right?

Then comes the confrontation proper.

Sometimes acknowledging or predicting the confrontees defensive reactions in advance and letting them know you realize the difficulty they may encounter in coping with the situation can defuse some of those reactions. This approach may be particularly effective if time is promised, and scheduled as part of the structuring, for the confrontee to respond and a contract for the structure is agreed on. Doing so may mitigate some of the feeling of being attacked and take off some of the pressure to react immediately. However, predicting a reaction in advance can backfire— may seem like mind reading. This is where the perspective gained by taking stock can provide the basis for the best choice of content and wording.

There are three cautions to heed in preparing and delivering the lead-in. First, do not make the lead-in too long. A long lead-in is like waiting for the other shoe to drop. Second, although it is important to acknowledge any uncertainty about the situation—that, particularly in an interpretive confrontation, you are sharing your perceptions—you do not want to negate the validity of those perceptions in advance. Do not take the confrontation back before you have done it. If you are not sure enough of your perceptions (or uncomfortable enough with your feelings), then do not confront. Third, make the lead-in stage distinct from the confrontation stage. Even if you have to say either to yourself and/ or the confrontee "OK, ready," separate the two.

Confrontation

Confrontation form, the rationale behind its development, and the empirical evidence supporting its use are presented in detail by Remer (1984), Watson (1983), and Watson and Remer (1984). For more extensive coverage the reader is referred to those sources.

Types of Confrontation

There are four types of confrontation messages. (We use the term *confrontation* in short to mean interpersonal confrontation between or among individuals with on-going relationships.) However, only two of these are legitimate, functional confrontation messages. The other two are what in mathematics are called *degenerate cases*. Degenerate cases are used to make a point by contrast. At present the term is particularly apt, as we see here. The four types are positive, negative, values conflicts, and constructive.

Positive Confrontation. Positive confrontations are essentially compliments in confrontation form. In a sense their goal is a behavior change, just as with all confrontations. They aim to increase or maintain the behavior on which they focus. In terms of behavioral theory they are reinforcing statements. They can be particularly effective because of their specificity.

What makes them confrontional? First they follow the confrontation form. Second, people are as uncomfortable with compliments as they are with any other legitimate confrontation. In fact, their reactions often border on defensive. These unwarranted responses must be dealt with by framing the positive confrontations properly.

Negative Confrontations. Negative confrontations are exactly what everyone fears when they think of confrontation. They have no, or only partial, form. Generally, they are a type of emotional purging that may serve a purpose for the moment, but are detrimental to all involved in the long run (i.e., they are impulsive rather than spontaneous acts).Calling someone an "SOB" may let him or her know you are upset but do not do much to change the situation unless you have a desire to distance yourself or end the relationship. It can accomplish that goal. Negative confrontations always harm the relationship(s) in which they are used (e.g., Boser & Poppen, 1983).

Values Conflicts. Values conflicts exist. They are part of life and will continue to occur as long as people have different expectations, needs, and enculturation. They cannot be addressed through the confrontation process. Thus, they are not legitimate confrontations, even if they are disguised in confrontation form. However, they can be identified by trying to use the constructive confrontation form. Then other means must be used to address them, a topic not within our purview.

When two people want different things in a situation—in our case particular actions to occur—but neither desire is more legitimate than the other except in the perception of the person wanting it, there is a values conflict. If someone trying to confront cannot find a legitimate consequence then a values conflict is occurring. For example:

"When you don't get your haircut when I ask you to, I feel hurt because I think you look better in short hair."

This is indicative of a values conflict. It smacks of "I want what I want." Maybe I think I look better in long hair. On the other hand:

"When you don't get your haircut when I ask you to, I feel angry, because the long hair clogs the drain in the shower."

This is a legitimate, observable confrontation. In between, in a way, is the legitimate interpretive confrontation:

"When you don't get your hair cut when I ask you to, I feel hurt, because I think you're angry at me and expressing it indirectly."

How is this confrontation not a values conflict? How is it legitimate? These questions are the point of the interpretive type of confrontation.

Constructive Confrontation.   Confrontation can lead to either a destructive win-lose confrontation, or a more mutually beneficial and constructive interaction facilitating personal growth can take place (Deutsch, 1973). The use of constructive confrontation is not comfortable and should not be. The discomfort engendered is both necessary and functional. The discomfort conveys the importance of the interaction to the long term health of the relationship, motivates both (all) participants and heightens the sensitivity of the confronter (a valuable condition throughout the entire confrontation process). The emotions involved are usually termed *negative,* though *uncomfortable* is also a better term for them as well. These confrontations are not negative in that they can, if done properly, lead to a positive outcomes (i.e., they are spontaneous rather than impulsive actions). They are designed to ask for a change in a behavior that will have an enhancing, long-term effect on the relationship, thus the label *constructive.*

There are two types of constructive confrontation: observable and interpretive. The positive impact of the observable kind is fairly obvious, but becomes clearer later when we discuss the contract to which it leads. The effects of the interpretive are less clear.

Interpretive confrontations were designed to lead to behavior change and/or to clarification of the status of the relationship (Remer, 1984).

They are (a) direct communications of the confronter's perceptions, (b) an explicit recognition that perceptions are the focus involved, and (c) an acknowledgment that because perceptions are matters of interpretation, they might be mistaken. These confrontations invite discussion. Interpretive confrontations may or may not lead to the same kinds of contracts as observable ones, but they will always lead to some change in the relationship.

The effects of both interpretive and observable confrontations will be constructive, at least as viewed from the mental health perspective/value of facing reality. This statement does not mean they will "save" a relationship, quite the contrary. What may be uncovered, particularly through an interpretive confrontation, could be a values conflict or a shift in the commitment of a significant other. What comes out might lead to a disengagement, a redefinition or even the end of a relationship. However, the confrontation does not create these realities, they are present and causing frictions regardless of whether they are examined and faced or not. We believe ignoring these sources of irritation will only prolong the process of redefinition and thus, be more detrimental to the individuals involved. Like the Fram Oil Filter Man says: "You can pay me now (for a $5.00 filter) or you can pay me later (for a $500 new engine)." In our judgment a shift now, even a break, although painful, is less so than either a break later or the energy wasted in trying to maintain a facade.

Confrontation Form

A key ingredient in the success of confrontive interactions appears to be structural specificity. Structured confrontation approaches have been associated with stress reduction and less threat in conflictual situations (Cohen, 1959). Several structured approaches have been proposed (e.g., Gordon, 1970; Ralph, 1981). A structured form for confrontation is helpful. Confrontations are composed of three components: a description of a problem behavior, a report of a feeling response that the confronter has to the behavior, and a consequence of the behavior to the confronter. They usually, and most effectively, take the form:

> "When you (confrontee)   (description of behavior),
> I (confronter) feel   (feeling state(s)),
> because   (consequence to the confronter),"

Although this exact form and/or order may not be absolutely necessary, retaining it serves to ensure that all components are present, which has been shown to be most effective (Remer, 1984; Watson & Remer, 1984); the confrontation is concise; it is distinctly separated from the components of other confrontation process stages; and the skill developed in its use transfers most readily across incidences where it is employed. The benefits of staying with this structure outweigh any seeming artificiality. At least until one is thoroughly familiar with it and skilled in its use, we suggest using the form verbatim.

Understanding the rationale behind the formulation, component by component, is necessary for using self-talk to overcome reservations about its use. Accordingly, we can now look at each component separately.

Behavior.   A complete description of the behavior, including the salient aspects of the context in which it occurs, allows a specifically applicable contract for behavior change to be negotiated. The description also serves as a basis for raising the confrontee's awareness, judging the severity of the problem and evaluating how effective any intervention has been. Generalizations can be made to other similar situations to which the contract may apply and discriminations can be made between situations where it does not. An additional benefit is that the confronter is forced to examine the context and decide what is the real focus. This knowledge can be used, through self-talk, to direct the energies for change to where they are warranted. The reasons can be illustrated by comparing two possible behavior descriptions:

"When you leave the dishes in the sink, . . . " and

"When you leave the greasy dishes in the sink for an hour when company is coming soon, . . . "

The former is a behavioral description, but very general. The latter not only tells what the behavior is but also identifies both a specific context and provides a better basis for understanding why the confronter might be reacting to the behavior in a particular manner. The contract for change that results from a more specific description is more focused. Consequently, it has a better chance of succeeding, because it is not asking for an overwhelming, broad, general change.

Feeling.   The feeling component is a simple direct report of the internal state of the confronter when the behavior occurs. As such it should be owned (Gordon, 1970), that is, worded "I feel." This component is necessary because it provides the impetus, the energy, for both the confrontation and the change of behavior (Yalom, 1975).

In many ways, feeling expression is the most troublesome aspect of confrontation. It can be a source of discomfort for both (all) the parties involved, particularly if any or all are not used to such expression. Some confronters have a hard time even identifying, let alone expressing, what they are feeling. If they are able to do so, their repertoire is exceedingly

limited, and thus their impact is as well. There is also difficulty in compre-
hending and/or accepting that people may feel more than one thing in
a given situation (i.e., they are ambivalent or even multivalent) and that
it is perfectly acceptable to be so. Finally, people fear that expressing
their feelings will engender a defensive reaction, because it will be read
as blaming (which unfortunately it may be if not done correctly.)

Staying away from wording like "You made me feel . . . ", "It made
me feel . . . ", "One feels . . . ", and the like can help. Although there is
no guarantee the confrontee will not feel guilt (which is not the same as
feeling blamed, although they are often equated), will not respond with
"You shouldn't feel that way," "Don't feel that way," and so on, the
chances are better using the direct report form. If you do get one of
these responses, however, you are then well placed simply to say: "I'm
just telling you how I feel in the situation."

Finally, as indicated earlier, there may be multiple feelings attendant
on a behavior. Do not be afraid to express more than one. Although
there may be no choice about what feelings are triggered in a particular
situation, there is control over the extent to which they are felt (Ellis,
1977; Maultsby, 1975) and also over which are expressed and how.
Choose the most apt label, (feeling description), the combination, and
the order of expression that you believe will have the desired impact.
Effective ways of moving a confrontation along the assertiveness continuum are (a) choosing a stronger word to express the feeling involved, (b)
adding expressions of other feelings engendered, or (c) reordering the
feelings expressed to alter the impact.

Consequence.   The consequence component is designed to convey the
impact on the confronter caused by the behavior. In this respect it is intended to be quite different and separate from the feeling expression. As
originally conceived, this component included only observable, objective
consequences (Gordon, 1970). However, Remer (1984) and Watson and
Remer (1984) expanded the definition to include the impact on confronter's interpretation of the behavior because these types of consequences
seem more prevalent and equally important. Both lead to a discussion of how
much of the problem is owned by each of those involved in the confrontation.
In addition, the interpretive type, because it is focused on perceptions and
self-talk already, is directly amenable to self-talk interventions. The consequence component takes one of two forms, observable (previously termed
consequential) or interpretive. As a result they lead to two different types of
confrontations, labeled correspondingly. Examples of each are:

"When you leave the dirty dishes in the sink overnight, I feel disgusted,
because they attract roaches." (Observable)

"When you leave the dirty dishes in the sink overnight, I feel troubled and put out, because I think you do not care as much about your obligations around the house as I do about mine." (Interpretive)

The former consequence is verifiable; the latter requires confirmation or input from the confrontee about the degree of its accuracy. Each may lead to different outcomes as we see when we discuss different types of confrontations or when we discuss contracting.

Identifying the consequences of a behavior may or may not be easy to do. The consequence must be to the confronter for the confrontation to be legitimate. Recognizing it (or them because there may be more than one, perhaps different, kinds involved) is essential to conveying an adequate justification, motivation for the confrontation. An observable consequence may be easily delineated if it exists, which is all too infrequently. Interpretive consequences may be more prevalent, but the difficulty in conveying them may be more in the intrapersonal dynamics, the willingness to examine and face one's own expectations and values and their effects on one's perceptions.

The most common problems in formulating the consequence component are being honest with oneself in the interpretive case, owning or identifying the personal ramifications in either case, and learning to keep feelings separate. Feelings are often confused with thoughts or beliefs (i.e., people say "I feel that the behavior is bad" or they say "I feel angry because I feel put upon"). In the case of the former error help and practice is necessary to find the attendant feeling; in the latter the confronter must learn to keep the components uncontaminated.

Cautions.   Sometimes when being confronted a person may respond by "counter confronting." ("The best defense is a good offense)". If the person you are confronting responds: "Well you do X," "You do that too," or something similar, it is best not to get into an argument. We suggest acknowledging that the confrontee may have a point or, in fact, may be right. However, that friction can be dealt with once the present confrontation has been completed. Suggest that you will be willing to do so then.

If the person persists, it may be a better strategy to do the other confrontation first. Doing so may be a good chance to model how to accept and work with a confrontation. Make certain, however, that you both agree to return to and work out the original confrontation. Then be sure to do so. Otherwise the confrontee has effectively side tracked the interaction from its intended focus.

Active Listening

The active-listening state is integral to making confrontation a productive process. The ratio of time spent invested in active listening to that in actually confronting is easily 5:1, if not more. Not only is active listening a stage itself, but the skill is also used throughout the entire process. Besides being essential for mitigating the defensive reactions of confrontees, its use provides a means of clarification and understanding that are the foundations of all stages. In fact, it is an exceedingly useful tool in many situations beyond confrontation.

Active listening consists of three phases: paying attention to the message a person sends and interpreting it, feeding what is heard back to the sender, and receiving feedback about the accuracy of the message received. The process continues to loop until the feedback from the sender indicates that the message has been received with the desired degree of accuracy.

Paying attention to the message sent may not be as easy as it sounds. Messages are sent on three levels: verbal, vocal, and nonverbal (Mehrabian, 1971). If all three levels are consistent, there is usually no communication problem. However, if the levels are inconsistent, in other words if the messages of the three levels conflict in some way, the overall message is ambiguous. The nonverbal level message then usually takes precedence (i.e., is the one believed most). Active listening is designed to relieve the ambiguity. This goal is achieved through the looping. Not only is the message sent clarified for the receiver, but the sender is also forced to consider what it is that is really meant, which can be more than one thing or not entirely in the sender's awareness.

Active listening responses, to be most effective, should be phrased tentatively to invite feedback. Thus, although trite now, wording such as "What I hear you saying is . . . ", "If I understand you correctly you mean . . . ", or "You seem to be saying that . . . ", are good introductions to the *rephrasing* of the message receive. The emphasis is to indicate that active listening is not simply parroting back what is said, but is necessary to initiating the feedback process and arriving at a consensus regarding the meaning of the message. Rephrasing recognizes that even the same words have different denotations and, more importantly, connotations to different individuals. What is required is a "negotiation for meaning" until that goal is reached adequately (it never can be reached in an absolute sense even when communicating with oneself because of natural processes such as maturation).

Why do active-listening responses work? In addition to clarifying meaning—in and of itself essential—they convey an interest and an investment of time and energy in another person; being heard accurately is validating of one's thoughts, feelings and perceptions; and just having someone focus their undivided attention on you for a few moments is personally affirming. All in all, actively listening to someone is quite a gift, in more ways than one—one that can be given and that can be developed.

Usually people have predictable, similar reactions when confronted. Knowing what to expect can be particularly helpful in the listening stage, both for allowing an easier switch of roles and for preparing for a specific reaction. There are two useful characterizations of confrontees' reactions, both are process descriptions. First is Piaget's (1954) accommodation and assimilation; second is Kubler-Ross' (1969) description of the grieving process.

Piaget (1954) indicated that learning takes place in two stages: accommodation and assimilation. First information is taken in; although it is not truly integral to the individual. Then, over a period of time, it is assimilated—digested and made part of the cognitive structure. This view explains why, no matter how open an individual is, there is some adjustment to the confrontation. It also helps explain why some confrontations are accepted more readily than others—the information meshes with or at least is not significantly discrepant from already present perceptions. However, this conceptualization does not deal with the emotional aspect.

Kubler-Ross' (1969) grieving model gives an excellent idea of the emotional adjustment through which a confrontee must go to accept a confrontation. Viewing confrontation as a loss of present self-concept, the reaction follows these stages: (a) shock/denial, (b) anger, (c) depression, (d) bargaining, and (e) acceptance, although not necessarily in this order or linearly. If you look back at when you have been confronted you may be able to see this progression in your own response: (a) "Who me?", (b) "How dare you say that about me?!", (c) "God. I'm a horrible person to do that," (d) "Wait a minute, it's not all my fault", and (e) "Well I can handle the part that's mine. I just goofed." If you have some idea what someone is going through (their self-talk) and where they are likely to get stuck—what stage(s) are hard for them—you can listen more effectively.

A few last notes on the active-listening process, first the looping should not stop until both (all) parties involved are satisfied with the product. If there is any question, continue to loop. What this requirement usually means is that the active listener, generally the most skilled of the participants, must look for cues (hesitancies, tones of voice, etc.) from the others (i.e., actively listen during the active listening) and to his or her own internal reactions. Finally, as mentioned previously in discussing preparation, it is imperative in order to be a good confronter, to develop and practice the skill of switching between roles. Confronting mode does not "feel" gift-giving (unless your powers of self-talk verge on or step over the bounds of self-delusion); the active-listening mode should not "feel" insincere or punitive. Separating the two and being clear about what role you are playing at any given moment can best be accomplished through the use of self-talk (for more on active listening see Rogers, 1952).

Contract Negotiation

The purpose of the entire confrontation process is to secure a change in a behavior that is causing friction between or among people. All the stages, when executed properly and carried to their fruition, are building toward negotiating a viable, mutual contract aimed at alleviating the problem.

Establishing a viable contract depends on the type of confrontation in which you are engaged. Objective confrontations lead to one type of contract, interpretive confrontations usually, although not necessarily, lead to another. The former produce contracts directly geared to immediate behavior change, primarily the responsibility of the person producing the problematic behavior. Here the other(s) involved are supporters, encouragers, and reinforcers—generally resource people. This circumstance is usually so because the consequence is irrefutable and compelling and the behavior is under the control of the confrontee and no one else.

Interpretive confrontations, on the other hand, because of their admitted subjectivity, more often lead either to exploratory contracts, contracts where all parties are more directly involved in altering the problem situation or may even lead to contracts with the confronter doing the bulk of the changing. Here one person's part of the contract might be focused on awareness of the behavior (perhaps by allowing the other person to point it out in some unobtrusive way when it occurs, without recriminations), whereas the other person might agree to work on the self-talk affecting a possible misperception. In any case both own a fair share of the problem.

Contracts can be exploratory, that is, their goals can be to establish whether a problem exists as far as those (any one of those) involved are concerned and/or to establish who owns how much of the problem (Gordon, 1970). Most problems are not simply the fault of any one person, and thus cannot be solved by one person alone. Exploratory contracts provide an excellent basis for negotiating a long-term, mutual one. Viewing contracts along a continuum of active behavior change interventions, exploratory contracts, like behavioral baselining (Watson & Tharp, 1985), can be seen as essential first steps to raising the level of awareness. Without awareness of both the behavior and its context (its ABCs—Antecedents–Behavior–Consequents) lasting behavior change is virtually impossible.

There are two keys to having the contract carried through. One is its mutuality, everyone must be actively involved in some way. We do not mean to imply that there must be a *quid pro quo,* although such an arrangement, if acceptable to everyone, is fine. However, the probability of success is increased dramatically if there is a sense of cooperative involvement established, even if the extent of one person's commitment is to acknowledge and encourage, through some overt action, the successful attempts made by the other(s). The other key is being open to negotiation, keeping a mind open to any and all acceptable solutions, particularly those not your own.

Another point that must be stressed is the sheer pragmatic approach to problem solution. The goal here is not to win an argument but to relieve the stress and friction. Any workable plan should be voiced, considered adequately and, perhaps, tried. Brainstorming techniques are useful here, if only as guidelines (see Parnes, 1977). In Gordon's (1970) parlance, the contract should be a win–win proposition.

The contract does not have to solve the entire problem at once. A series of contracts, each built on the foundation of previous successful attempts, cannot only provided surcease, but can also build the bonds of the relationship in general and the sense of confidence in the power/ability to cope with other difficulties when they arise. Certainly a number of small, but important gains are preferable to one big attempt that proves only partially successful.

Finally, once a contract has been negotiated to the point of being agreeable to all concerned (an excellent opportunity to use the active listening skills already acquired), it should be stated aloud, or better yet written down, so there will be no mistake about the specifics or the commitments included. We also suggest that the time length of the contract, if it is a trial run, the criteria for judging its success, when evaluation/follow-up will occur and, perhaps, contingency plans (the next or alternative steps to be taken) be included.

At this point some examples of possible contracts might be illuminating. Looking back at the confrontations discussed previously we have the following possible contracts:

Re: Greasy dishes
When company is coming within a hour, Sally agrees to put off reading the paper and to do the dishes immediately after dinner. Rob agrees to remind Sally once, right after dinner, about the evening's plans and at other times to allow Sally to read the paper before she does the dishes.

They agree to try this contract out for a month, or four occasions. If the dishes are washed, put away, and the kitchen straightened, they will continue the contract. If not, they will discuss possible alternative remedies at that time.

Re: Dishes etc.
Archie agrees to keep a record of the number and kind of tasks

for which he accepts responsibility around the house and the amount of time it takes him to complete them after he accepts the undertaking.

Edith agrees to record similar information regarding her household chores and also to note the number of times she notices Archie doing both assigned tasks and other ones as well.

They agree to get together in 1 week on Tuesday 8 P.M. for 1 hour to analyze and discuss what they have found. They will then determine how much of a problem exists and who will do what to alleviate the situation.

Re: Haircut and Gummed Up Drains
Greg agrees to go out within the next 2 days to buy a shower cap, like the one used by his sister, Jan, for the days he does not wash his hair, just as she does. He also agrees to clean the hair out of the drain immediately after taking a shower on the days he does wash his hair. His father, Mike, will compliment him on his maturity and sense of responsibility after each time the contract is met (and may even let him have the car more often).

They will talk again after dinner 1 week from today to assess how the plan is working or if there are any problems. If Greg has not gotten the shower cap or has failed to cleaned out the drain more than once, he will have his hair cut the next afternoon or offer another alternative to try that must be acceptable to his Dad.

Re: Haircuts
Marcia, Jan, and Cindy talk with their mother, Carol, about the length of her hair. They would like it shorter and more stylish. Carol likes it as it is and has been for the last 20 years. Finding no consequence to them other than being embarrassed to have an out-of-date mother, they recognize this as a values conflict and decide to seek family therapy as a way of ameliorating the frictions.

Follow-Up

Follow-up is the final stage of the confrontation process. In theory, it can continue, probably intermittently, forever, as long as the contract negotiated is in force. It encompasses all subsequent actions or interactions that happen as a result of the confrontation and evaluation of both the negotiated contract and the confrontation process. At a minimum it can serve as a reminder to everyone involved that their commitments continue.

There are two purposes to the follow-up stage. First is to reach closure to the confrontation proper and subsequent contract negotiation (i.e., bring the present enactment to a close). Second is to ensure that other necessary interactions will occur, in a way providing a warm-up for future enactments.

To provide closure certain actions should take place. The contract as negotiated, with all it specifics, should be explicitly stated aloud. Criteria by which the success or failure of the contract will be judged should be established if they have not been already in the contract negotiation. Reservations, reactions, or questions of everyone involved in the confrontation regarding the contract or the process itself should be expressed and addressed to the satisfaction of all concerned. Achieving this end may require looping back to any previous stage that has not been adequately completed either because of error during its implementation or because new contingencies have arisen. Once this goal has been accomplished, a verbal or written commitment of each person involved in the contract should be obtained. Finally, if not already agreed on, a time to review, evaluate, and possibly revise the contract should be set. If there are responsibilities involved with the evaluation, such as finding a room or sending reminders to people, these should be explicitly addressed as well. As far as possible, nothing should be left to chance.

When the evaluation takes place, to ensure best results there should be sufficient warm-up. First check to see that everyone is there who is involved. It may be necessary to reschedule to another time if there are more pressing concerns distracting or drawing off resources. (However, if a pattern of avoidance occurs that issue may have to be dealt with directly, requiring another confrontation.) When everyone is present be sure everyone understands the purpose of the meeting, briefly recapitulating the salient aspects of the process that has occurred to date if necessary. Restate the contract, each person's responsibilities as agreed on, and the criteria for evaluation. Then proceed to the evaluation.

Using the contract and the criteria, assess its degree of success. On that basis review, and, if deemed necessary by *anyone* involved, revise the contract, essentially looping back to the contract negotiation stage, or other stages, whichever seem appropriate to address the problems that have arisen. It is best not to get into blaming or recriminations, but to take a nonjudgmental, nonexcuse-accepting stance (Glasser, 1975). Look at the problems that have prevented the successful execution of the contract and to overcome problems, restructure the contract in a way acceptable to everyone. However, particularly in the case of someone not carrying through repeatedly on a commitment as a result of an objective

Preparation	Lead-In	Confrontation	Active Listening	Negotiation	Follow-Up
• Judge worth of relationship	• Prepare confrontee	• Present succinct, direct statement of perceived situation	• Switch roles to that of listener	• Find acceptable plan for solution	• Restate negotiated contract
• Decide level or type of confrontation	State importance of person or relationship	• Convey concern about confrontee's behavior	• Convey Understanding	• Establish contract	• Confirm verbal or written commitment
• Review knowledge of self & other(s)	• Reinforce previous coping capabilities	• Coincides with intital phase of enactment	• Help clarify	• Focus on future changes	• Express reservations or questions
• Choose time, place, & context	• Acknowledge discomfort		• Validate confrontee's reactions	• Take first step toware closure	• Set time to review & revise
• Plan wording of confrontation & lead-in	• Suggest structure for confrontation		• Lend support	• Catharsis of integration	• Set criteria for success
• Prepare to switch from confronter to listener	• Warm-up to enactment phase				• Evaluate
• Consider changes & contracts					• Take related actions
					• Coincides with closure phase of enactment

Warm-up ———— Enactment ———— Integration

FIG. 11.3 Six stages of confrontation.

confrontation, a new, interpretive confrontation may be in order. If the contract has succeeded, a new contract, simply restating the old with a new time for further follow-up will likely be sufficient.

As indicated earlier follow-up can continue forever. Realistically, formal follow-up of old successful contracts tends to be dropped after a period of time. Still, it is a good idea and good practice to do informal follow-up, using self-talk and/or overtly. Doing so serves to review the process, reaffirm the relationship, and build confidence in everyone's abilities to handle future difficulties—in a way serving as the preparation for future situations.

SUMMARY/CONCLUSION

The confrontation process is more involved than many imagine. This complexity can add to the anxiety that the idea of confrontation itself provokes. For these reasons, teaching confrontation skills is both necessary and, when done effectively, rewarding.

We have broken the process down into six stages (see Fig. 11.3). Further, the stages are presented with rationales to make each a somewhat separate learning unit. They need not be addressed in any particular order nor to the same extent. The skills learned in each apply to situations other than confrontation and, thus, can be useful elsewhere and practiced separately. How you move through them is up to what the client already knows well—existing resources and skills. All stages should be incorporated in the training, however, for all must be present to produce a whole, spontaneous interaction—a complete, effective confrontation. Although what we have presented need not be followed verbatim, we hope the structure presented will serve as an aid to facilitate both teaching and learning of these skills.

REFERENCES

Alberti, R. E., & Emmons, M. L. (1974). *Your perfect right: A guide to assertive behavior* (2nd ed.). New York: Impact Press.

Bass, E., & Davis, S. L. (1988). *The courage to heal: A guide for women survivors of child sexual abuse.* New York: Perennial Library.

Boser, J., & Poppen, W. (1983, March). *Multidimensional communication in youth–adult relationships.* Paper presented at the annual convention of the American Personnel and Guidance Association, Washington, DC.

Carkhuff, R. R. (1969). *Helping and human relations* (Vol. 2). New York: Holt, Rinehart & Winston.

Cohen, A. R. (1959). Situation structure, self-esteem and threat-oriented reactions to power. In D. Cartwright (Ed.), *Studies in social power* (pp. 35–52). Ann Arbor, MI: University of Michigan.

Coser, L. (1956). *The function of social conflict.* New York: The Free Press.

Deutsch, M. (1973). *The resolution of conflict: Constructive and destructive processes.* New Haven, CT: Yale University Press.

Egan, G. (1986). *The skilled helper* (3rd ed.). Monterey, CA: Brooks/Cole.

Ellis, R. (1977). Rational-emotive therapy: Research data that support the clinical and personality hypotheses of RET and other modes of cognitive-behavior therapy. *Counseling Psychologist, 7*(1), 2–42.

Filley, A. C. (1975). *Interpersonal conflict resolution.* Glenview, IL: Scott, Foresman.

Glasser, W. (1975). *Reality therapy: A new approach to psychiatry.* New York: Harper & Row.

Gordon, T. (1970). *Parent effectiveness training.* New York: Wyden.

Hollander, C. E. (1968). *A process for psychodrama training: The Hollander psychodrama curve.* Littleton, CO: Evergreen Institute Press.

Jakubowski, P. A. (1977a). Assertive behavior and clinical problems of women. In E. I. Rawlings & D. K. Carter (Eds.), *Psychotherapy for women* (pp. 147–168). Springfield, IL: Charles C. Thomas.

Jakubowski, P. A. (1977b). Self-assertion training for women. In E. I. Rawlings & D. K. Carter (Eds.), *Psychotherapy for women* (pp. 168–193). Springfield, IL: Charles C. Thomas.

Kubler-Ross, E. (1969). *On death and dying.* New York: MacMillan.

Mahoney, M. J. (1974). *Cognition and behavior modification.* Cambridge, MA: Ballinger.

Maultsby, M. C. (1975). *Help yourself to happiness through rational self-counseling.* New York: Institute for Rational Living.

Mehrabian, A. (1971). *Silent messages.* Belmont, CA: Wadsworth.

Meichenbaum, D. (1972a). Cognitive modification of test-anxious students. *Journal of Consulting and Clinical Psychology, 39,* 370–380.

Meichenbaum, D. (1972b). Ways of modifying what clients say to themselves: marriage of behavior therapies and rational-emotive therapy. *Rational Living, 7,* 23–27.

Meichenbaum, D. (1976). Toward a cognitive theory of self-control. In G. Schwartz & D. Shapiro (Eds.), *Consciousness and self-regulation: Advances in research* (pp. 223–260). New York: Plenum.

Meichenbaum, D. (1977). *Cognitive-behavior modification: An integrative approach.* New York: Plenum.

Moreno, J. L. (1985). *Psychodrama: First volume.* Ambler, PA: Beacon House.

Napier, A. Y. (1988). *The fragile bond: In search of an equal, intimate and enduring bond.* New York: Harper & Row.

Newell, S. E., & Stutman, R. K. (1988). The social confrontation episode. *Communication Monographs, 55,* 266–285.

Papa, M. J., & Pood, E. A. (1988). Coorientational accuracy and differentiation in the management of conflict. *Communication Research, 15*(4), 400–425.

Parnes, S. J. (1977). CPSI: The general system. *Journal of Creative Behavior, 11*(1), 1–11.

Parsons, R. D., & Meyers, J. (1984). *Developing consultation skills: A guide to training, development, and assessment for human service professionals.* San Francisco, CA: Jossey-Bass.

Piaget, J. (1954). *The construction of reality in the child.* New York: Basic Books.

Putnam, L. L., & Poole, M. A. (1987). Conflict and negotiation. In F. M. Jablin, L. L. Putnam, K. H. Roberts, & L. W. Porter (Eds.), *Handbook of organizational communication* (pp. 549–599). Beverly Hills, CA: Sage.

Ralph, K. M. (1981). *The ABCDE message: A structure for assertive communications.* Unpublished manuscript, Lancaster County Mental Health/Mental Retardation Drug and Alcohol Abuse Programs, Division of Consultation and Education, Lancaster PA.

Remer, R. (1984). The effects of interpersonal confrontation on males. *American Mental Health Counselors Association Journal, 6,* 56–70.

Rogers, C. R. (1952). Barriers and gateways to communication. *Harvard Business Review, 4,* 46–52.

Watson, J. J. (1983). *Interpersonal confrontation and the expression of anger.* Unpublished doctoral dissertation, University of Kentucky, Lexington, KY.

Watson, J., & Remer, R. (1984). The effects of interpersonal confrontation on females. *Personnel and Guidance Journal, 62*(10), 607–611.

Watson, D. L., & Tharp, R. G. (1985). *Self-directed behavior: Self modification for personal adjustment* (4th ed.). Belmont, CA: Wadsworth.

Witteman, H. (1988). Interpersonal problem solving: Problem conceptualization and communication use. *Communication Monographs, 55,* 336–355.

Yalom, I. D. (1975). *The theory and practice of group psychotherapy* (2nd ed.). New York: Basic Books.

Author Index

Subject Index